THE GLEN ┊ AN GLEANN
Recollections from a Lost World

THE GLEN ¦ AN GLEANN
Recollections from a Lost World

Séamas Ó Maolchathaigh

Translated and edited from the Irish by Mícheál Ó hAodha

ARLEN
HOUSE

THE GLEN ¦ AN GLEANN
Recollections from a Lost World

is published in 2014 by
ARLEN HOUSE
42 Grange Abbey Road
Baldoyle
Dublin 13
Ireland
Phone: +353 86 8207617
Email: arlenhouse@gmail.com
www.arlenhouse.blogspot.com

978–1–85132–104–9, paperback

International distribution by
SYRACUSE UNIVERSITY PRESS
621 Skytop Road, Suite 110
Syracuse, New York
USA 13244–5290
Phone: 315–443–5534/Fax: 315–443–5545
Email: supress@syr.edu
www.syracuseuniversitypress.syr.edu

Typesetting by Arlen House
Cover image:

based on *An Gleann Agus a Raibh Ann*
by Séamas Ó Maolchathaigh

CONTENTS

Droichead na nGabhar – Goatenbridge

Baile na hAbhann – Newcastle

Cnoc Lochta – Knocklofty

Bóthar na Coille – The Wood Road

An Baile Gaealach – Irishtown

An Sean-Phóna – The Old Pound

An Chathair – Cahir

Cloichín – Clogheen

Cloichín an Mhargaidh – Clogheen

Tearra – The Tar River

An Chúirt Dóite – Burncoat

An Droichead Mór – The Big Bridge

Méar an Eolais – The Finger Post

An Teach Mór – The Great House

THE GLEN ⁞ AN GLEANN
Recollections from a Lost World

My Earliest Memory

The task I've set for myself here is – with God's help and praise and with much gratitude to him, and if He leaves my memory to me long enough – to tell the story of Gleann Chárthainn and the people who lived there when I was young – as best I can. I've had a long life. My children and grandchildren are grown-up men and women now.

That tells you how many peaceful summers, tough winters I've had since the day I was baptized in the church at Baile na hAbhann. I'm the oldest person still living in An Gleann now other than my equally-elderly neighbour Dic Ó Siadhaile, carpenter, and a man who is nine months older than me. And now that I've mentioned him, I have to admit that it was Dic who kept on at me to write this book. He is partly responsible, therefore, if this book turns out to be a failure on my part. From my very first day at school in Baile an Droichid, there weren't three lads who were closer friends than Dic and I, and Seán Baróid. May God have mercy on poor Seán; he's gone on the way of truth for many years now, but I will mention him often in this narrative. If you added all of the times I've spent outside An Gleann during the course of my life together, it wouldn't come to more than six months altogether; as a consequence, there are few events that occurred here that I didn't witness or that I didn't hear all the details about. Now that I am old and feeble, it gives me great pleasure to travel back along memory lane and to remember all the kind and wonderful people who lived here in An Gleann, when I was young. They were the happiest of days, those days when I was young and innocent and entirely unaware of the hardships and sufferings of this life. If anyone who reads this story after I am gone enjoys it or finds some satisfaction in it, I only ask that they say a prayer for the soul of its narrator. No-one should expect a neat and finely-wrought story from me because I'm only a novice when it comes to the art of story-telling. A 'bromach' (colt/boor) is what Dic Ó Siadhaile calls any chancer who works with wood but who has never learned his trade properly. And that is exactly what I am too when it comes to the writing project I have undertaken here. I would be ten times more adept and knowledgeable if I was working with the spade, the shovel or the ploughshare itself. I'll give the story of this book my best shot, however. No-one can ask for any more than this – that a person does his best.

The oldest memory that I have is of sitting in the lap of my mother and looking frighteningly at a huge fire and the flames climbing high into the air from it. Our barn was on fire. It was my aunt Máire who had caused the fire by accident. She never forgave herself for it either. My aunt Máire was a wonderful woman. I thought this when I was a child and I still think it now. She was wiser and more sensible and more stubborn than any other woman I ever met in my life, and that is saying something. That's why she was so ashamed at how simply she had set the barn on fire. She was going out with the buckets of gruel to feed a group of banbhs when she heard a hen calling from beneath a bush at the edge of the garden. She left down the two buckets and went over to find the hen as she was afraid that she might be laying her eggs outdoors. It was high-summer and everything was bone-dry. Not a drop of rain had fallen in the previous three weeks. When she had first filled the buckets of gruel inside at the hearth, a small red cinder had got into one of the buckets. This cinder had jumped from one dry piece of ground to another until a pile of dried ferns that was lying against the side of the shed caught fire. When my aunt turned around from looking for the hen, the fire was already licking the edge of the shed and even King William's army itself couldn't put it out. An old machine and various other unused items were in the shed and soon went up in flames. I don't remember everything about the fire now; I was so young and I was so frightened by the sight of this huge blaze. I often heard the story of that fire recalled later down through the years, however, often from my aunt Máire herself. Indeed, she often told this story against herself – and she never told it without saying how embarrassed she felt about this bizarre accident.

I don't remember my poor father at all. He died when I was just a year old, one night in the month of May when he went to check on the sheep. A few of the sheep were lambing and he stayed outside for too long. It was hailing and very cold and he got an awful wetting. He got very sick and only lasted ten days before he died. My mother was one of the Fogartys from Leacain on the northern side of the mountains. She was living in Lios na Faille for just two years when my father died and she was devastated. Although she lived to be nearly 80 years of age, she was never really the same again; she often felt lonely and down after he died.

My grandmother, my aunt Máire, and my mother and I all lived in the one house together when I was a child. It was my aunt who did most of the work around the house. My mother focused on sewing and knitting and that type of thing and I often saw the tears in her eyes as she worked. My aunt Máire was one of my father's sisters; she was ten years younger than him, she said. There were three other siblings between my father and her but all three died within the space of a week with the red fever – 'God between us and all harm', as the old people used to say. She was seven years younger than my mother but, that said, I obeyed my aunt a lot quicker than I did my mother. I was a lot more afraid of my aunt than I was of poor mother. My aunt Máire was always telling my mother that she had me spoilt rotten. I could have torn that whole house apart and my mother wouldn't have laid a finger on me. I used to test my aunt's patience to the limit and play tricks on her, I'm sorry to say, partly because my mother let me away with murder. That said, I was very fond of my aunt despite her attempts to discipline me and if I ever found myself in trouble or in an unusual bind of some sort, it was to my aunt that I went first, rather than to my mother. I might have been just a child then but in a strange kind of way, I think I already understood that my mother had enough troubles of her own without me adding to her worries in any way. I don't remember that there was ever a cross word exchanged between my aunt and my mother in all those years. I think my mother understood that my aunt was always right. Aunt Máire was a great worker around the house. She'd have a job done while another woman would still be thinking about it. Even out in the fields, binding corn or planting small potatoes, for example, she could match any man work-wise. All I have to do is close my eyes and I can see my aunt again now as plain as day. It is as if she was here again moving up and down the same kitchen that I am writing these words in now, her back as straight as a whip, her perfect nose and her curly-black hair. She was always happy and full of the joys of life, her teeth shining bright. I can see her walking up and down the floor of this kitchen as if it was only yesterday, the heels of her shoes tapping out their swift rhythm as she went about her daily work.

I wasn't sent to school until I was seven years of age and I had a lonely enough life when I was a young child. I didn't have any brother or sister and there was no other child living close to me that I could play with. I used to play by myself most of the time. A small stream ran downhill alongside the ditch that ran parallel with the boreen outside our gate and many's the hour I spent playing out there, building little bridges and walkways across the stream and trying to catch the small trout, the loach and the eels that swam there, albeit that I was afraid of the eels. There was algae in the stream also, little thin filaments that would have reminded you of the hairs on a horse's mane and I used to imagine sometimes that they were alive. Liam Beilbhí used to tell me that these filaments were actually pieces from the manes of real water-horses and that they actually came alive after they had been in the water for a long time. To test out his theory, I actually placed some ribs of hair from our mare beneath a rock in the river. I kept a close eye on these ribs of hair for days on end but even if I'd stayed there forever, they would never have come alive I'm afraid. Although I was very young then, I had my doubts about Liam Beilbhí and his stories about those supposedly magic filaments of water. He told me to be careful when I was walking barefoot in the water and to watch for what was called the 'conach' in Irish – because it would attach itself to my feet and suck out my blood. I never actually saw any of these 'conach's' in the stream and it was when I was older that I learned what Liam Beilbhí was referring to; he was referring to the creature that is called a 'leech' in English.

I was very interested in all the wild birds that were in the area when I was young, the sparrows, robins, thrushes, blackbirds, wrens, fieldfares and lapwings, and the same with the swallows and the larks during the summer. My aunt Máire taught me the names of all the different birds. Liam Beilbhí made a cage for me to catch the birds in and the special stick for the springing trap that ensured they were trapped once they went in. I'd have it set up outside in the garden when the weather was frosty and it was mainly sparrows and robins that I caught with it. I even caught a few blackbirds in it at one stage and I was thinking of getting a special box made to keep them in but my aunt Máire persuaded me to set every bird, whether big or small, free from the cage. It was always said that you should never trap a small bird or keep it in a cage so that it was unable to fly, and that it was better to kill a bird rather than do this. My aunt's words influenced me greatly and, ever since then, I've always hated the sight of a bird trapped in a cage. It was with awe that I listened to the call of the first cuckoo each Spring. You'd hear the cuckoo calling every day during Summer here in An Gleann. There were plenty of trees and wooded areas in An Gleann and such places are always a favourite haunt of the cuckoo. My aunt Máire explained to me how the cuckoo doesn't make its own nest but lays its eggs in the nest of another. As a child, I was always hoping to find a nest with a young cuckoo in it but I never did. It wasn't until I was a middle-aged man that I came across a young cuckoo in a sparrow's nest in the wall of the hayloft. Buachaill an Dreoilín ('The Wren's Boy') is what one of these sparrows is called here in An Gleann. Old-Risteard Ó Siadhaile, the carpenter, and Dic's father, often came to our house visiting and socializing when I was a child. He, my grandfather, and Liam Beilbhí, the man who worked as a labourer for us, would be chatting and storytelling around the fire. Ghost stories and the like were the main stories sean-Risteard told and he was a great man to tell a story. I remember that my aunt Máire was always mocking and joking about all his stories relating to spirits and ghosts. She could never understand, she'd say, how everyone only ever saw these ghosts when they were on their way home from the pub but no-one ever saw them on their way there. I didn't understand it at the time but she meant that it was the drink that was responsible for these apparitions and ghost sightings, of course. I would be sitting on the inside of my grandfather, right in the corner, as sean-Risteard told his stories and I believed every word of them, even if my aunt Máire didn't. In fact, I was so frightened on listening to these stories that I wouldn't dare venture outside the door of the house once night fell for fear that 'Petticoat Loose' might grab me by the back of the head; not for all of Déamar's gold would I have stepped outside on those evenings. After my grandfather died, sean-Risteard didn't come visiting in the evenings to us anymore. In fact, as I got older, it was me who went to Ó Siadhaile's house fairly often on winter evenings instead. Other neighbours would always be there too and normally sean-Risteard told the same stories that he had related previously in our house. The Ó Siadhaile's house became a great house for callers and socializing, and I was often in a cold sweat after listening to an evening of sean-Risteard Ó Siadhaile's spooky stories. He shouldn't really have been telling stories that were so vivid and frightening when there were children like me present. The country people aren't as given to ghost stories today as they were once, although there a few people here in An Gleann who still love them. I suppose that older customs and traditions always survive longer in a place as remote as Gleann Chárthainn. The glen here is surrounded by mountains on each side, the highest ones on the west and the north, with the ones to east and the south slightly lower. From the window of the kitchen here I can see Cruachán and An Dá Maoil. These mountains are the highest in the vicinity of An Gleann. When there is rain on the way, the first sign you see of it is the mist drifting in a south-westerly direction across the shoulder of Cruachán. The fog comes in small ethereal wisps in across the mountains here and many's the time I spent stretched out on the kitchen table, my two elbows on the window ledge and my hands propped beneath my chin as I stared up at the hills.

As the seams of cloud drifted in one after the other across the hills, I imagined them as the riders of white horses, cantering quickly across the horizon. Where had they come from? Where were they going? And why the great hurry? These were the questions I tried to find answers to. The layers of cloud came closer and advanced in greater numbers, moving ever-closer together until before very long, the entire hill was hidden beneath a veil of mist.

I imagined that those hills had a soul, a soul that became lonely like me from time to time. In the end, Cruachán and I were soul-mates and had an intimate bond with each other, so that the mountain was the first thing that I checked upon every day, when I got out of bed and went to the window. I thought about that mountain a lot during those fine summer days. What lay on the other side of it? I'd hear my grandfather's talk of Tír na nÓg (The Land of Everlasting Youth) and although I didn't understand everything that he told me about that world of wonder, I still imagined sometimes that I could just about see it in the distance, way beyond the peak of Cruachán. The fact that I was alone and had no other children for company was the reason for many of these thoughts. I think it is a bad thing for a child to be raised all alone like this. Such a child has too much time alone with his thoughts and spends too much of his living moments in that lonely inner world of the mind and of memory. There are elements of such a lonely childhood that stay with someone for the rest of their lives. Such an individual has too fertile an imagination and is prone to worrying about things that never actually happen. Not unnaturally, I didn't understand any of this when I was a child, and only came to such a realization years later.

When I stood in the strip of clay that led into the field on the other side of the road, I'd spot the young Burkes from Mónach Buí out playing together in the field behind their house; there were four of them, two boys and two girls, and I'd hear their shouts and laughter. I'd have given anything to be over there playing with them and I'd envy them their life of play and company and compare it to the lonely days that I had all on my own. I never once thought of heading down to play with them, however. They were just four fields away, but I knew that we in Lios na Faille didn't mix with the Burkes of Mónach Buí. That's just the way things were. Although we too were Burkes – the Burkes of Lios and Séamus de Búrc was my father's name, and although both our families were related to one another far out – we didn't associate with one another. Not when I was a child, and not for many years afterwards. I didn't understand what had caused the two families to fall out with one another the first day ever, not until Risteard Ó Siadhaile explained the story to me many years later.

MY FIRST SUIT OF CLOTHES

I was gone seven years of age when I was first sent to school. The first thing I had to get for this was a new suit. I hadn't ever worn trousers any time prior to this. The boys didn't wear trousers here in An Gleann that time, not until they were seven or eight years of age. They wore coats or dresses, the same as the girls. There was a big difference between those days and today in terms of the clothes that young boys wore. No sooner are young lads out of the cot now but they are wearing trousers. Not everyone had shoes and socks then either. I remember one lad who went to school with me regularly and he never had any socks or shoes. He walked along the furze track that his father had laid as a path through the fields and the skin on the soles of his feet were so tough that no thorn would pierce them. That wasn't the case with my feet, however, as I always had socks and shoes on me. I might take them off the odd time during the summer, but I wasn't much good for walking in my bare feet. I just wasn't used to it and my feet were too tender.

In those days, the tailor went around from house to house working. Ruaidhrí Eoghain was the tailor who made my first suit of clothes. I remember him well as he often worked in our house. A small swarthy stump of a man, he wore a grey-flecked beard and because he was lame, he used a walking stick. Ruaidhrí Ó Corbáin was his name but everyone referred to him as Ruaidhrí Eoghain or the lame tailor. It was always behind his back that they called him this, of course. They were afraid to say it to his face, in case they got a belt of the stick down across the shoulders from him. Either that or he'd give them a good tongue-lashing straight to their faces, one that they wouldn't forget in a hurry. Despite this, the local blackguards and wits were always trying to get a rise out of him whenever they got the chance. Here's one story that I often heard about Ruaidhrí Ó Corbáin. During the war between the French and the Prussians, he was drinking in Marty's pub one day in Baile an Droichid. He was very hostile to the Prussians. As he left the pub, half-drunk, he came across Peaid na Brídighe and Tomás Dhomhnaill – two chancers who were always clowning around the parish – they were hiding in behind the ditch on the other side of the road, as Ruaidhrí walked past. When he was gone about fifty yards up the road, they shouted out at the top their voices. 'There's the Prussian!' Ruaidhrí came to a stop and shouted back 'There's the Frenchman' and he walked back to where the first shout had come from. The shout came from in behind the ditch again – 'There's the Frenchman!' but Ruaidhrí couldn't see anyone because they were hiding. 'There's the Frenchman', he called out again but he couldn't see anyone and so, in the end, he went back up the road again. No sooner was he gone up the road but the shout 'There's the Prussian!' came out again from behind the ditch. Ruaidhrí responded and down again with him and he shouting out 'There's the Frenchman' three or four times. He was so mad that he threw his hat down on the road and jumped on it with fury and threatened bloody murder on anyone who took the Prussian side in the war. In the end he had to leave without getting any satisfaction, however. He was fifty yards back up the road again and the lads shouted out 'There's the Prussian' again and back down with Ruaidhrí again. Up and down the road the poor man went, hobbling along on his lame leg; he was at this for the guts of half of an hour before the two blackguards decided to leave him alone.

My aunt Máire bought the material for my suit in Clonmel and it was left wrapped in paper, on the top of the cupboard at home for a few months, until the tailor next made his rounds. I'd look up at it first thing most mornings, and hope that this was the day when the tailor would make his appearance. Eventually, on the morning when he did arrive, we heard him call out in greeting to us from the threshold of the front-door. His voice was rough-sounding and deceptive. When you first heard his voice, you imagined that he was a big monster of a man – that was the kind of voice that he had. But when you actually saw him then, you realized that he was a very small man; he was barely five feet tall. He was also scrawny and thin. You could say that his voice and his body didn't go together really. Once he had his breakfast eaten Ruaidhrí stood me in the middle of the floor to take my measurements. Chatting to my grandfather all the while, he praised me as he measured me up and down – telling me that I was a great boy and how alike my poor late father I looked. He whispered the measurements to himself as he talked – 'eight-and-a-half inches', 'fourteen inches' and so forth. It would be later before I understood the meaning of these figures and measurements. Ruaidhrí was illiterate but he was able to read the marks and figures on the measuring tape. All told, the poor man's measurements were probably not the most accurate in the world. Back then, however, especially in a place as remote as An Gleann, people weren't too worried if their clothes were a bit uneven in length here and there. When he was finished measuring Ruaidhrí would spread his new cloth out on the table, drawing lines on it with a piece of chalk. Then he cut out the pieces of cloth he required using a big scissors. Once he had the cloth cut to his satisfaction, he would remove his shoes and sit up on the kitchen table to begin his sewing. I always marvelled at how agile he was and the way he tucked his legs crossways beneath him. I used to try and imitate him sometimes but I couldn't seem to manage it for very long. My legs would cramp up within a matter of minutes. Ruaidhrí didn't have a sewing machine; no-one had head of such a device at this time and so he did all his sewing by hand. Despite her best efforts, my aunt was unable to explain to me why the tailor's thimble was open at the end of it. Ruaidhrí would chat away non-stop as he worked. He'd have all the news from the parish and if he found himself on his own, you'd hear him humming songs tunelessly to himself – 'Seán an Bhríste Leathair' (Seán of the Leather Trousers) and 'Aonach Bhearna na Gaoithe' (The Wind-Gap Fair) were the two tunes he always repeated. He lived on the northern side of the mountain in Leacain and when he was working anywhere in An Gleann, he always called in to visit us on his way home.

I looked great once I had the suit on, although I felt very strange. I felt like I was stuffed tight into myself somehow in a way that you didn't up feel when you wore the coat-dresses. They felt much looser and freer. That said, I was more than willing to put with any initial discomfort I felt in the new suit. After all, I felt like a real man now. When I stood there, hands in my trouser pockets, I felt as big and as important as Dónall Ó Briain. That in itself was more than enough to compensate for any discomfort I felt with the new clothes. I can't remember now what colour that lovely suit was but I still remember the smell of the cloth. Strangely, even today, all these years later, all it takes for me is to get the smell of new clothes in a shop somewhere and all those memories come flooding back. I am immediately transported back to my childhood long ago – to the same kitchen where I now sit writing these words. I see it all clearly in my mind's eye, the tailor sitting astride the table and me standing proudly in my new suit in the middle of the kitchen floor. Even if it is just for half a minute I feel proud as punch all over again, the same pride that came over me all those years ago. It is strange how some memories remain with people and return even years later. Often these memories are just minor details or incidents while the most important recollections of all have disappeared, as if in a dream. Stranger still is the way that the simplest taste or smell, or musical tune can bring the past back to life again. An incident or event that occurred even years ago can re-surface as fresh and new as if it happened only yesterday. When I was about ten years of age, Dic Ó Siadhaile, Seán Baróid and I went out to Cúil Mhóin (the turf-back) picking blueberries. We each had a tin can and we weren't long finding them. We ate our fill of them. Eating blueberries can give you a mighty appetite. Their effect is as bad as the 'féar gorta' (hungry grass) that can come over you all of a sudden when you are out in the hills. As a consequence, we were all very weak and dizzy with the hunger by the time we got home to the Baróid's house. The sun was going down in the evening sky and Seán's mother was washing butter in a big vat outside the dairy. She had just finished making the butter and understood our plight immediately. 'I'd say that you're hungry children' she said to us. 'You wouldn't say 'no' to a cut slice of bread and butter, I'd say'. She went into the kitchen and returned with three large slices of soda bread and a knife. She took some butter from the vat and spread it thickly across each slice. At that moment, I felt certain that I had never eaten anything as tasty in my life as that bread just then, smoothed as it was with fresh butter. Even today, sometimes, when I taste fresh butter, an image comes into my mind of that afternoon long ago. I see Seán's mother, her sleeves rolled back on her arms and she stirring the butter with the churn-stick and Seán himself standing in the lea of the front-door, the red rays of the sun shining across his face, Dic Ó Siadhaile crouched near the door, hunkered down near Seán's feet. As for me, I'm leaning against the upturned donkey-cart just opposite the two lads. All three of us are eagerly chewing our food and not a word out of any of us.

It took me just a few days to get used to my new suit and it was decided that I would start school on the following Monday in Baile and Droichid. Baile and Droichid is two miles from our house. I was very familiar with it as we regularly passed it on our way to Mass on Sundays. On Sundays, we attended Mass in Baile na hAbhann which was three miles north of us. There were just a few Sundays in the previous three years that my mother and my aunt hadn't brought me to Mass with them on the horse and cart. The white mare would be out in front and us sitting in behind on the cart, small piles of hay beneath us. I hated the thought of school. As mentioned earlier, I had very little experience of other children and I was really shy and fearful of going in amongst a group of children who were strangers to me. I couldn't understand for the life of me why we needed to bother with school at all. It made no sense to me and I was more than happy to stay at home – even if I was the lone child in the household. I was quite happy to spend my days collecting birds' nests and playing in the stream at the side of the boreen, staring out at the hills roundabout. Of course, there had been times when I'd spotted the young de Búrca (Burke) children out playing in the fields near their house and would have given anything to be out there playing with them. My attitude towards company had hardened at this point, however, and I was generally quite happy to stay at home on my own – anything, rather than have to go to school. When you get older, you have a different perspective on things and a clearer picture emerges of why certain things are obligatory and beneficial in this life that didn't seem that way at the time. It is different when you are seven years of age, however. Often, young children have private worries in their heads, worries that they never share with anyone else, because no-one would understand them. For example, when I told the adults in the house that I was quite happy to stay at home with them and not to bother with school at all – they just laughed and teased me. Little did they know that, this teasing and slagging really hurt me to the quick. It was like a spear going through my heart. I had no option but to grin and bear it, however; I knew that none of them would take a blind bit of notice of my pleas to them. In the end, my fate was sealed. I had to go to school and that was the end of it.

My First Day at School

On the Sunday evening before school, my mother and my aunt had a row about who would bring me to school the next day. My aunt said that my mother should accompany me to school, by rights; in the end however, my aunt gave in to my mother's requests and said that she would bring me to school. My mother 'buttered her up' until she agreed to do so. This resolution to this discussion gave me peace of mind because I preferred to have my aunt with me anyway. I knew that I would feel more secure in myself if she accompanied me on that first stressful day going to school. I got little sleep the night before that first Monday. The morning duly came around and I put on my new suit. After breakfast, my face and hands were washed and my hair was combed. My schoolbag was placed on my shoulders and off we went – my aunt and I. We walked down the length of the boreen until we hit the main road. A few hundred yards from the corner where the two roads meet was the house where Risteard Ó Siadhaile, the carpenter, lived. His son Dic was already standing on the edge of the road, waiting for us. Dic was nine months older than me and had already been attending school for two years. I often met Dic at Mass or on our way home and we often gave him and his mother a lift on our cart. Despite this, I was still fairly shy with him on such occasions. I tended to be very shy in the company of other people until I got to know them well. This would be a personality trait that would follow me all my life. Because of this, some people considered me a dour and stand-offish type of person when it was actually my shyness that held me back. People can't really change the true nature of their personality or the character that they are born with.

The three of us set off along the main road, Dic chatting incessantly to me. I wasn't very talkative at all, however; I was really anxious and upset and I just couldn't really focus on what he was saying or get any words out. It felt like we'd only been travelling for a short time when we were suddenly crossing the bridge and the school loomed before us, right there at the edge of the road. It consisted of a large building that had once been used as a mill. The bottom end of the school skirted the road and it was this end that was the entrance to the boy's school. The name of the school was written in English in white paint, across a blackboard which was attached to the wall about a foot above the schoolroom door. The girl's school was upstairs from the boy's school on the first floor. A door led up to this from the bottom of a stone staircase. There is no trace of that old school left now; a new school was built in Baile an Droichid more than twenty years ago. When we got there, my aunt told Dic to ask the schoolmaster to come out for a moment. The racket that came from inside the classroom when the door opened frightened the life out of me. We stood outside and a few minutes later the schoolmaster appeared, shutting the door behind him. He shook hands with my aunt. 'How are you Miss Burke?' he said. They chatted together in English for a short while. The schoolmaster was a low-sized, stocky man, who sported a short black beard that was flecked with grey. His hair was fairly long at the back. His name was Seán De Paor (John Power) but the schoolchildren always referred to him as An Paorach (Power). That is what everyone in the local community called him, although they never called him that to his face. My aunt and he chatted for a while as I stood close to her, a tight grip on her dress, all the while. She told the schoolmaster my first name, my surname and my date of birth and she apologized to him for not sending me to school earlier, explaining that I wasn't strong enough to make the daily journey to and from the school prior to this. When she was finished speaking with him, she shook hands with the schoolmaster and said goodbye, telling me to be a good boy as she did so. Then she left. As she turned the corner and disappeared out of sight, a wave of sadness overwhelmed me. It was as if a great darkness had engulfed my world and drowned out the light forever. The master took me by the hand and led me into the classroom. You'd have sworn that I had two heads, the way all the other boys stared at me as I made my way into the class. My face reddened with embarrassment. The master brought me over and put me sitting next to Dic Ó Siadhaile. I don't remember too much about what happened for the rest of the morning and until we were let out to play at lunchtime. The big lads kicked a football around in the field behind the school while we younger lads played outside on the road. I had a few slices of bread and butter in my small schoolbag but I didn't feel very hungry. Very few children had butter on their bread back then; most children just ate their bread dry. If anyone had a halfpenny in their pocket back then, they'd use it to buy half-a-loaf of bread in Máire an tSuibhnigh's shop. The truth is that halfpennies were hard to come by for most schoolchildren in those days, however. Indeed, I was a rich man myself that first day at school because I had four pence in my pocket. My mother had given me two pence as I left the house that morning and Liam Beilbhí, our workman, had given me a penny. Dic's mother had also given me a penny returning from Mass the previous day. Dic brought me into Máire an tSuibhnigh's shop and I bought two pence worth of the sweets then known as 'steotar'. You could get two large rocks of these for a penny. Back in the school, some of the pupils were asking me for bits of these rocks and I would gladly have given away both of them in their entirety as I was afraid to refuse these other children – except that Dic Ó Siadhaile shooed them all away, all except two or three people who were relations of his. Seán Baróid was included among them. That was the first time I ever met Seán Baróid but from that day on he and Dic and I were bosom buddies. Dic was still very young then but he already burned with the energy and love of life that has characterized him right up to the present day. He threatened bloody revenge that day on anyone who dared make life difficult for me from then on. We were called back into the classroom after the break but I remember very little about that first day in the class; it's all like a fuzzy dream now. I know that I wasn't put learning any lessons that day. I was just told to sit next to Dic for the rest of the day. Wasn't I delighted when we were let out of class at the end of that first day and I spent the rest of the evening telling my aunt and my mother all about the school. A joke that was told against me for a good while afterwards was the fact that I expressed surprise at the strange 'lay-out' of the classroom on that first day – a room without a dresser or a table or a sink anywhere in sight. The next day I began my learning. My aunt Máire and my mother had been teaching me the basics at home for a good while before this and when the master saw that I was able to read most of the first book, he immediately put me into the first class alongside Dic and Seán and I was very happy about this. Seán was a good scholar. Poor Dic was always only average when it came to book-learning; he was very intelligent in other ways, however. He had an amazing knowledge and understanding of wild birds and animals and their ways. No-one could match him when it came to carpentry work; he was by far the best tradesman in the area. There are two wooden cart wheels still here in Lios na Faille that he made forty-eight years ago and they are as good today as they were on the first day. I got used to school after a while and I didn't want to stay at home at all after that. Schoolwork didn't faze me too much when I put my mind to it. That said, I was a bit lazy and often had a tendency to put things on the long finger. I never had any trouble keeping up with the rest of the class and I was happy enough with that. English was the language in which all the subjects were taught in schools then and the language that was used at all times. There were no schools anywhere then in which Irish was used. My aunt Máire, my grandfather and Liam Beilbhí all spoke Irish fluently although my mother wasn't as fluent as the others; everyone in An Gleann could speak Irish back then, however. It was the language that almost everyone still used then, other than some of the younger generation who were already attending school. What happened then was that the adults began to speak English to their children. This change between the generations killed the Irish language faster than anything else did. When my mother and my grandfather and my aunt were chatting among themselves, they only ever used Irish – particularly when they were discussing anything that they didn't want me to know about. They were only fooling themselves if they thought I couldn't understand every word that they were saying, however. Liam Beilbhí had a story about the day I'd fallen over while climbing the stile outside. I got a cut on my head and was bleeding. Liam was out in the meadow and he came running over when he heard me shouting.

'What happened to you in God's name?' said Liam.

'Dár cnís! (By the Holy!)', I called out, 'I'm dead'.

That was the exclamation that Liam always used and I'd picked it up from him. Although I still have the scar from that injury on the back of my head, I don't remember anything at all about that fall now. That's not surprising really because I was only four years old when it happened. At that time, Irish people had a very bad attitude towards the Irish language. They were ashamed of the language really. A few days before I first attended school, for example, I overheard my mother, my grandfather and my aunt Máire discussing me while sitting around the fire. 'He'll make a show of us when he's speaking Irish at school', my grandfather said. When I look back now, I think that the years I spent at school in Baile an Droichid were the happiest years of my life, even if I didn't realize it at the time. God granted me a good intelligence and the schoolwork was never a big hassle for me. Despite his crankiness I can honestly say that Power, the schoolmaster, never once used the stick on me for not doing my homework. That's not to say that he didn't give me a hiding a few times for other reasons, needless to say.

Power had a bad temper when he got annoyed. Mind you, he often had good reason to get angry. After all, in Baile an Droichid school, he had to deal with some of the biggest blackguards that ever walked the earth. When I was at school there, there were at least four or five lads and you wouldn't have put anything past them. If you didn't impose some discipline on them, God knows what they'd have got up to. Sometimes, Power went too far, however. He was particularly tough on anyone who was absent from school, for example. He'd nearly kill the poor devils when he got his hands on them. He would make the child who was to be punished climb onto the back of another so that he'd have a better angle to beat them from. Then he'd grab a hold of the child with the left hand and lash them on the backside with the stick that was in his right hand. At that time, many of the schoolchildren had various patches and bits of pieces of cloth sewn over the backside of their trousers deliberately to take the sting out of the lash of the stick. Power's wife taught in the girl's school that was upstairs on the first floor of the school building. She was a kind and gentle person. Her pupils were very fond of her and she rarely laid a finger on them. Some of the culprits who were being beaten by Power used to take advantage of her kind nature by roaring out at the top of their voices and pretending that they were in even worse pain than they actually were. They'd let out these horrific screams and she would come rushing downstairs. No sooner did Power see her passing the window than he would stop using the stick on whoever he was lashing. The following story gives an insight into the type of man that Power was – the hard inner core there was to him. Two boys had been absent from school for a few days. Peatsaí Buitléir and Tomás Ó Muirgheasa; I remember both of them well. Peatsaí hated school so much that he once tried to break his foot beneath the wheels of the cart so that he wouldn't have to go at all. One morning, his father, Séamus Mór arrived with his mule and cart and Peaitsaí whom he had tied up with a rope in the back of the cart. Séamus Mór was a big rough man and he was in a furious temper as he untied Peatsaí and led him into the school, holding him by the ear. He told the teacher in harsh voice that he wasn't leaving until he'd watched the master give Peatsaí a good hiding with the stick, one that would flay the skin off of him. The master put Peatsaí sitting down and then went outside the door to his father. Whatever he said to Séamus Mór seemed tó pacify him as he went home without seeing the beating. He was barely five minutes gone when Tomás Ó Muirgheasa's mother arrived to the school, holding Tomás by the hand. She began chatting to the master and implored him to accept poor little Tomás's apology for his misdemeanour and that he would be a good boy from then on.

The master didn't promise her anything and the mother eventually went on her way again. She was gone barely one hundred yards down the road when he gave poor Tomás an awful hiding. Worse luck for him, no-one came to save him. The schoolmistress didn't hear him at all. The schoolmaster didn't lay a finger on Peatsaí. Maybe Power knew what he was doing, however, and maybe there was a method in what he did that time – because I don't remember that either Peatsaí or Tomás ever went missing from school again.

Power was an excellent teacher. You'd learn things from him despite yourself, that's how good he was. If Power couldn't teach you, then no-one could. He'd explain something to you twenty times if he thought that you didn't understand it. If you pretended that you understood something or other when you didn't, however, and if he found out later that you hadn't understood it, he'd give you a tongue-lashing that you wouldn't forget in a hurry. And he was the man who could cut someone down with his words, I can tell you. That said, many of the pupils who passed through his hands were very successful in later life, both in Ireland and abroad, and afterwards I heard some of them saying that they had done well because of what they had learned at the school in Baile an Droichid and that they were very grateful for it.

As I mentioned earlier, they didn't teach any Irish in the school at Baile an Droichid then, and whatever I know about reading and writing Irish, it wasn't there that I learned it.

My First Trip to Clonmel

They promised me at home that I would be allowed to go to Clonmel as soon as I had started school. I had a few months of school under my belt before that promise was fulfilled, however. My grandfather had to go to Clonmel to get a pair of shoes made. I remember my aunt Máire and my mother debating – as usual – who would accompany my grandfather on the journey. My mother made every excuse under the sun as to why she couldn't go, however, and my aunt had to give into her in the end. Unless it was really urgent, my poor mother never really wanted to leave the house or go to Clonmel. I myself knew for a week beforehand that I'd be going to Clonmel on the following Saturday and so I spent all that week boasting with my small friends at school about the impending trip. Dic Ó Siadhaile told me that he was going there the same day also with his father. His father was going to Clonmel to get a load of timber and Dic had to keep a hold of the mules' reins while his father was getting the timber in the mill. The noise of the saw would have frightened the mule otherwise, and she'd have bolted. Dic had been in Clonmel many times previous to this. Compared to me, he was a seasoned traveller.

Liam Beilbhí and Dic's father both gave me a penny to buy a loaf of bread for the Mayor's dog. My grandfather and my aunt Máire described the Mayor's dog to me. They told me that it was the custom then that everyone visiting Clonmel for the first time had to give a loaf of bread to this dog. Dic, the blackguard, also warned me that this dog was as big as a calf and that if I didn't have the loaf of bread ready for it, that it would eat me instead. I wanted to bring a loaf of bread with me from the house at home but my aunt Máire said that that wouldn't do at all – that I had to buy the loaf in the town.

I was up early that Saturday morning. I don't think I slept much the night before, to be honest, I was so excited about the trip. It was a beautiful morning, the sky clear and cloudless.

We were due to leave the house at eight o'clock and Liam Beilbhí already had the white mare harnessed and the cart ready for the road, and a bag of straw lying across the cart as a seat. My aunt Máire sat up on the bag of straw and I sat opposite my grandfather, my legs stretched out in front of me. I wanted to take in everything around me as we moved through the countryside and I suppose that I felt sitting out in front with my grandfather was better than sitting on the back with my aunt Máire. Off we went down the boreen, the white mare trotting along at a lively pace. Soon, we were out on the main road and I was really excited. At long last, I was on my way to Clonmel. Passing Ó Siadhaile's house, Maighréad told us that Dic and his dad had left an hour earlier. I was delighted to hear that Dic was ahead of us. Both of us would have a great time together once we met up in Clonmel. Wasn't Dic really lucky that the Mayor's dog wasn't worrying him the way it was worrying me? We moved down through the bottom of the glen and out Bearna an Mhadra (the dog's gap) and from there we passed close to An Tonnóg and onto Baile an Droichid. The old school was silent and deserted and there was no-one in the village except Seáinín Ó Deá who was standing in the doorway of the shop leaning against the lintel. The blacksmith was building up the fire in the forge. He was working the bellows and the smoke was billowing thickly from the chimney of the forge. As we passed the door of the forge, I saw the red flame of the forge-fire reflected in the blacksmith's face.

We continued on to Baile na hAbhann and every step of the road was a source of great wonder to me. I couldn't have been happier as I studied every tree and bush along the way. I knew the road as far as Baile na hAbhann like the back of my hand since I travelled it every Sunday on my way to Mass but once we crossed over the bridge, it was as if I was in a 'foreign' country. I'd often marvelled at the size of this bridge from a distance but now I was actually passing over it for the first time. It was much bigger and had more arches than any other bridge I'd ever seen; it was even bigger than Droichead na Cille in An Gleann. If you looked sideways, you could see an Droichead Mór from Ard an tSean Phóna and count the bridge's five 'eyes'. As we trotted along, my eyes surveyed the entire countryside – the houses, the big fields, the crossroads and the water-pump at the edge the road. I was fascinated by all the sights we passed and I had my poor aunt Máire and my grandfather tormented with questions about everything we saw, especially the water-pump, as we didn't have anything like this in An Gleann; neither did we have need for such a pump. My grandfather liked nothing better than describing all the sights and the history of each place, we passed through. He was explaining everything in minute detail and it was my aunt who could appreciate all this information better than I did given that I was still just seven years of age. I was too distracted to take in everything that he said that day. In later years, I would glean much more knowledge about many of the places that we passed through that day and I have included some of that history in the pages of this book.

My grandfather showed us the remains of a 'big house' with a long 'avenue' leading up to it, the avenue surrounded by fields on each side. The house had a run-down look and abandoned look about it. About half of it was just an empty shell now with the roof gone; there was no-one living there anymore. He told us that the people who lived there once had owned a carriage pulled by four horses. They'd once had their own private grounds for hunting in and had also owned hundreds of acres of land around the area. It was they who had built the wall that skirted the road on the northern side which was a mile long. The iron gates leading into the land had pillars topped by semi-circular-shaped pieces of stone and yet the walls that skirted the fields within were all falling down in places and had rough gaps knocked into them now where there should have been gates. The other walls that had once had pillars at regular intervals were now pillar-less and where once there had been great iron gates, there were now only new-built ditches made of random rocks. The Butler-Lowe's had once owned this estate. They had lived the high life of pomp and extravagance however, and had become bankrupt in the end. Eventually, they'd lost everything that they'd owned under the 'Encumbered Estates Act'. One of the men in the family had enlisted in the army as a regular soldier. When they'd read out the names at roll-call, however, he wouldn't answer to the name of 'Richard Lowe'. He refused to do so, insisting that they use his double-barrelled surname. Eventually the army colonel heard what was going on and he ordered that the man's full name be called out each time. He was always called 'Richard Butler Lowe' from then on. After my grandfather had finished telling us this anecdote, he pointed an iron gate out to us that was on the western side of the road which had a series of rocks leading up to a small plinth to its side. He told us that there used to be a spirit (ghost) living at that gate and that it was this ghost that had broken Micil Mhártan's leg one night when, on returning from the fair, he had challenged her to a fight. I knew Micil Mhártan. He was lame and always carried a stick. I hadn't known until that day what had caused him to be lame however, even if I had heard Risteard Ó Siadhaile describing the ghost of Geata na Staighrí many times. The next 'big house' that we passed was the residence owned by the lord at of Cnoc Lochta. It was situated a little way in off the road near the banks of a river. My grandfather said that the castle there was still owned by the lord of Cnoc Lochta but that his antecedents had been much richer than he now was. Like many of the English gentry in Ireland, they had blown all of their money on parties and debauchery. The last of them who had once owned considerable wealth, a Colonel Green had been big into gambling. He'd once bet a thousand pounds on a card-game and on a horse-race. Years later, one of his sons was reduced to waiting with the horses and carriages outside the hotels in the town and doing card tricks at race meetings to make a living. The next big bridge we crossed over was Droichead Áth na Scairbhighe and then we skirted along by the river on Bóthar na Coille. This road passed through a big wood for a distance of about three miles and it was a really lonely stretch of road. There is another road that goes from Cnoc Lochta to Clonmel other than this one, a road that passes on the northern side of the river. Bóthar na Mainistreach is what they call this latter road because there was once a big abbey there which the English destroyed. It wasn't my grandfather who told me this story and I'm not sure that he knew anything about this to be honest. It was years later that I heard about this. The truth is that we learned nothing at school in those days about life in the older Gaelic Ireland. I remember the names of two houses that skirted Bóthar na Coille then – 'Tigh na dtrí dhoras' (the house with the three doors) and 'Tigh beag na Coille' (the small house in the woods) is what they were called. The first house was a big house, big and long. It had three doors or entrances and three families lived there. It is still standing there today but there are only two entrances to the building now. That house was situated between the woods and the bridge. As indicated by its name, the second house edged the road but was deep in the middle of the woods. It was in a very lonely spot because there were no-one living within a few miles of it no matter what direction you travelled in. The man who lived there was charged with looking after the woods. There is nothing left of that house now except the ruins of one low wall.

We kept going and the first sign of the big town that I saw was the church-spire. As we came closer to the town, I saw hundreds of slate-roofed houses. My eyes were agog as we arrived into the town. There seemed to be crowds of people everywhere on the streets, moving to and fro. It was hard to know where everyone was going and what they were all doing. We passed beneath a great arch and then we were on the main street of Clonmel. My grandfather drove the white mare in beneath a narrow arch and along a side-road. We dismounted inside in a wide meadow that had stables on either side of it. My father unharnessed the mare and led her into the stables while my aunt Máire took me by the hand and brought me down through the town. She kept a firm grip on my hand. There wasn't a word out of me. I just stared at everything around me, like someone who has just awoken from an amazing dream. My aunt Máire and I walked down this street and then the next, turning a corner here and a corner there. I began to get nervous that we wouldn't be able to find our way back again to where we had left the horse and cart. My aunt knocked on the door of a house and we were let in. The woman who owned the house was a maker of women's clothes and hats. She gave us a great welcome and told my aunt that I was the spit of my father. I can't remember what brought my aunt to this house but one thing I do remember distinctly is that there was a big tropical bird with a great twisted beak sitting on a perch up in the corner of the room, a chain attached to its foot. The thing that amazed me more than anything else about this bird, however, was that it was able to speak. The woman spoke to the bird and the bird was able to answer her. It frightened the life out of me to be honest. In the years since, I've seen parrots a couple of times and I've heard some of them saying things but I'll never forget the sight of that parrot on my first-ever trip to Clonmel. My aunt and I came down the main street again and we met up with my grandfather. Risteard Ó Siadhaile and Dic were with him. My aunt Máire bought some sweet cakes that had currants in them for Dic and I while my grandfather and Risteard went into the pub. My aunt told Dic and I to stay where we were and to wait for the two men to come out of the pub again; she headed up the street to somewhere else. The men were only inside a short while and when they came out my grandfather said that he had to go over to An Baile Gaelach [Irishtown, Clonmel] to get a pair of shoes made. Risteard said that he'd bring me and Dic up to see the train station while he was gone. Dic had been to the station before a few times and on our way up there, he tried to explain to me what a train was. I'm not sure that I took too much notice of him, however. I was too busy taking in all the other sights that were around us on the streets of the town. On arriving at the station, we went out onto the platform. Risteard was explaining how the train runs along on iron rails but, I don't know whether I was listening to him as dutifully as I should have been. I remember that he pointed out a white timber board that was like a sign hanging from a high pole. He told me to keep an eye on this timber board because when it fell down, the train was about to arrive.

Eventually the white board fell to the side and then I heard a sound like thunder and the ground shaking beneath my feet. A few moments later and I witnessed the most frightening thing that I'd ever seen. This enormous monster let a screech out of her that resounded in my ears and into the station she arrived in a cloud of smoke and steam. She came to a stop right opposite where we were standing. I don't remember rightly what happened then except that the doors opened and people came out of this great machine. Other people then climbed onto the train once the others had left, the doors closed and she let another screech out of her. Off she went on her way again, emitting those giant puffs of smoke. The sight of this great noisy machine had given me such a fright that it was a while before I was able to talk again. The many wonders that I witnessed in the train station that day remained a great source of conversation for me back home for months afterwards.

After the train station, we met with my grandfather and my aunt Máire and the three of us went to get our dinner in a small café that was situated in a basement, just below the level of the street. I don't remember what we had to eat that day; I suppose I was so excited at all the new wonders of the world that were everywhere around me that I didn't pay much attention to the food. Many of the townhouses in Clonmel had basements beneath them in those days. You could get food in some of them and in others there were tinkers and cobblers, and other similar tradesmen working. Nowadays, the same use isn't made of the basements in the townhouses anymore. Many of them are boarded up although you see the odd one that a pub might use to store their barrels of beer in.

After dinner, we met up with Dic again and his father told me him to bring me down to the quay, to show me the boats. The quayside on the river there wasn't far away and there were two big boats in on the quayside. Like the train, the boats too were a great marvel to me at that age; I had never seen a boat before and we watched as a group of men carried bags full of coal from one of them. They carried the bags of coal across the road to the tall buildings opposite the quay. People were coming and going from these tall buildings; it was a hive of activity and noise with horses-and-carts and people moving here and there and carrying thing. Dic and I walked down along the length of the quayside until we came to some huge mounds of timber. The last time he'd been on the quayside in Clonmel Dic told me, he'd seen men transferring these stores of timber onto one of the boats there. We were close to a big tall bridge there when I saw something else that amazed me. About twenty horses were walking along the edge of the river pulling a large boat or barge in unison. They passed beneath the bridge, one man standing in the prow of the boat and holding a long timber pole or tiller that was attached to the end of the boat and directing everything. I later learned that he was steering the boat and ensuring that it stayed in a straight line in the middle of the river.

I've been down along the quayside in Clonmel in the intervening years but the sight of the riverbank now only makes me sad. Today it is so empty and lonesome compared with the day when I was there as a boy when the place was a hive of activity. Now, the grass has invaded the quayside. Most of the tall buildings alongside are all boarded up and abandoned now, some of the windows sealed off with wooden boards while others just have big empty holes. It is years since any of the big ships carrying coal and the like that I saw that day have passed along the quayside. The only signs that they were ever there are the remains of the mooring posts along the quayside where the boats were once secured. I suppose those boats became too slow and too cumbersome for the life that we now live today.

On returning from the quay-side, Dic and I met up with my grandfather who had the mare harnessed and ready for the road. Sean-Risteard was up on the cart which was loaded down with timber. They were both full of chat and I knew by the two of them that they were well on it or 'maith go leor' after their few drinks in the pub. I'd often seen Liam Beilbhí after a few drinks and he was full of chat and fun like they were after he'd had a few drinks at the fair also. My aunt bought a 'pouch' of sweets for both Dic and I and when everything was ready, we set off for home again. I sat next to my aunt Máire on the bag of straw and we hadn't gone too far along the road when I felt my eyes closing despite myself. I leaned my head against my aunt's shoulder and fell into a deep sleep. I didn't wake again until I heard the wheel of the cart on the road and we were within one hundred yards of our house at home. Liam Beilbhí was waiting for us in the meadow and he took the mare from my grandfather and stabled him.

'Yes now, little Séamus', he said to me, 'did you give any loaf of bread to the Mayor's dog?' It is hard to believe it but I hadn't even thought of that scary dog even once during the whole course of the day. The first I remembered about it was when Liam Beilbhí reminded me of it again; it was amazing really considering how much worrying I had done about that dog in the preceding weeks. I had been so taken in by all of the wonderful things that I saw that day that I clean forgot my worries concerning the dog. Needless to say, I found out later that all this stuff about the Mayor's dog and the loaf of bread was a just a load of codswallop that many young lads heading to Clonmel for the first time were told. This is a joke that you wouldn't hear anymore around the place.

There was probably never a traveller who returned from America or Australia who was as full of stories as I was for the first week or two after that first trip to Clonmel. The regular audience for my stories was my mother and my little pals at school. Over the years I've travelled to a good many places throughout Ireland – albeit that I was never abroad – and I've seen many beautiful sights on my travels – but these were all as nothing compared to that first-ever trip to Clonmel.

THE DEATH OF MY GRANDFATHER

I was attending school for about a year-and-a-half or so when my grandfather died. Needless to say, I didn't understand what death was, given that I was still just a child. Unfortunately, I have become too familiar with the nature of death in the intervening years. Many's the energetic young lad and girl in the bloom of their youth whom death has taken from us here in An Gleann over the years, never mind all the frail older people for whom death was probably partly a relief from all the tragedies and hardships of life. Death stole many of my closest relatives and friends and the only person left now from my generation is Dic Ó Siadhaile. Dic and I are like Oisín after the Fianna have gone. The two of us are out of step, so to speak, with life as it is lived around us today. We don't understand this modern lifestyle and it does not understand us either.

I remember that my grandfather took to his bed a few days prior to Christmas. It was the first time I had ever seen him sick or weak. The priest visited him and I remember everyone in the house and two or three of the neighbours watching over him for a couple of nights in succession. I was sent to bed, as I was too young. I remember waking up one night in my bed up on the loft and listening to the murmur of voices below me. I listened carefully and was surprised to hear the adults praying.

The door of the bedroom was half-open and a light was shining up from the kitchen downstairs. I got out of bed and went down the stairs in my night-shirt. There was no-one in the kitchen and I tiptoed over to the door of the room where my grandfather was. My mother was reading aloud from the prayer-book that my aunt Máire used when she went to Mass and my aunt was holding a lighted candle which she had placed in my grandfather's fist. Sean-Risteard Ó Siadhaile was sprinkling holy water from a bottle around the room and Liam Beilbhí was on his knees next to the bed and answering the Litany that my mother was reading from the book. My mother was reading from the book in English but I still remember that Liam Beilbhí's responses were in Irish. He kept repeating 'déan trócaire air, déan trócaire air' ('Have mercy on him, have mercy on him') in Irish. I can't remember now whether it was in Irish or English that the others responded to the prayers. No-one noticed me at the door. My mother finished the prayers and my aunt stood up, the lighted candle in her hand. The room was deathly quiet. I peered over at my grandfather. There was no movement out of him whatsoever. You'd have thought that he was in a deep sleep. The next moment, he began to pick at the bed-clothes with his fingers. A few minutes after this he gave a great sigh as if he was stretching himself out in the bed. No-one said a word for the next few minutes and then my grandfather opened his mouth and his eyes. Then he went completely still.

'He's gone', said Liam Beilbhí.

A terrible fear came over me.

I ran out into the kitchen and up the stairs and in under the bedcovers. I covered my head completely and began to shake with a fear that I did not fully understand. For a long time that night, I heard people coming and going in the room beneath me. Eventually however, I fell asleep. When I awoke, it was a bright day outside.

When I saw my grandfather the following morning, he was stretched out on the bed and wearing the brown habit. It was strange to see him lying there without the slightest movement out of him, a man who was always so full of life and energy before this. I couldn't understand what had happened. I just couldn't comprehend it properly at all.

My aunt Máire and Risteard Ó Siadhaile went to Clonmel with the white mare and the cold-box to get food and other supplies for the wake. For the rest of that day, the neighbours were in and out of the house on a constant basis, the women especially. I don't think there was any woman living in An Gleann who didn't visit the house at some stage while the wake was in progress. It was late that night by the time Risteard and my aunt returned from the town. The cold-box was full of food and I noticed some planks of wood on top of it. It wasn't long before the house began to fill with people. The majority of the people who came to the wake that night were young men and women. Dic Ó Siadhaile and I spent the night going in and out of the house, carrying water and turf scraws and blocks of timber for the fire. Just behind the door to the wake-room was a table where Micil Mhártan sat, cutting pieces of tobacco and filling clay pipes with it to divide out amongst the assembled people. The men smoked tobacco while the women took snuff from a plate. Before long, the kitchen was clouded with pipe-smoke. Every now and then, the snuff would be divided out amongst the women inside in the wake-room. There was no wake held in An Gleann when I was young that Micil Mhártan wasn't in charge of proceedings – i.e. in charge of the pipes and the tobacco. This is another old custom that disappeared a long time ago – even in An Gleann – the handing out of the pipes and tobacco to the people assembled there. That was a nice custom I think although it may have been the expensiveness of the tobacco that killed it off in the end.

They didn't play any games at my grandfather's wake although when I was a child, I heard the people talking sometimes about all of the games and amusements that were common at wakes years earlier. People sang songs at the wakes also although this was a tradition that was already in decline in An Gleann even when I was young. They didn't have any games or amusements at the wakes of anyone whose farm was a substantial size by this time, and although my grandfather was a good age by then, he had inherited the farm in addition to the necessity of providing for two women and a child. Needless to say, it was years later before I understood anything about these aspects of rural life then.

Dic Ó Siadhaile and I didn't rest for the rest of that night. We were in and out and keeping an eye on everything that was going on. We also spent a good bit of the night out in the shed watching Risteard the carpenter making the coffin. It was the planks of timber that I'd seen on the back of the cart that he was using for this job. A few other men were with him while he was doing this job and truth be told, the crack was better out in the shed than it was in the kitchen of the house. Risteard was a great wit once he had a few drinks in him. He and the other men who were with him were slagging one another and verbally sparring. It was like a competition to see who was the wittiest or the best speaker and the funniest story-teller and it was great to listen to them.

Whiskey was divided out amongst those who were assembled two or three times during the course of that night. Two people went around dividing it out, one with the jug and a glass in hand and the other holding a candle. The candle was lit so that the pourer could see what he was doing when he poured the whiskey into the glass. As each person was handed their new-filled glass they uttered a prayer – 'May God have mercy on he who is gone' or 'The blessings of grace on the soul of the departed' or some other similar prayer. That was what they would say before knocking back the whiskey. Everyone attending the wake was given tea also, although tea wasn't anywhere near as common in Ireland then as it is today. People often built up big debts so as to have the best of everything at the wake of someone belonging to them. They'd never want it to be said that they didn't wake their relative with style or give them a proper sending-off. The same is true today, of course, and it will probably always be this way as long as the human race is on this earth.

My grandfather was waked on Christmas Eve. About ten o'clock that evening, when everyone was gathered for the wake, it began to rain. From that moment, until the light of the following morning, the rain pelted the earth without cessation. It was so heavy and the night was so dark that no-one could leave the house. I often heard them talk about this at home in later years.

They would hold a Mass or sometimes, two Masses in the house of someone who had died, prior to their burial. The morning of the funeral was when one of these Masses was held. There was no Funeral Mass the day that my grandfather was buried because it was Christmas Day. People believed it a sign of good fortune to be buried on Christmas Day. They saw it as a sign that the person was well-prepared and ready for the next life. The people were also happy if one of their relatives was buried on a Sunday, as that meant that they had a big funeral.

When the funeral left our house on Christmas Day, Peigí Beag (Small/Young Peigí) and the carpenter's wife stayed behind to look after the house. I wasn't allowed go to the funeral and so Dic Ó Siadhaile stayed behind to keep me company. We had great crack that day, playing games and amusing ourselves without anyone bothering us and asking us to do different jobs around the place. If I'm honest, I have to admit that I wasn't thinking too much of the departed that day. Of course, that's normal for a young person and no-one should find fault with them for thinking that way. Young people soon grow up and have enough of the worries and sadness of this world to bother them. We found a piece of timber that was left over from the making of the coffin and that had the shape of a gun about it. Dic planed it so that it was smooth and also used his father's chisel on it. He put a spike in it as a 'trigger'. This 'pretend-gun' gave us hours of fun for months afterwards. In fact, that gun is the thing that I remember most clearly now about my grandfather's funeral.

Another memory I also have is of Dic and I swiping a pipe filled with tobacco on the night of the wake. We told Micil Mhártan that we were bringing the pipe out to one of the adults and he handed it to us without a question. We hid the pipe out in the shed and after the funeral had left the house, we dug it out again and brought it back into the house. Peigí Bheag and Maighréad an tSiúinéara ('the carpenter's Maighréad') were sitting at the fire upstairs and we had the kitchen downstairs to ourselves. I tried smoking the pipe first. I sparked it up the way I'd seen Liam Beilbhí do a thousand times and took a few big puffs out of it. Next thing, I felt really strange. It was as if the kitchen was spinning around me and the floor was moving up and down; I felt sick and got into a cold sweat. Dic noticed what was happened and he grabbed a hold of me and brought me outside into the fresh air. He kept a tight hold of me as I was so dizzy that I was sure I was going to fall over. We went down to the haggard and I threw myself down on a pile of hay there. I felt like I was dying. A few moments later, I threw up. I felt much better after that but I won't forget until my dying day that awful feeling of nausea and sickness that came over me. One good thing came out of that incident, however. I never smoked a pipe from that day until this.

I still remember clearly how lonely the house was for a long time after my grandfather's death. The sight of his empty chair in the corner where he sat every night was very sad. The small hole in the hearth where my grandfather kept the pile of rolled-up papers that he used to light his pipe was the same as before but my grandfather wasn't there anymore. My grandfather had never taken a stick from the fire to light his pipe as was Liam Beilbhí's habit; instead, he always used these rolled-up pieces of paper as a taper. His pipe and all the rolled-up pieces of paper remained in their place near the hearth for a long time after my grandfather was gone.

My aunt Máire and my mother were always telling me that my grandfather was now up with God and the Glorious Virgin in the Heavens but, to my young mind, this didn't tally fully with what had happened. What I couldn't understand was how he was now buried out in a hole in Cill Dubh. Did he miss us out there the same way that we missed him? Or was he like someone who is in a very deep sleep and who can't feel or remember anything? Thoughts such as these frequently occupied my mind at this point, thoughts that I would have been embarrassed to share with anyone else, as I felt sure that they might tease me about them. I didn't understand what death was and I was trying to work it out for myself in my young mind, with little enough success.

As with most youngsters however, I didn't stay sad for too long. The feeling of loneliness and grief disappeared gradually over time and my memory of grandfather faded as the days went by so that in the end, I thought about him only rarely. When I did think of him, it was with a sense of loneliness; there wasn't the same hole in my heart that was there in the first weeks after he died however.

PATTERN DAY IN BAILE NA HABHANN

The Pattern Day in Baile na hAbhann was always on the Feast of the Assumption. There were originally spiritual and religious rituals as associated with this pattern long ago; but they were all forgotten by the people by the time I was a youngster, however. By then, it was just a day for fun, sport and drinking. There was always a big crowd there. The people came from all over to attend it, from anywhere within a radius of five or six miles.

I remember saving my pennies for a month or so before the Pattern and if I had even a shilling in my pocket by Pattern Day, I considered myself a rich man. I'd have enough to buy two dozen sweets and biscuits, and maybe even a bottle of lemonade. The people would have their stands ready by the time first Mass began at nine o'clock. There was always one stand there every year that backed Seán an Bhácúis' house and it was always the finest stand of the lot. The woman who owned this stand was known as Máire na gCácaí (Mary of the Cakes) by everyone in Baile na hAbhann and she came from the city. She was a big, fat woman who was always full of good humour and fun and I still remember her stand well, it was brilliant really. It had a canvas awning as a roof so that the rain never fell on any of her wares. And, as a child, your eyes just widened with amazement at the variety of magical items that she sold – multi-coloured sweets in glass jars,

jars of sweets coloured red and white that were known as 'steotar' when I was a child, sweets that were amazingly-presented and laid out in their glass containers, big, rich sweet-plums, red apples, golden oranges, and all sorts of 'lucky bags' filled with secret surprises; bottles of lemonade and other fizzy drinks – and lots of other items that I can't remember now.

We were all fascinated by the secret packages or 'lucky bags' that hid what they concealed – usually some sweets and a present of some sort. Those who were in the know claimed that the lighter the bag, the better the present. As soon as someone bought one, there were immediately five or six people gathered around them checking to see what he or she had got. Sadly, many of the lucky bags were like life itself; they promised a great deal but when you opened them they never lived up to the sense of expectation.

There were other smaller stands at the pattern and traders who went around selling from a basket. The 'thimble-man', the 'loop-the-loop' man, and the three-card trick man were all there, as was the man who could put a small match standing on a piece of clay and balanced a coin on it. Another group were always gathered in the corner next to the bridge where there was a game set up that involved throwing sticks at a range of standing bottles and trying to knock them down. Everyone who paid a penny could play; they were given three sticks and if they managed to knock a bottle and break it they got three more chances – and so on.

Some of the men who played were half-drunk and they wouldn't have hit a barn door never mind the bottles! There was a man there with another booth; he had a game where you had to shoot small arrows from a gun at a board. There was always a big crowd gathered at that booth and people competing to see whose shot was the most accurate. At every stand, the fairground people called out at the top of their voices and sang the praises of their particular booth or stall, each of them trying to out-do the others and get the people to play their games. It was a real cacophony of sound and confusion. It was the best feeling in the world just to walk around the Pattern-field while chewing a few sweets or an apple and just to take in all the sights. It was brilliant to be a youngster like me on a day like that.

Both of the pubs in Baile na hAbhann were packed to the rafters with people drinking on Pattern Day. The crowd even spread into Peaid Mór's front-field outside and people sat here and there in groups or under the trees, enjoying their drink, some of them sharing a half-barrel of porter. By afternoon, when everyone was 'well-on' you heard singing sessions coming from both pubs. The down-side was that the local 'toughs' always started fighting each other once they had too much to drink and they often belted each other out on the road outside and on the way home from the Pattern. Many's the man who got a mark or an injury on Pattern Day that stayed with him until the day of his death. I myself saw Sean-Cruthúr Garbh ('Old-Rough Conor') on one particular Pattern Day thrown against the wall outside Peaid Mór's pub, a cut across his head that was more than four inches long. His face was covered in blood and at first, I thought that he was dead, because he wasn't moving at all. He was struck with the bottom of a half-gallon tin can and it was probably his own fault too, as I often heard it said that Cruthúr got very aggressive when he was drunk. I remember coming across Cruthúr again just a week later and he was walking around without any bandage or anything, the wound still plain to see on his head. Nowadays, if someone got a cut like that, they'd be at least two weeks in hospital.

Old-Cruthúr was tough and was over seventy years of age by then, but he was as healthy as a trout most of the time. He lived in the old barracks, a house that was situated the furthest south of any in An Gleann, close to Barra an Bealaigh where the road passes across the mountain. He had three sons who travelled out around the country to work for farmers. They only came home when they got a holiday and then they'd head off to the pubs drinking with their father. They were all fond of fighting and on their way home from the pub, the four of them would be drunk. If they weren't fighting others, they'd be belting each other.

Many's the hour that Nóra, Cruthúr's wife, spent sitting on a big rock just inside the gate of their house, her heart in her mouth as she waited to hear her sons or her husband returning along the road after a drinking session. The local tinkers would always attend the Pattern at Baile na hAbhann, their wives and donkeys in tandem. There weren't too many pattern days that they didn't have a fight amongst themselves also, with the ash plants and the soldering irons used as weapons. It was often all-out war between the McCarthys and the Lennons and the 'peelers' would have to break them up and send them away. It wasn't always easy either for the 'peelers' as there were old enmities and feuds between these two tribes going back many years and any time they met up at a fair or market it would be war between them. One afternoon on Pattern Day the 'peelers' had driven the Lennons back one road and the McCarthys back the other way when word came to their barracks that a fight had broken out among the McCarthys themselves back near the old church. The sergeant himself went out to see what was going on and just as he came on the scene the Cárthach Mór (Big McCarthy) struck his wife behind the ear and she fell down in a heap on the ground.

'You're after killing her now', said the sergeant.

'Would you don't be talking rubbish' said Big McCarthy, 'I know right down to my fingernails how much punishment she can take'.

It was true for him. Within a few minutes, his wife was sitting back up on the road and she tearing strips off her loving husband once more. It was the sergeant himself who told me that story.

All the fighting and trouble put an end to the Pattern in the end, however. I was at the Pattern when I was twelve years of age and actually witnessed the last fight ever there, the one that signalled the end of Baile na hAbhann Pattern forever. One of rough Cruthúr's sons was going around challenging everyone he met to a fight. Two of the peelers came down from the barracks and arrested him. When Cruthúr and his other two sons heard that the peelers were outside the pub and had just arrested him however, they came running out of the pub and jumped the two peelers. They were forced to release their 'prisoner' and even had to pull out their batons to protect themselves. Next thing, two of the Condons from Baile an Droichid who were closely related to Cruthúr's wife joined the fray. Four extra peelers arrived from the barracks to help their comrades and after much arguing and fighting, all six men were taken to the barracks and locked up. The two Condons and Cruthúr's three sons were each given two-month prison sentences. Because of his age, Cruthúr was only sentenced to one month in prison, although he died about six months after coming out of prison that time.

It was at Sunday Mass following that Pattern that the parish priest gave a blistering sermon about what had happened at the Pattern. He said that the Pattern had originated as form of devotion to the Glorious Virgin and that it had been like this going back seven generations. The present generation had brought dishonour and disrepute on the Pattern with all the drinking and fighting, he said, and if God granted him that he was still alive by the following year, there was no way that a Pattern would be held in Baile na hAbhann that year – or any other year either.

What the priest vowed came to pass. The following year, on the Sunday prior to Pattern Day, the priest told the community to go home straight after Mass on the holy day and not to hang around in the streets afterwards. He himself was in Baile na hAbhann one hour before Mass and he sent all the stall-holders and those with the gambling games home. For as long as that priest lived, there was never again a Pattern held in Baile na hAbhann. Subsequent to his death, there was a brief revival in the Pattern for a couple of years but it declined each year again until, in the end, it just petered out completely. Many people don't even remember now that there was a Pattern held there at all.

Before finishing up with this discussion, I have to tell the story of the prize-money that Dic Ó Siadhaile and I once won on Pattern Day there. This happened on the same day that the fighting took place between the Connors' and the 'peelers'. There was a man there who always had a gambling stall set up for the day. He'd have a small playing board set up on which a thick white sheet of paper was tacked down with a series of small tacks. He had eight squares drawn out on this piece of paper and he also had four other boxes on which were drawn the Ace of Hearts, the Ace of Clubs, the Ace of Diamonds and the Ace of Spades. He had three dice, each of which was about a cubic-inch in size and he had these same card-values drawn on the different faces of the dice. You bet your penny on whichever box or square you wanted and he shook the dice inside of a small tin-can and tossed it out onto the board. If you bet on the box titled the Ace of Spades, for example, and the Ace of Spades came up on the dice, then you got your penny back and another, extra penny in winnings. Also, if the three of Spades came up after you tossed the dice, you got the penny you'd put down as a bet back in addition to three-pence in winnings. Dic Ó Siadhaile and I were watching this game for a while; there was a big crowd, both young and old, crowded around the dice-man. Some people were trying their luck with the game while many others were just onlookers, the same as Dic and I. 'Let's get out of here' Dic whispered in my ear, after a few minutes. We pushed our way out through the crowd until we were alone.

'Listen to this', said Dic. 'I was watching those dice carefully and noticed that the Ace of Hearts and the Ace of Clubs always face one another on each of those dice of his. It was the same with the Ace of Spades and the Ace of Diamonds. I'm fairly small and every time he shakes the dice, and just before he places the tin-can and the dice face-down on the table, I can see which number is likely to come up on the dice. If I see the Ace of Hearts on the dice inside in the can, then the Ace of Clubs is going to appear face-up when he throws out the dice onto the board. It's the same with the Ace of Spades and the Ace of Diamonds but we won't analyse it too much now. How about we go back and stand opposite one another on different sides of the playing board. I'll stand next to the stall-owner and whatever I place my penny on, you do the same and we should be able to win ourselves a tidy sum'.

I wasn't so sure that this plan of Dic's to trick the gambling stall-owner would work but I told him that I'd do what he said. The two of us squeezed our way through the crowd and took up our positions, one of us on each side of the board, Dic standing right next to the gambling-man. The stall-owner was calling out to the people and boasting and telling them to play his game. He was telling those people who were gathered around to put down their pennies. He shook the dice out inside the holder and placed the dice-holder face down on the board. Anyone could place their money on the table right up to the point when the dice were revealed. Dic didn't place his penny-bet on the board until the dice were tossed and about to be revealed. He bet a penny and I placed my penny on the same colour as him. We did this three times and were successful each time. We lost on the fourth throw. Twice more I won my bet and then we lost once again. This time Dic placed two pence on the diamond and I followed him putting down my two pence. The dice threw up two diamonds. When Dic saw two of any colour he always bet two pence as he was sure that one of them would definitely turn up, and sometimes even the two of them. Our luck continued and the dice-man couldn't understand what was happening.

'You two devileens are the two luckiest bucks I've ever seen', he said.

I have to bring this story of mine to an end, however. It's already dragging on a bit. I stuffed myself with cakes and oranges that day and downed it all with three bottles of lemonade. And despite all of this, I still had ten shillings and three pence in my pocket coming home and Dic Ó Siadhaile had in and around the same himself.

Years later, when Dic and I were grown up, I'd often ask him whether what we had done that day was honest at all; but he'd just laugh and tell me to cop onto myself. 'Huh! You fool', he'd say. 'Sure, wouldn't he have played the exact same trick on you if he had got the chance? Don't the likes of him make their money from trickery and deception? Believe me, there's nothing wrong at all with playing a few tricks on the likes of them yourself, if you can get away with it'. Maybe Dic was right; then again, maybe he wasn't.

SEÁN MAC CRAITH

One beautiful Autumn evening, I was sitting on the verge near the front gate and looking down across the glen. I had just returned from the Baile na hAbhann Pattern. It was the same day that the Cruthúraigh and the Condúnaigh were arrested and when Dic Ó Siadhaile and I had tricked the man who ran the gambling stall. I was feeling bloated after eating so many sweets that day and I was tired also after walking over and back across the road during the Pattern and then the five-mile walk home again afterwards from Baile na hAbhann. Dic and I had got a lift to the Pattern from sean-Risteard on his mule and cart but we hadn't come home with him as he had left again around four o'clock in the evening, which was too early for Dic and me. Another reason we hadn't returned with sean-Risteard was that there was a big group of us from An Gleann walking home together and, as a consequence, the walk didn't seem half as long as it really was. Girls and boys as young as ten years of age would often walk to and from the Pattern or the fair in those days and no-one thought twice about it. I don't think there are any youngsters today who would be able to walk such long distances.

As I mentioned, the evening was lovely with the sun low in the sky on the western side of Cruachán; the sun was a blood-red colour. Whatever way I glanced up, I noticed a man descending Bóthar na Faille, a road that turns southwards through Bearna an Bhainbh and between an 'dá Mhaoil' until the ground begins to level out on the southern side of the mountains. This was the way that most people travelled through the mountains long ago, years before they made the road through Gleann Chárthainn.

I was watching the man as he came closer but I couldn't make him out. It was hard to see him at all as I was looking straight into the sun. As he came closer, I noticed that he seemed to be carrying a fairly large canvas pack under his arms and a walking stick in his other hand. When he reached where I was sitting, he stood right opposite me and removed his hat, wiping his brow with a red handkerchief. He was a well-built man who was reasonably tall; he had a very kindly and gentle look in his eyes. Clean-shaven, his hair was as black as pitch except for the occasional streak of grey running through it here and there.

'Dia dhuit a bhuachaill mhaith' ('Hello, my good boy'), he said to me in Irish.

'Dia is Muire dhuit', I replied.

'Praise be with you, but you have sweet Irish. You wouldn't happen to know whether your father might need a man to do some fixing or binding (sheaf-binding) around the place by any chance?'

The harvest had ripened early that year, a good fortnight before it normally did.

'My father is dead', I said.

'Oh, may God have mercy on him', he replied.

'I think', says I, 'that we do need a man for work'.

'Liam Beilbhí, the man who was working for us, is sick in bed for the past three weeks and we have no-one now. But if you go inside to my mam and my aunt Máire, they'll let you know better'.

'Good boy', he said, 'I'll call in so'.

I went back into the house a little while later and he was sitting at the kitchen table drinking tea, and the great chat that my aunt Máire and himself were having would have convinced you that they'd known each other for years. They spoke to one another in Irish and the more I listened to him speak the better I understood his Irish. His dialect of Irish a little different from what we spoke here in An Gleann. This was how Seán Mac Craith came to Lios na Faille the first day ever. He stayed with us for a good while. I don't know what arrangement was made with him at the time but the small room at the top of the stairs near the end of the house was prepared for Seán and that was where he slept that night. When I woke up the next morning he was sharpening a spade out at the door of the shed. He went off cutting corn up on the 'stand', the field that was highest up on the side of the mountain. My aunt Máire worked behind him binding the corn for the day and when I came home from school, I was put making stooks of the corn. Seán Mac Craith spent the rest of his life with us here in Lios na Faille. He stayed here for twenty-two years until the Feast of the Assumption one year when the biggest funeral ever to leave Gleann Chárthainn went southwards to the graveyard in Áth-Mhéain where Seán was buried with his ancestors.

Whatever praise I could give to Seán Mac Craith, it would never do him justice. He was the kind of a person who was a real man, a gentleman down to the tips of his toes. He had no weaknesses. No-one ever heard him use bad language or engage in back-biting about others. He never insulted anyone or made little of them in his life and only spoke well of others. Two or three others tried to imitate his manners and his ways after he first arrived here, but they only managed it for a while. He never argued with anyone verbally but if someone pushed him beyond what he could take, they would get a belt of his fist and they'd know all about it. He was the type of man that you could have left all Déamar's gold in his care and he was so honest that he wouldn't have touched a farthing of it.

He was well-read in both Irish and English and it was Seán who first showed me how to read and write Irish, both skills which we learned nothing about at school in those days. Just a few months after he arrived to us, he encouraged me to try and get my hands on some of the Irish-language books produced by the Irish Texts Society and I got the first two books that they issued. He helped me reading the books until I was able to do it for myself. I didn't find the reading too difficult as my spoken Irish was already quite good. It was Seán too who first taught me the real history of Ireland when he gave me the book *The Story of Ireland* to read. To put it in nutshell, whatever is good or noble about me as a farmer and as a man – it is thanks to Seán Mac Craith that I have it.

Based on what I could tell from listening to my aunt Máire and my poor mother chatting, the people of Lios na Faille had every reason to be grateful to Seán also. It was he who ensured that we kept our farm after my grandfather died. After his death, we had been relying on different labourers to do piecework for us on the farm but as everyone knows some of these men had little interest in the work and were trying to do as little as they could for their day's wages. You can't blame them I suppose; that's human nature really. We'd do the same probably if we were in their shoes; that said, I wouldn't want to find any fault with them.

We had been doing fairly well while Liam Beilbhí was still able to keep up with the work. He had been working here since he was a child as had his father before him. Liam had too much work on his shoulders by then, however. It was as if it was his own farm, he had so many responsibilities. Liam was no good at the fair or at the market and after my grandfather died, my aunt Máire had to do all the buying and selling. Although I never heard anyone saying that she didn't do a good job of this – she was a very able woman – it would have been difficult for her to get the best bargains when dealing with cattle-dealers and jobbers, a class of people who spent all of their time buying and selling.

God was definitely looking after us when he sent Seán Mac Craith our way as he was a man in a hundred. There was no aspect of farming that he wasn't an expert on. He was a great harvester and he was the best ploughman ever to work in An Gleann. He could reap and stack and there are walls on the farm here that he built years ago and they are standing as good as ever. There was very little that he didn't know about the doctoring and care of animals either. He had only just arrived here when his reputation as a man who could cure any animal went out around the area; from then on, there wasn't a sick banbh or foal that he wasn't called to attend. It was the same in relation to the cow that had colic. He never refused anyone who asked him to come out and help them with their animals, even early in the morning. He never accepted a penny from anyone in lieu of his work either.

My poor father would have been hard-pressed to better Seán when it came to plans and schemes on how to improve the farm. Anything that I know about farming is thanks to Seán Mac Craith. He showed me how to do all the different jobs around the farm correctly and efficiently. He also taught me how to understand the underlying reasons why certain aspects of the farming process were done in the way that they were. To sum up, he made me into a more understanding and more rounded person and I never had as close a bond with anyone else in my life as I did with Seán Mac Craith. For as long as any of the Búrcaigh are living here in Lios na Faille, Seán Mac Craith will be remembered with fondness.

The Spring after he first came here, he opened the field called Páirc na Naoi n-Acra (The Nine-Acre Field), the field that is the furthest away from the farmhouse and the field with the best soil of the lot. We ourselves planted three acres of that field and rented out the rest. My aunt Máire wasn't too happy that we'd rented out the other part of it, apparently. She said that this had never been done before, as long as the Burkes had been in Lios na Faille. We didn't have enough stock to do otherwise at the time however; neither had we the monetary equivalent of such stock. It was Seán Mac Craith who advised us to break the entirety of that field and to rent out most of it then. We were lucky that potatoes were a good price that year and we had a great crop so that we did better out of this arrangement than we thought we would have initially. The following year we planted a crop of corn in that field. Needless to say, I don't remember any of these things but I often heard my wife and my aunt describe them in later years. When you're a young lad of twelve years of age, you don't take much notice of any of these decisions as relating to farm work.

The most difficult form of ploughing of the lot is when you are making ridges to sow potatoes. The ridges had to be ploughed with a wheel-less plough then which meant that every ridge had to be 'upturned' by hand. There are ploughs available today and they are so modernized now that even a schoolboy could plough the soil using them.

Seán Mac Craith had all the ridges upturned in the Nine Acres field but hardly anyone in the Gleann came to see his work; even though they were so neatly done. All I remember from those days are the numbers of people who were tilling land that was rented out and the 'meitheal's' that came together for the harvest.

Seán Mac Craith was his own man. He didn't interfere with the neighbours or their work in any way and rarely went visiting other houses at night. He'd usually stay in chatting with my mother and my aunt or would spend his evenings reading the newspaper. He used to get the *Shamrock* every week and he'd read the adventures of 'Mick McQuaid' aloud to us. He was very good at reading and he used to have us laughing at Mick's shenanigans and the funny things he got up to along with his friends 'Joe Doolan', 'Terry Geraghty' and 'Kit Culkin'. Seán would fix shoes or the horse harnesses and he could work leather as good as any shoemaker. The 'land question' was very controversial at this juncture and Seán had a great interest in it. He was very well-up on politics also. I couldn't say exactly what his political views were but I certainly got the impression that he had more time for the Fenians and their aims than he did for the Irish representatives who attended the English Parliament. He said that we'd never drive the English out of Ireland, if all we did was talk about it all the time.

When he first came to Lios na Faille, the locals in An Gleann were always speculating among themselves about where Seán had come from originally or why he had decided to leave where he was from the first day ever. They had all sort of theories on it but none that was accepted fully by anyone. I don't remember anything about the various suppositions they had in relation to Seán; all I know is that over time, the locals forgot about all of this and came to accept him as one of their own.

Seán was originally from a townland situated near the mouth of An Abhainn Mhór, a place that was within sight of the sea and a good many miles south of the mountains where we lived. Once he came to Lios na Faille, he never once returned to his home place. It wasn't because he didn't like his home place that Seán never returned. Indeed, you never heard any man who showed such love for where he had been born and reared as poor Seán did. 'The Glorious Country' is how he always referred to it, and there was nowhere like it anywhere else in the world in his eyes. The old people there were the kindest and most natural people you would meet anywhere, he said. In fact, there was nothing in Gleann Chárthainn that came anywhere near how nice the people were 'south of us' as he always but it. The people down there were the finest and the crops that grew there were the best of all. In fact, if Seán had any fault at all, it was this over-idealization of his home place. That said, there is no-one whom God has created that doesn't have some small fault or other.

We used to use that phrase 'south of us' as a nickname for him sometimes and this phrase was sometimes used by the people in the village to make fun of him behind his back. They would never have made fun of him like this to his face because Seán wasn't the type of man to take mockery like that lying down.

If he was so fond of his family and his home village, why did he leave the first day ever, never to return? It was many years before Seán told me the 'kernel' of this story; he told me to keep it to myself and I never did tell anyone else what that secret was; not until now have I put it down on paper for the very first time. The only person I ever whispered the story to was my wife Sibéal and whatever was my secret was hers also.

In fact, Seán told me his story at the same time as something similar happened to one of my closest relatives. The reason he finally unburdened himself of his secret was in part to try and assuage my sorrow and hurt at what had happened to my relative. It was the unpredictable actions of two particular women that destroyed both Seán and my relative. Here's the kernel of his story as Seán explained it to me: He had a nice farm once, about twenty-five acres of fine land next to Abhainn Mór. His only family were his mother and a younger sister. He and a local girl were fond of each other when they were going to school and everyone assumed that they would marry each other one day. He wasn't shy about saying that he wanted to see his sister settled or provided for before he brought another woman into the farm. His mother died then however, and his sister inherited her share of the farm. About a year later however, just when everything looked like it had worked out well, Seán's world fell apart. He ended up taking to the road shortly afterwards.

Three months prior to this, a man had returned from America and bought a big farm of land that had been put up for sale in that area. He had a fine house along with the land, a house that was situated on the other side of the road, across from where Seán Mac Craith's family lived. The farm had cost two thousand pounds which was an enormous sum of money for a farm in those days. This 'Yank' had a lot of money and he set about buying a large amount of stock and employing a big number of tradesmen to fix up his house. The returned emigrant was middle-aged and balding, his mouth filled with gold teeth. Anna Barún (Baron), the girl whom Seán had been so fond of for years, was a lovely girl, Seán said, and he never said a word against her even as he related his story to me. From the first day that he set eyes on her, the 'Yank' was cracked about Anna however, and was following her around day and night. Nearly every evening, he was up in the Barún's house chatting with Anna's mother next to the fire. The mother was a widow just as Seán's mother was, and Anna was her only child. Initially, Seán didn't think anything much about the way that the 'Yank' was always following Anna around the place and trying to get her attention. And anytime Anna mentioned the 'Yank' in conversation, she'd make fun of his gold teeth and his whiney accent. Seán didn't see Anna for a couple of days and, next thing, it was all over the parish that Anna Barún was to marry the 'Yank', that everything was already arranged and that they'd be getting married within the week. Seán went up to the house to find out was there any truth to this story. He spotted Anna through the window as he approached the house. She was with her mother in the kitchen but when he went into the house, she was gone. She had hidden herself from him in the back somewhere by all accounts. After saying 'hello' to the mother, Seán said that he wanted to have a few words with Anna but he could tell immediately from the hostile look on the mother's face that something was not right. She told Seán that he wouldn't see Anna that day or any other day either from then on. She also said that she would never let her daughter into a small scrap of a farm like the Mac Craiths owned and that she was going to somewhere far better. He asked again could he speak to the girl herself but the mother told him to get out of the house. She slammed the door behind him. Anna and the 'Yank' were married four days later and they went to Cork on their honeymoon. Poor Seán's heart must have been torn apart because even when he told me the story, many years later, he was still very upset about it. I told him that he was better off that he hadn't married this girl, that she didn't deserve a man as good as him anyway, and that he shouldn't be still tormenting himself about it all these years later. Seán was loath to blame Anna Barún for what happened, however. He blamed the mother's greed for all his woes.

Now that she was married to someone else, Seán just couldn't face it every day when he saw Anna pass by. He would have stayed put but he couldn't be sure that he wouldn't do something terrible to the 'Yank' whenever he finally ran into him. He made his decision and went to Youghal where he arranged with a solicitor to get the farm and everything that went with it signed over to his sister. He told the solicitor to post all the relevant documents to his sister and to explain his decision to her. Then, without so much as a backward look, he took the road north and followed it out through the mountains. After wandering from place to place for some time, he eventually wound up in Lios na Faille. He arrived in our place on the Feast of the Assumption and for as long as he lived with us, no matter the weather, there wasn't a year that he didn't climb to the top of the mountain at An Maoil Mór after dinner and look out southwards towards the sea. Every year, he would spend the whole of that day looking back in the direction of 'Dúthaigh na Glóire' (The Glorious Country), not returning home until sunset.

BAILE NA HABHANN

As evident from its name, Baile na hAbhann is situated at the mouth or jetty of a river. It is three miles north of Baile an Droichid. It is here that the local church is and this meant that the people of An Gleann would have to travel about five miles to go to Mass on Sundays and on holy days. The parish has two churches; the other church is situated in Gleann na bhFiúr six miles east of Baile na hAbhann.

When I was growing up, the village of Baile na hAbhann consisted of one main shop, two pubs and a few small huckster's shops in Baile na hAbhann. The main shop sold everything that would ever be needed by country people. The best pub there was owned by Peaid Mór Ó Sé; Peig Paor had a small narrow and darkly-lit pub on the corner near the church. The 'Peelers' Barrack was there on the main street also to keep us all under control for Seán Buí (i.e. England) and there was a bakery and a forge on that main street also. Baile na hAbhann was a great place for drinking in the past, at least that was what I heard. The land around about is the finest land you can get anywhere and yet a number of the biggest farmers in the area lost everything because of an addiction to alcohol. These farmers could be found in the pub even when they should have been outside and busy with the harvest. There was no law then against drinking on a Sunday and there were a lot of men in the parish who attended first Mass and then went drinking in the pub for the rest of the day; they'd stay there drinking all day until they were kicked out of the pub at ten or eleven o'clock in the evening. As mentioned earlier, Peig Paor's pub was on the corner near the church and some of the biggest drunkards in the parish used to listen to Mass from up on the first floor of this pub as it had a view of the church door. When they saw the people in the church kneel down, they too dropped to their knees around a table that was in the middle of the room. Then, when the congregation rose to their knees again, they too would stand up and have a drink. Peig Paor was to blame for the fact that she let them in when the Mass was on. From what I heard, she never had much luck for it. Over time, she lost whatever she owned and she ended up in the Poorhouse in the end. Peaid Mór's descendants still own his pub today. Baile na hAbhann school was about a quarter of a mile from the village; it was situated on a height up at Sean-Phóna (The Old Pound). There were two men and two women working there when I was young. The school is still there but the boys and girls are mixed together in the classes now and there are only two teachers there now, one woman and one man. The population of this area has declined greatly since I was a child.

It was in Baile na hAbhann church that I was baptized and it was there too that I made my Holy Communion, my Confirmation and it is where I was married. I remember the very first day that I went to Mass; I was more interested in the sight of the altar boy with his lighted stick or taper than I was in anything else, to be honest. A few days later, Little Peigí and my aunt Máire were out in the shed cutting sciollán's and once everything was tidied up after the dinner my mother went out to help them. I was left alone in the house by myself and I went into the parlour and took the two brass candlesticks from the mantelpiece there. I put candles that I found in the cupboard into each of the candle-holders and placed them on the ledge of the dresser. Then I got a long thin stick and attached a scrunched-up piece of paper to the top of it to act as a taper. Then I lit this paper-taper in the fire and went to light the two candles as I'd seen the boy in the church do. My mother came into the kitchen unknown to me and she burst out laughing.

'In God's name child', she exclaimed. 'What are you doing?'

I was too embarrassed to reply.

She told Little Peigí and my aunt the story when they came into the house later at tea-time, and Peigí told me that I'd be a priest when I grew up.

'Maybe. God willing', my mother said.

Little Peigí's prediction proved false however. I wasn't worthy of being a priest. It wasn't God's will.

Football matches between the schoolchildren at Baile na hAbhann school and Baile an Droichid school were often held. Nowadays people refer to football as 'peil' in Irish but back then, people only ever used the word 'caid' for the game. It was strange but although the boys were regularly out hurling on the road with bits of ash plants as hurleys, there were never any hurling matches organized between the schools. I remember my grandfather saying that hurling was the only game played by grown men in that area prior to the Famine, when the potatoes all went black, but that after the Famine, hurling was a game that only young lads played. Although there were twice as many pupils attending Baile na hAbhann school as there were attending the one in Baile an Droichid, we won the football matches more often than we lost them. I remember one year in particular, when we played one another twice but it was a draw on each occasion. All the local people were really wound up about this and it was decided to settle the matter with a match between the grown-up lads from both schools. The enmity between both sides got out of hand during the match and it ended up in a fight. The priest later spoke out from the altar and it was many years later before another match was organized between the two sides. There weren't any definite rules in the matches back then; there was more wrestling and pulling and dragging amongst the players than anything else. The object of each side was to overcome the opposition so that they got the ball from their end of the field to the other. The game was played from end to end, from one ditch to another.

The 'Great House' owned by the local landlord or 'master' as he was called, George (Seoirse) Langley was situated about a half-mile east of Baile an Droichid village. This house was built on raised ground near the banks of the river and surrounded by a copse of fir-trees. Iron bars protected the windows that were as thick as shovel-handles with a gap of about six inches separating each bar. He also had frames made of iron built into the doors and windows for protection. It was like a fortress or a prison. Today, it is just a roofless ruin. I can barely remember George Langley now. He used to travel around in a carriage, himself and his daughter together. He sported a short grey beard and always wore a two-peaked hat – or top-hat. He was lame in one foot and I don't remember that anyone ever saw him walking. 'Leainglí na coise' (Langley of the foot) is what the people called him behind his back. The Langleys of Baile na hAbhann were descendants of the British who received Irish land during Cromwell's time. The Langleys were tyrants without mercy and George Langley was one of the worst of the lot. He kept his tenants under such tight control that no-one could plough a field or even cut down a bush without first asking him for permission. If he noticed the slightest improvement on the house or smallholding of one of his tenants he would increase their rent straight away. I heard the old people tell how Langley's wife spotted a farmer's wife in the city one day wearing a new bonnet and cape. There was no way that any of her tenants was going to wear clothes that were anywhere near as nice as her own and when she got home that day, Langley's wife insisted on increasing the rent paid by that woman's husband by an extra five shillings per acre. Whenever the tenants paid their rent they were forced to queue outside the 'Great House' for hours – until George Langley decided to see them. It didn't matter what the weather was like. Langley deliberately always kept them waiting longer when the weather was bad. Once, a tenant of his was very sick in bed on the day that the rent was due to be paid and so he sent his son with the money instead of him. When the boy got there, Langley asked him where his father was and why he hadn't come himself to pay the rent. The boy told him that he was very sick in bed.

'He was drinking last night, I suppose', said Langley. 'You bring that money back home with you again and you tell your father that he has to present me with the money himself personally'.

The sick man was so afraid that he had no choice but to get out of bed and go to Langley's house himself to pay him. That poor man was dead a week later. No mercy was shown to anyone who was late with the rent. He just threw them out on the side of the road straight away. I remember as a very young boy seeing furniture including bits of beds and chairs thrown on the side of the road when we going to Mass one Sunday. This was outside a house in Cúil na Gréine, north of Baile an hAbhann. A family had just been evicted; from what I heard, that entire family emigrated abroad. Langley evicted many families such as this one and he also had a rule that if the man-of-the-house died before his wife did, then the widow and her children had to leave their smallholding. It didn't matter whether she had the money to pay the rent or not or how many children she had. He just threw them all out on the side of the road anyway.

And there were some of the tenants who didn't do themselves too many favours either, as they weren't very honest. There was hardly any farm that Langley evicted people from that there weren't people willing to take the place of the people who'd been evicted. I often heard people saying that some of the tenants used to watch each other like hawks and if they saw someone else whose smallholding was struggling, they'd be up to Langley trying to make secret deals with him whereby they would get this land when the other poor people were evicted. There was no talk of the 'Boycotting' that time or for a long time afterwards either. Personally, I think that that is how most of the antecedents of the big farmers around here managed to get their smallholdings in the first place. I've often thought since that it was amazing that no efforts were made to drive the likes of Langley and his like off the land at all, especially in counties such as this one, and reclaim it from them – as happened in many other Irish counties.

Before the 'peelers' came to Baile na hAbhann, Langley was the 'law' here and every holy day and holiday he would arrive over in the afternoon and clear everyone out of the pubs and no-one would say a word against him, they were that afraid of him.

He never needed to call to more than one pub because his arrival was enough to get everyone in the pubs to go home immediately. They would leave immediately and maybe it wasn't such a bad thing that he cleared everyone off home those evenings as there were many people who were very addicted to alcohol then. All the same, it shows the power and control that Langley had over people. The Irish people then were just slaves who were as oppressed as much as any of the black people in America were at this juncture.

The area that was An Gleann here wasn't part of Langley's estate. The Baron family who lived in Youghal were the landlords who controlled us here and Richard Baron was the last of them. He sold his estate to the tenants here when the first Act was implemented in Ireland allowing local people to buy their smallholdings back from the landowner. He still had the rights over the 'game' however and the Barons still hunted in this area until about ten years ago, when the last of them died. The Barons were Catholics. I suppose that Cromwell hadn't considered it worth his while taking their land off them as it consisted of mountainous glens for the most part.

I often heard the old people saying that it was An tAthair Tomás Ó Floinn (Father Thomas Flynn) who first challenged Langley's control of this area and the landlord's oppression of the people here. I don't remember this priest because he died the year that I was born. Langley always had between eight and ten men working for him here in Baile na hAbhann where he farmed about one hundred acres. The men had to work every holy day and I'm fairly certain that he didn't allow the men go to Mass on those days. In fact, he used to 'rub their noses in it' because he would deliberately make sure that they were working on some job in and around the church on those very days and when Mass was being held.

It was actually a holy day the first time that An tAthair Tomás Ó Floinn said Mass in Baile na hAbhann. It came to the time for second Mass and Langley was outside monitoring a group of men who were knocking an old wall that was directly opposite the gates to the old church. When the new parish priest arrived at the gate and saw what was going on, he jumped down from his horse and handed the bridle to the man nearest to him. Over he went to Langley and he stood in front of him and stared him straight between the eyes for a moment or two.

'Langley', he said, and there was fire in his voice, 'don't let me see something like this going on again for as long as I'm parish priest; otherwise, I'll leave a mark on you that will be a thousand times worse than that lame leg of yours'. He didn't say anything else but turned on his heel and went back in through the gates of the church. Langley didn't say a word in response. When the priest came out again after Mass, Langley and his men were gone and he never organized any work on a holy day after that, not unless it was a job that was absolutely necessary. Needless to say, I don't remember this whole incident as I wasn't even born then but I heard the old people tell these story a hundred times or more. You can still hear people telling this story in An Gleann here today. Apparently, Langley wasn't quite as harsh with the people after this incident as he had been before.

When he (Langley) died a few years later, his daughter inherited his estate as she was his only child. She never married and was a kind person who was never cruel to her tenants. She gave the people every chance to pay their rent and never evicted anyone for as long as she lived. Every Christmas, she would divide clothes, blankets, tea and sugar out among the poor of the parish. I still remember her well, driving around in her open-topped carriage, the same carriage she travelled alongside her father in when she was young. 'Miss Tessy' is what the people called her and they had great respect for her, despite the fact that her antecedents were a bad lot.

After her death, the estate was divided out amongst the tenants under the Land Purchase Act but the house and about one hundred acres went to some distant relative of the Langleys. This relative seldom visited the estate but he had a steward who looked after the farm for him. The 'big house' was burned to the ground during the 'Black and Tan' War and it's just an empty ruin now. This farm eventually came into the possession of the Land Commission and they divided it out amongst the former tenants and built new houses for them. Langley was a very powerful figure in this parish once. He was an unmerciful tyrant who now lies buried in the old chapel that is surrounded by a big iron railing and which is overgrown with weeds, nettles and other bushes. I'd say that no-one ever said a prayer for him, not since the day he died. Little did he think when he was at the height of his pomp and glory that one day he would only have the owls for his night companions and the swallows for company during the day. The wheel of life is always turning.

AT SCHOOL IN BAILE AN DROICHID

Baile an Droichid is about two miles from Lios na Faille. There is one walk-way or bridge over the Tonnóg river there and it is from this bridge that the place got its name. The school and Máire an tSuibhnigh's huckster shop were on one side of the bridge and the pub owned by 'Léan Mháirtí and Jim a' Ghabha's forge were on the other. Except for the old ball alley that was behind the school, there was really nothing else in Baile an Droichid then. Today, there is still a small shop there in the place where Máire a t-Suibhnigh's shop once stood and the forge is still there. A new school was built on the far side of the road opposite where the old school once stood but there are no traces of the old school or the pub left now. The rocks that were used to build the old ball alley have been used for other building projects as relating to the road years ago.

The years that I spent at school in Baile an Droichid were the happiest and most pleasant years of my life, although I didn't understand this at the time. No-one realizes just how happy their childhood is until the real worries and troubles of life hit them. That was how it was for me anyway, and I'd imagine it's much the same for most people. When people are young, they have no shortage of hobbies or past-times. They get a sense of enjoyment from every aspect of life, even the tiniest and most ridiculous of games. That's how it was for me and the other lads who went to Baile an Droichid school with me anyway. If I could only remember all the tricks and games that we got up to back then, I could fill a book with them now. There were a lot of tricksters and jokers around when I was going to school and it would be hard to match them as regards some of the pranks they got up to.

We played sports depending on what season it was and what the weather was like. We played hurling out on the road in the winter-time, using old rough-shaped sticks as our hurleys. Our ball was a round-shaped piece of wood about the size of your fist that was referred to as a 'Cat'. We didn't have the word 'sliotar' back then in An Gleann. The best sticks for hurling back then were made from furze bushes. A travelling 'show' used to visit Baile na hAbhann every winter for a week and they had a game which involved throwing a small wooden ball at a series of figurines or little men that stood together on a plank at the back of the cabin or booth. You had to stand about ten yards away from the figures when you were throwing and you got three wooden balls for a penny. For every figurine that you knocked over, you won another penny or you were given three more throws for free. These figurines were not easy to knock over however, as they were quite heavy at the base. Some of the other figurines comprised a kind of a thin iron spike that was surrounded by feathers but which you had to hit directly on the spike; otherwise, they wouldn't fall either. The reason I mention this game as played in the booth of the travelling show is that every year, some of the older lads from school would invent various plans and tricks to try and steal a few of these small wooden balls so that they could use them later for hurling.

These wooden balls were dangerous too because if you give one of them a good puck it would fly like a bullet. One day, one of them flew in through the window of

Máire an tSuibhnigh's shop and in addition to breaking the glass window-pane, it also smashed a plate on the dresser in her kitchen. There was war afterwards about this at school and Power asked us all loads of questions about what had happened; he never did find out who was responsible for breaking that shop window and plate, however. In the end, all hurling was banned for the rest of that season.

We also had a football or what the old people referred to as a 'caid' from time to time, although it was difficult to find a field to play in. Thinking of those wooden balls and the hurling now puts me in mind of many funny incidents that happened all those years ago. One day we were out playing on the road with one of those wooden balls when a lad named Peaitsín Ó Briain was hit in the face with one of them. He was bleeding profusely and Power put him lying on the flat of his back on the road; he placed a small smooth stone inside the collar of his shirt and against the back of his neck in an effort to staunch the flow of blood but this didn't work either. There was an elderly woman who used to wander from place to place in those days whose name was Nóra or Nóra na Ceirte ('Rags Nóra') as she was better known. She was a big fat woman who suffered from chest complaints and she was always wheezing and short of breath. She also always wore a pair of men's shoes for some reason and she had some kind of ailment on one of her feet that meant it was always wrapped bandage-like with cloths of some form or another. This was the reason that she was known as 'Rags Nóra'. She happened to come by just as Peaitsín was stretched out on the road and bleeding heavily. She went over and looked at him. 'Cuirigí cac muice leis' ('Put some pig-shit on it (i.e. to stop the blood') she said and went on her way. As I alluded to previously, Power, our teacher, didn't have any Irish and when Nóra siad that, three of four of us started laughing.

'What did she say?' Power said to us in English.

None of us said anything; it was as if we were embarrassed by what Nóra had said. 'What did she say?' said Power again in angry voice.

There was a young lad from An Gleann here by the name of Seán Ó Gráda and he explained to Power what Nóra had said in as diplomatic a way as possible. Power didn't say another word but just turned on his heel and went back into the school. Peaitsín's nose had stopped bleeding by now and we brought him up to the stream where he cleaned it with the water. Then we went back playing hurling again. Nóra's cure for the bleeding nose became one of those witticisms that were regularly used by every blackguard in the area for years afterwards. At some stages of the year, we used to play buttons a lot. We were really competitive in these games of ours to see which of us won the most buttons. I remember that I had more than one hundred buttons on string at one point. There was no old pair of clothes anywhere around the house that I hadn't swiped the buttons off for those competitions.

Others were at the same trick. I often saw other children tearing a button off their shirt or jacket or off their trousers so as to play the buttons game, and after they had lost all of their other buttons in the games. There was even the odd child who would sell buttons to you if you needed them. Twenty buttons and one additional 'gilt' or brass button for a half-penny was the going rate then. That said, the children rarely bought buttons since the halfpennies were hard to come by. The 'gilt' was the brass button that had a particular sheen on it; it was ideal for playing the 'bob' as it had weight in it. I remember seeing those brass buttons on the short king-corduroy trousers that Bil Learaí and Liam Buitléar wore. Both of these men wore those knee-length trousers until the day that they died. On those trousers there were four gilt buttons on the outside of each knee. Come the first of March, all of the young children who were able to make them spin had a 'top' to play with. You could buy a 'top' for a penny in Máire an tSuibhnigh's shop. They were coloured green or red but it was only the youngest kids who were interested in the coloured ones. The older lads went for a different type of spinning 'top', one that you had to get the blacksmith to make a small spike for. Many's the sliver of metal that was swiped to make these spikes because once you had one of these, the 'top' could really spin powerfully. Some of the schoolchildren got these little 'spikes' made at home but they were never as smooth or as powerful as the ones that were pre-made and that you bought in the shop. Poor Jim a' Ghabha, the blacksmith had to listen to endless cajoling and blathering from schoolchildren who were hoping that he'd make them one of these rods. Jim was a right trickster himself because he'd often make one of these spikes and then throw it out to one of the children standing around the forge-door. Then, when the child picked up the rod which was still burning-hot from the fire and flung it away as quickly again with a yelp of pain, Jim would break his heart laughing. There was a special skill to the way that this rod was made so that it inserted into the 'top' correctly and worked well. If it inserted totally straight, the 'top' wouldn't 'sleep' when it spun; nor would it feel 'light' enough when you placed it in the palm of your hand. A 'top' that went to 'sleep' so that you didn't even notice it was spinning anymore was called a 'gleoisín' (babbler/chatterer) whereas a top in which the rod had been inserted incorrectly and which spun unevenly was called a 'gigiléir' (jiggler). The best wood to make a 'top' from was the wood that came from the wild-apple tree or the 'crab-apple' as it was known. This wood was very tough and wouldn't break easily. A 'crab' top and a well-made, unbreakable rod; if you had these two elements in your 'top', you had one of the best spinning tops going.

We would play ball against the gable-end of the school sometimes and the older lads would play this all-year round. The girls had their own games that they played and we boys often played together with them. That said, I don't remember now what games that both boys and girls played back then. As you'd expect from schoolchildren our age, we never stopped playing tricks on each other and on other people. There were a couple of kids in my class and the devil himself wouldn't have been a patch on them as regards inventing tricks and playing them on other unsuspecting people. Donncha Pheigí was the most accomplished joker in the pack, and to look at him you would have thought that butter wouldn't melt in his mouth; he was that innocent and baby-faced. He was a picture of innocence, with those blue and twinkling eyes of his and the mop of blonde hair. He had a saint-like look about him almost; anyone who thought that Donncha Pheigí was some kind of a saint would have been badly-mistaken, however.

As mentioned earlier, Máire an tSuibhnigh's small huckster shop was across the road and directly opposite the school. Máire was married to Seáinín Ó Deá, a small stocky man with protruding ears. The poor man had a tough life because his wife was very domineering and controlled him completely. She was a big, swaggering woman with a rough voice and she was the boss, both inside the home and outside. I suppose that this is probably the reason that their two sons were always known as Seán Mháire and Micil Mháire respectively. Poor Seáinín didn't really count at all. Their shop didn't have a great deal of stuff for sale and whatever money they made from it was made almost entirely from what they sold to the schoolchildren across the road. Sweets, loaves of bread, apples and plums when they were in season; tobacco, clay pipes, shoe-laces and other small knick-knacks of a similar type; these items made up the bulk of their sales.

It was easy to wind up poor Seáinín and unsurprisingly, nothing pleased the schoolchildren better than to make him angry or get a rise out of him. He owned a small white dog that had very long hair-like fur and one day Donncha Pheigí threw the dog into the sewer at the school and pulled it out again. Once the dog went across the road to the shop, what did he do but promptly give himself a good shake right in front of Seáinín who complained to the headmaster about this and we were all given a good grilling to try and find out who the main culprit was in relation to this. Needless to say, no-one had seen anything or knew who the culprit was! There was a lintel of sorts leading down into the sewer and another day Donncha Pheigí drove a line of young ducks belonging to Máire an tSuibhnigh down along the lintel and into the sewer-water below. This caused a right war altogether but once again, no-one was found out or paid the price for it. That time, it was Máire herself who arrived at the school to complain to the schoolmaster. He was never very friendly with her, however, and it was for this reason, I suppose, that Power didn't make much effort to find out who was responsible or punish them.

Máire an tSuibhnigh owned quite a lot of fowl, including ducks, hens and turkeys. I don't remember that she had any geese. They'd always be waiting outside when we children came out to play during our school breaks hoping for some pieces of bread from us. They timed their appearance at exactly the same time as we got our break. Even the crows in the trees always gathered in the trees outside the school at the right time also. And isn't it amazing also that none of these birds ever appeared on the days that we were off school? I often heard Jim a' Ghabha saying that the crows never gathered outside the school on Saturdays or Sundays, nor any time that the scholars were on holidays. I suppose every living creature has its own sense of things. What reminded me of Máire an tSuibhnigh and her fowl was the trick that Donncha Pheigí played on the ducks sometimes. He'd get a piece of twine a few feet long and he'd tie a bit of bread to either end of it. Then he'd throw it out to the ducks. Everyone who has seen ducks eating knows that they have a particular way of gobbling food. No sooner was the twine on the ground then two ducks had jumped on either end of it and gobbled the pieces of food. Next thing, the two ducks would be pulling against one another until the strongest of the ducks pulled the twine and the piece of bread from the throat of the other. Next moment, another duck would jump on this piece of food and gobble it straight away and the whole pulling-against-each-other game would begin all over again. You couldn't help but laugh at the crazy shenanigans of the ducks as they each pulled the twine, one from the other!

Donncha's trick with the ducks and the twine would have repercussion for all of us, however. One day he was doing this trick with Máire's turkeys when a cockerel turkey swallowed the two pieces of bread and managed to wrap both ends of the twine around his throat in the process. When Máire found the poor turkey it was practically half-strangled already. We went back into our classes after the break and Seáinín Ó Deágha came racing in after us issuing threats to all and sundry about what he would do to the blackguards who had done this; he also left the schoolmaster under no illusions about what he thought of him and the fact that he didn't 'lay down the law' more forcefully with his students. Power said nothing. He went over and grabbed Seáinín by the shoulders and shoved him roughly out the classroom door, slamming the door behind him. Power didn't know what had brought Seáinín into the school and he didn't ask us children either. The following day however, he warned us to put an end to the twine trick, or that we would face serious consequences.

I remember another trick that was played on poor Seáinín. He used to bring turf home from Móin a' Bhráca on the south-eastern end of An Gleann using his black mule and cart. The mule was very temperamental and one day he had tied it to the gate outside the meadow just as we came out of class to play at break-time. Donncha Pheigí called two or three other pupils over to him. They undid the axles on both sides of the cart and moved the cart slightly. Once Seán had eaten his dinner, he came out and untied the mule and sat up on the cart. The mule had a habit of shooting forward when it set off and that is exactly what happened. The only problem was that the wheels were left behind! Once the mule heard the unusual noise the cart made on the road, it became even more agitated and bolted even faster, its legs flying high in the air and Seáinín had a hell of a job trying to stop her and get control of her again. I don't know whether poor Seáinín ever realized the trick that had been played on him because he wasn't a very astute man in that sense. Whether he did or not, he certainly never complained to the schoolmaster about us anyway.

We played lots of tricks on other people and on each other in those school-going days of ours in Baile an Droichid and many's the fuss we caused; most of those tricks are gone from my memory now all these years later, however. That one trick that Donncha Pheigí played on poor Seáinín Ó Deá is still as clear in my mind now as if it had only happened yesterday.

The Blondies

The only people still living in Gleann Chárthainn now who remember the Blondies that once lived out in Gleann na Faille are carpenter Dic Ó Siadhaile and myself. Gleann na Faille runs for a distance of about three miles between the mountains. It is a narrow and lonely glen. The mountains are high on both sides and a cascading river runs through it, the rush and noise and spume of which cascades over the rocks. The north face of the glen rises vertically into the sky. The mouth of the glen here is high but the ground dips as you go further into the glen and the water here slows and becomes less agitated in its movement. On the other side of the mountain slope was a woods when I was young. It was a lonely and enchanting place and on a piece of level ground in there is where the Blondies lived. You'd never have thought that people would choose to live in such a lonely and isolated place. Our house was nearest to theirs and we were more than three miles away. The only road into this place was a rough mountain boreen that followed the course of the river. This road saw some improvement when they decided to chop down the woods there and use it for timber during the war. The Blondies were long gone by then, however. The place where the trees once grew there on the side of the mountain is a big space of pockmarked ground now – the surface of the hill would remind you of an emaciated or half-plucked chicken that has lost most of its feathers. There is hardly any growth there now, just the odd small wasted-looking butt of a tree, half-eaten by the occasional goat that wanders that way. The only remnants of the Blondies place now are the walls that circumvented their smallholding and the bits of rock that mark the spot where their house once stood. Back then, the walls of the cottages were built with rocks and the roof of the house was made of heather. The old fields are all over-run now with heather and the western gorse and the bracken, the same fields that I remember crops of potatoes and rye growing in one time.

I remember Tomás and Martán and Seán Bán and Cáit Mhór (Big Kate), the mother. I don't remember Old-Blondie – the father – at all. He was dead before my time. I still remember well the first day that I ever saw their house out there in Gleann na Faille however. Cáit Mhór was standing in the front door and I remember thinking that she was the tallest woman I'd ever seen in my life. It was for good reason that they called her Cáit Mhór. Her hair was beetle-black and her skin was sallow. She held herself as erect and straight as a whip.

That day when I was out on the mountain, I was with Seán Mac Craith and we were looking for a ram that had gone astray just a few weeks after it was bought and brought to Lios na Faille. As we passed the Blondies' house, Seán greeted the mother but her reply was dour and rude. Seán didn't bother asking her whether she had spotted the missing ram but when we had passed the house, he started questioning me about her. He said that he'd passed their house one day recently as he'd passed over the mountains but he hadn't seen anyone at home there. I told him what little bit I knew about the Blondies – the mother and her three sons – and that was little enough in itself and only based on bits and pieces that I picked up about them at home.

The three sons were very similar in appearance to their mother, all three of them over six feet tall and swarthy with black hair. Their looks didn't tally with their family nickname at all, seeing as none of them had blonde hair – although I often heard it said that their father Tomás Bán Ó hIfearnáin – had very blonde hair indeed. The sons followed their mother's colouring. They were their own people and kept very much to themselves. They didn't socialize with any of the other people in An Gleann and the only time they had any interaction with them was at a funeral or at a wake, occasions that they always diligently attended. They kept quite a large number of sheep on the mountainside and they spent all their time looking after them or cultivating the small patch of ground they owned near their house. I remember seeing the three sons passing our gate outside, each of them carrying a big bag of wool, on their shoulders. They would bring this wool into Baile na hAbhann whenever the wool merchant from Clonmel was visiting and buying it there. They used to keep hounds and they would hunt hares with them and I heard that they had guns and shot many grouse out on the mountain and woodcock in the woods.

This was an era when the local landlord considered all the game to be his by rights and he would gladly have turfed them out of their smallholding if he had got the chance. They had a lease that couldn't be broken so easily however, and he failed to get them evicted. I heard sean-Risteard Ó Siadhaile saying that it was their grandfather, known as Tomás Bán, who had first settled in the area. People used to say that the 'Blondies' weren't too particular about swiping other people's sheep when they wanted to have some lamb for their food, although I never heard that anyone ever proved anything against them in this regard. Personally, I don't think there was any truth in this rumour.

They rarely attended Mass except for Christmas Day and Easter Sunday and it was hard to blame them on this front seeing as they would have had to walk ten miles or so from their house to the church in Baile na hAbhann. That said, the sons nearly always passed down along Bóthar na Faille every Sunday and holy day, all three of them clean-shaven and wearing their best clothes as they went drinking in 'Léan Mhairtí's pub. It'd be late that evening when they'd make their return journey and when my aunt Máire caught sight of them she would get angry and say that they'd come to no good in the end. She was angry of course because she knew that they hadn't attended Mass although they'd been able to spend the day in the pub. My aunt Máire was a devout woman and she hated to see people making little of the Sabbath or the Lord's Day. Her prediction that they wouldn't come to a happy end eventually proved right but to explain how this came to pass, I first need to tell the story of how Seán Baróid, Dic Ó Siadhaile and I discovered the tomb-like cave beneath the waterfall at Poll an Easa.

The river in this area runs southwards through An Gleann Láir and there is another one that flows westwards through Gleann na Faille; these two stretches of water come into contact with one another about a half-a-mile from our house. The flow of water from Gleann na Faille was always much stronger than the other one but they would always meet close to a place called Dá Ghleanna. Here the water from Gleann na Faille falls down over a rock-face about eight-foot high and mixes with the other currents. The pool into which this water falls is called Poll an Easa and every summer a good many of the local lads used to go swimming there. The water in this pool wasn't more than three or four foot deep and the lads used to have some crack seeing which of us was able to stand under the waterfall without falling over from the power of the water. Of the lads who went swimming there every summer, there were none who were there as often as Seán Baróid, Dic Ó Siadhaile and I, I'd imagine. If the summer was very dry the river was reduced to a shallow stream of water and there was just a trickle of water coming down over the waterfall there. It wasn't difficult at all to stand beneath the waterfall on a day like this, when the summer was very dry and we went swimming in the pool below. Anyway, one day I happened to go in behind the falls and, completely by chance, I happened to glance in a certain direction underneath the rock-face there. Whatever way I looked up, I spotted what I thought was a chink of light coming from somewhere inside the great rock there. The rock-face was covered with moss and lichen and whatever was in there was well-hidden beneath all the undergrowth that covered a thick lip of drooping rock. I called the other lads over and we peered into where the light was coming from. They were as surprised as I was at this discovery and we chatted for a while about what might be in behind the rock there. We began to peel away some of the lichen and moss and the hole where the light came from soon became much bigger. After a few minutes, it was big enough to crawl into. 'Let's go in and see what's in here', said Seán Baróid, a lad whose courage never failed him. He climbed in first and Dic and I followed him in, each of us walking on all fours. We found ourselves in a chamber or cave that was as big as this kitchen; the roof of it was actually far higher than it originally looked and we could stand up in it quite easily. 'My God!' Look at *this* boys!' Seán said giving a shout. Strangely, it wasn't dark inside in the chamber. Sunlight spilled in from four or five different cracks high up in the wall of the cave. It was one of these rays of sunlight that I had orginally spotted from the outside. Another incredible thing was the sight of so many swallows' nests on the inside of the chamber and the birds were flitting in and out of the cracks in the wall there. We had often spotted the swallows disappearing through the fissures high up in the rock which formed the waterfall but none of us had any idea that they had a whole series of nests built in there. The floor of the chamber was covered in small stones and gravel and there was a big flat ledge of rock shaped almost like a table in the middle of the room. Further in, and directly opposite the entrance to the cave was another chamber, but we didn't venture any further to explore it that day. Hardly any of us said a word for the first few minutes that we were in the cave. We all just stood there and looked around us in amazement. Next thing, Dic Ó Siadhaile let a curse out of him. 'Well, my soul from the Devil, but who would have guessed that there was a place like this hidden just behind the waterfall!' We began to shiver then since we didn't have any clothes on and we said we'd better go out again. The heat and the light of the sun outside was a huge change compared to the cold inside in the cave.

We decided that we wouldn't tell anyone about this cave beneath the waterfall although we returned there often in the following weeks. We brought a candle in with us the next time to check out the other cave or passageway inside but we soon discovered that it was entirely blocked up with gravel just a few feet inside the entrance.

Over the years, Risteard Ó Siadhaile, Dic's father, was often going on about the cave called Uaigh na Caorach Glaise and Liam Beilbhí would explain how it had got its name – in fact, myself and Seán Baróid went down with Liam Tóibín, the schoolmaster, to see that cave years later – but I can honestly say that it was nothing compared to the excitement of that moment when we discovered this cave beneath the waterfall and climbed into it for the first time that summer's afternoon long ago.

In spite of our solemn promises that day not to tell anyone about the cave, our secret was soon out – and it was I who was responsible for revealing it too. This is what happened. One day around the end of September, just a few weeks after we'd discovered the cave beneath the waterfall, a rumour went around An Gleann that the Blondies had been arrested. Seán Mac Craith was the person first to tell us this story, a story he'd heard down in the forge Micil Dhuinn's forge in Cill Dhubh. They'd been arrested in their house in Gleann na Faille the previous night by all accounts. The 'peelers' had even brought them past our house the previous night although we hadn't heard anything outside. My aunt Máire did mention that she had woken the previous night at about two a.m. because she'd heard the dogs barking and making noise. I must have slept very soundly that night because I never heard anything.

The 'peelers' had only managed to apprehend two of the sons, however, Mártan and Tomás. Seán Bán had managed to get away and they couldn't find him anywhere. The two 'Blondies' they arrested were brought to the prison in Clonmel, accused of making and using counterfeit money. Apparently, 'Léan Mhairtí had become suspicious of a shilling coin that one of the brothers had used to pay her with in the pub and she'd shown it to one of the 'peelers' who was a regular customer of the pub. The 'peelers' had arrived unannounced in the middle of the night and attempted to arrest the three men but Seán Bán had managed to evade capture. While searching the house, the police had found other false coinage and a device used to make counterfeit money; the latter was hidden in the roof of the house.

The police were out hunting Seán Bán, day and night, for the next fortnight or so but they couldn't find him. They searched every house in An Gleann including our house. In fact, they searched our house three times – most likely because we lived closest to the 'Blondies'. There was no sign of Seán Bán anywhere, however. He had completely disappeared; it was as if the ground had just opened and swallowed him up. If anyone did know where he was hiding, they certainly never said anything. And even if the neighbours had often been negative about the 'Blondies' prior to this, now that they were in trouble, they empathized with them and were on their side. Even my aunt Máire was very critical of 'Léan Mhairtí for selling the 'Blondies' out like this, especially after all the money they had spent in her pub over the years.

Around this time, a black-face sheep of ours got separated from the flock and went missing. One day Seán Mac Craith sent me up the mountain road to see could I find her. I went about a mile up the mountain but I saw no sign of her there and when I was coming back down the mountainside again I followed the course of the stream. At one stage, I spotted a man standing on a height in a south-easterly direction from our house – in the place called An Cnoc Dubh. He was far off in the distance so I couldn't make out who he was, although he had the look of a 'peeler' to me. I didn't take too much notice of this lone figure either as the 'peelers' had been so active in the area in the preceding weeks that it didn't come as a surprise anymore to see them around the place. I followed the river downhill until I came to the far side of Poll an Easa. The terrain dips greatly here as you go deeper into the glen and where I was walking now was an embankment at a level of about twenty feet above the surface of the river. The area was thick with undergrowth on both sides of the water with gorse and brambles everywhere. There were lots of blackberry bushes here and I was sauntering along at my leisure, picking and eating blackberries as I went. I took my time, examining each blackberry I picked momentarily to make sure that there were no flies or maggots in it. If the root area between the berry and the bush was white and unbroken you always knew it was safe to eat the blackberry because no maggot had broken its way through the surface and buried itself inside in the fruit.

I was walking along slowly like this when I heard the sound of something coming against me through the bushes. Someone was crashing their way through the gorse and the brambles. I stopped and peered out ahead of me. Next moment, who emerged from a patch of thick brambles but Seán Bán? He was bathed with sweat and was breathing very heavily. He had obviously been running through the undergrowth at speed and was completely out-of-breath. For the first minute or two, he could barely get a word out – he was that exhausted and out-of-breath. From that day to this, I have never seen such a hunted look on the face of man nor beast. 'Wh … ere are they?' he managed to blurt out eventually, raising his hand in the direction of the top of the river. I knew straight away who he was referring to and I moved up through the bushes and the gorse until I had a better view over the whole of the glen. I peered out from behind a big clump of gorse bushes and looked around. Then I spotted three 'peelers' making their way down along the mountain road. They were about a half-a-mile away. The man on the crest of An Cnoc Dubh was still standing in the same place I'd originally seen him, a vantage point from which he could see the entire countryside beneath him. All of a sudden, he began to walk downhill very quickly however, as if making directly for where I was. Seán Bán was in right trouble now. I said to myself. If he followed the river for another few hundred yards, the ground gave way to an area of level ground which was flat and treeless, the riverbank bare of all bushes and gorse. He couldn't stay where he was either because the 'peelers' would search the whole area very carefully.

I stood still for a few seconds and then remembered … 'My God, there's the cave beneath the waterfall', I thought to myself. I ran back down and found Seán Bán again. He was lying flat on the ground; he looked completely exhausted, as if he didn't care what happened to him anymore. I put my hand on his shoulder'. 'Come on, get up quickly', I said. 'They're coming. There's a hole down here, inside underneath the waterfall, and they'll never find you there'. He looked up at me. He looked confused as if he couldn't understand what I was saying. I had to repeat it to him again. He got up then and followed me. I showed him the cave in behind the waterfall then and told him to climb in. In he went and I returned to where I had been earlier, and began casually picking the berries once more. I wasn't there very long when one of the 'peelers' stood opposite me at the edge of the river.

'Young boy', he said, 'did you see anyone near the bank of the river here a few minutes ago?'

'Yes. I saw someone here a good while ago', I said

'Which way did he go?' said the peeler.

'I'm not sure', I replied. 'I heard someone bursting through the gorse and I was afraid; so I hid myself. He went past me but I couldn't see the person. I was too afraid to look out and see who it was'.

The peeler believed me, by all accounts. While he was talking to me the other two peelers appeared on the opposite bank of the river and he told them what I had just said. The two left then, following the course of the river down into the glen. The third man stayed up on a height for a little while and then followed the other two down, albeit moving more slowly. They must have thought that they had Seán Bán and that he wasn't going to escape them this time. They searched every patch of gorse and every bush carefully on their way down. They stayed there searching until night fell but they had to give up in the end and go home.

As soon as the 'peelers' had left me to go searching, I went straight home. As soon as I found him, I told Seán Mac Craith about the cave beneath the waterfall and what had happened with Seán Bán and the 'peelers'. Once he got over his initial shock, Seán said that we had better go and see whether Seán Bán was alright. Seán told my mother and my aunt Máire and they got some food and other things ready for us. Then we waited until darkness fell and we were sure that the 'peelers' had gone home. The two of us set off up the mountain. Seán was carrying a few blankets, some bread and butter, and a bottle of milk. I had a candle and a packet of matches wrapped in paper. When we got to the waterfall, I showed Seán the secret cave and we both went in. I went in first and lit the candle. Poor Seán Bán was fast asleep, stretched out on a stone slab. He was so exhausted and worn-out that we actually had a job waking him up. Seán had to shake him back and forth a few times before he came to and his eyes opened wide with surprise. He recognized me then and grabbed hold of both of my hands tightly.

'You're your father's son', he said.

He looked over at Seán then. 'You're Seán Mac Craith', he said, 'I've never spoken to you before'.

'That's me', said Seán.

'Here, eat and drink some of this. You need it badly I'd say'.

Seán Bán drank half the bottle of milk but he didn't eat anything. Seán Mac Craith gave him the blankets and we left him the candle and the matches and then returned home. Before leaving, Seán told him that he'd return again in the morning to see how he was.

I hardly slept a wink that night, I was that excited about everything that had happened. This was some story to tell Seán Baróid and Dic Ó Siadhaile the next time I met them. Seán Bán spent eight days in that cave and during all that time, the 'peelers' searched every nook and cranny on the mountain during daylight hours. At night, some of them hid in the ditches watching out and listening in case Seán Bán reappeared when it got dark. They questioned me three times about what had happened that day but I stuck rigidly to my original story. They had no choice but to give up in the end. They couldn't for the life of them understand where Seán Bán had gone. The neighbours said that what had happened that day was that the soldiers had approached the Blondies house from the southern end of the glen but Seán Bán had managed to get away from them. They had followed him as he ran away down the glen and they were sure that they had him at one stage. They would have got him too, if Seán Baróid, Dic Ó Siadhaile and I hadn't discovered that cave beneath the waterfall a few weeks earlier.

Seán Mac Craith was the one who went out to see Seán Bán while he was hiding; needless to say, he had to be very careful when visiting him as there was no knowing where the 'peelers' might be hiding or watching out. He bought clothes and shoes and anything else that Seán Bán needed. He got the money for the clothes from Cáit Mhór after he went to her and told her where her son was hidden. In the end, Seán Bán managed to evade capture. He escaped across the mountains and down to Youghal Bay where, with the help of a relation of Seán Mac Craith's, he managed to get across to England on a coal-ship. A month later, Mártan and Tomás Bán went on trial in Clonmel. Each of them were found guilty, of course, and both of them were 'transported' to a penal colony for seven years. The day after the court case, Cáit Mhór went down on her two knees in the middle of the road as she passed 'Léan Mhairtí's pub and cursed 'Léan's seed, breed and generation. Whether this curse came to pass or not, there is no-one related to 'Léan Mhairtí living in Baile an Droichid now and there is no trace of the pub there now either.

A while after this, Cáit Mhór sold all the sheep that they kept on the mountain and left Gleann na Faille. In fact, we bought a lot of her sheep from her and she even gave me one of them as a present. She had received a letter from her son Seán in England. The letter had actually been sent to Seán Mac Craith although there was no news for Seán himself in it. The years went by, and as is normal, people rarely mentioned the 'Blondies' – except occasionally, when they were visiting and telling stories in one another's houses. I grew into a man and had my own share of life's troubles to worry about. Then, ten years – almost to the day! – that I'd first shown that secret cave to Seán Bán, a small package arrived in the post to me, as addressed to Lios na Faille. I could tell from the post-mark on it that it had been sent from Australia. I opened it and inside were two gold watches, complete with golden chains. My name was written on a piece of paper that was around one of the watches and Seán Mac Craith's name was on the other; there was nothing else written in the letter. Seán was out in the shed when I brought the package out to him to show him the two watches. We knew that Seán Bán had sent us them and our respect for him was even greater than it already was – especially considering that he had remembered us so many years later and the help that we had given him when he was in trouble. Whatever other faults he might have had, Seán Bán had a good heart. That watch is in my pocket now as I put these words down on paper; I sent Seán Mac Craith's watch to his sister's son after he died. He told me to do that when he first became sick.

A few years later, rumours reached us in An Gleann that the 'Blondies' had done very well for themselves in Australia and owned hundreds of acres of land and thousands of sheep. I don't remember whom we heard this story from first. After that, I never heard anything more about the 'Blondies'.

HOW POWER ENDED UP BROKE

The parish priest who was in Baile na hAbhann after An tAthair Tomás Ó Floinn died was a very impetuous and hot-tempered man. He was easily angered and everyone was afraid to cross him. I remember him on the altar at Sunday Mass and he frightened me with how angrily he spoke about something or other that had happened in the parish and which he wasn't happy about at all. He'd speak Irish or English depending on what suited and he was fluent in both languages. I remember him reading the Gospel from the Mass Book on Sundays. He would hold out the Mass Book in his hands and read the Gospel in either Irish or English, translating directly from the Latin with ease. He was known for his charitable nature and no poor person ever left his door without receiving alms from him. He gave everything away and when he died there wasn't even enough money left to bury him.

Many different priests were in this parish at different stages when I was growing up. They were all fine men, upstanding and devout. The odd one of them had his own faults but just because you wear a black soutane doesn't mean that you don't have the same human nature and weaknesses as anyone else. There was none of them as hot-tempered or fiery as the man whom I'm referring to now, however. The local people used to tell stories about how, every so often, he got into a right temper for one reason or another. Here's one of these stories:

There was a widow living in Boithrín na Cille about a half-a-mile away from the crossroads. The house where she lived is still there to this day and her descendants still live in the area. One of her sisters died over in England and she adopted her sister's only son and looked after him – although she had three children of her own and wasn't well off. When this lad that she'd adopted got older, his health was very poor. He had tuberculosis or 'an Díce' as the people of An Gleann used to call that awful disease. One Sunday when he was quite sick, he coughed up a load of blood and his aunt thought that he was about to die. She sent someone to get the priest and told the messenger to hurry as there mightn't be much time. The parish priest said the two Masses in Baile na hAbhann that Sunday and had just returned home when the messenger arrived to his house; the person with the message had to go to the other end of the parish to reach the priest's house. The younger priest (curate) had been called out to give the Last Rites to someone else who was dying and so the parish priest had to return to Gleann Chárthainn which was a journey of about eight miles from his house. When he arrived to the widow's house, what did he see but the lad whom he'd been told was dying, sitting in a chair close to the fire. It seemed to the priest that he had a healthy glow on his face. The priest got into a temper and he didn't even give the poor widow a chance to explain the situation. He just laid into her verbally. 'A farthing on it that I'll give you a good lash of the whip', he said storming out the door again. One of the neighbours claimed afterwards that the priest's parting words as he left the house were 'My curse on you'. It is very difficult to believe that the priest could have said such a thing. I don't believe that he ever said those words but two or three of the neighbours who were present that day, claimed that he did and people still tell this story here in An Gleann. For rural Irish people then, there was nothing worse in this world than a priest's curse. The priest was only halfway home that day, when the boy who was sick coughed up a huge amount of blood. An hour later and he was dead without receiving Confession or the Last Rites. The priest was really upset when he heard about the boy's death and he wouldn't accept a penny from the widow for any of the Masses that were offered on behalf of the dead boy.

There was a house on the other side of the boreen, just down from the widow's house. The man there was a labourer and he lived there with his wife and four children. They had a small girl who was about five years of age, and from what I heard she was so beautiful that you couldn't but stare at her. On the afternoon of the boy's funeral, some blackguard tied an old tin-gallon can to the tail of the mule belonging to the local carpenter. The mule ran off down Bóithrín na Cille at quite a pelt, the sound of the can on the road, frightening it and making it run even more quickly. By chance, the labourer's little girl ran out the gate of her house onto the road just as the mule came racing past. The mule hit her and she was killed instantly.

Micil Mhártan's house was about two hundred yards down the boreen from the widow's house. The only people living there were Micil and his wife Cití. Their three daughters all lived in America. The old couple were reasonably well-off because their daughters used to send them plenty of money back from America. On the night following the little girl's funeral, Peaid Philib from Cúl na mBroc was out on the east side of An Gleann. He was walking home about midnight, having spent the afternoon drinking in Baile na hAbhann after the funeral. He always took his time and was usually late going home. It was just as well for Micil Mhártan and Cití that he was like this because as he was returning along the road that night, he noticed that their house was on fire. The flames were bursting up through the roof from inside the house and Micil and Cití were shouting inside. The kitchen was ablaze and they couldn't get to the door to escape because the smoke was so thick.

Peaid Philib put his shoulder to the front door and tried to break it in but it wasn't easy because it was well-secured from the inside with a timber cross-beam. On his third charge against the door, Peaid managed to smash it in and pull the old couple to safety. They were really lucky as the rest of the house went up in a big ball of flame just seconds later. By now, some of the other neighbours had gathered; everything was burned to the ground however – everything except for a few bed-covers that someone pulled out through a window using a pike. All the locals were convinced that it was the priest's curse that had caused all of these terrible things to happen, especially given that Micil Mhártan's wife and the mother of the small girl who was killed were both in the widow's house the day that the priest got angry. A number of the neighbours went to the priest and insisted that the priest come back to the area and remove the curse. Incredible as it may seem, the priest did actually come back and he spent a half-an-hour reading from his holy book while walking up and down the boreen. I am repeating this story now exactly as I heard it told many times; in fact, this story is still told in An Gleann even today. There are still people here also who believe that it was the priest's curse that caused these tragedies in the area. I find it very difficult to accept that there is any substance to such a belief, however.

It was this same priest who put an end to the Pattern at Baile na hAbhann and he was definitely right to do that in my opinion, as it had just become an occasion for drinking and fighting. I still remember the time that the Pattern was prohibited but I have no memory of the incidents where the little girl was killed and the old couple's house burned down. Any images I have of these tragedies come from my own imagination I suppose, and as based on the many times that I heard others describe these terrible events.

In my final year attending Baile an Droichid school, I remember how we all noticed that the relationship between Power the schoolmaster and the parish priest had become strained and acrimonious. The older lads in the school would often wonder what was going on. When the priest arrived into the school on a visit, he barely said 'hello' to the schoolmaster and the schoolmaster barely acknowledged him either. In the end, they stopped speaking to one another completely. I remember the parish priest taking over the class that the master was teaching a couple of times without even asking the master beforehand. The parish priest would take the class to teach them the Catechism. They used to teach prayers and the Catechism in the church in Baile na hAbhann in between the two Masses on a Sunday also and the teachers from both schools would be in attendance. If the teachers didn't show up, the parish priest used to get really angry with them. It wasn't always that easy to get to the church from An Gleann then because it was over four miles away, but the priest didn't accept any excuses for being absent. He came to the school each week without fail and he'd question the pupils to check whether they had been at the prayers on the previous Sunday. He had a short whip with a small knot or notch on the end of it and anyone who didn't know their prayers would get a couple of lashes of the whip across the hands. The cord on the whip would wrap itself around and the knot would get you on the back of your hand. Many's the messer who had welts on the back of his hand after he was finished with them.

Seán Ó Gráda was going out one day just as the parish priest arrived at the school on horseback. He told Seán to mind the horse as he went into the school. He wasn't long inside when Seán heard the whip and the roaring coming from inside. Seán hadn't been at the prayers himself the previous Sunday and he was so scared about what the priest might do to him when he came out that he let the horse go by accident. Off went the horse and it took the priest a half-an-hour to catch it again. Everyone had to go out and help him get the horse under control again and the priest was so angry that day that I'd say he'd have flayed the skin off Seán Ó Gráda if he'd got his hands on him. He must have forgotten about it fairly quickly, however. Seán didn't receive any punishment for what had happened and the schoolmaster never said anything to him about it either.

I remember as clearly as if it were yesterday the day that Power was kicked out of the school. We were only just back in school a few days after the Autumn holidays when it happened. A group of us were gathered at the school in the morning waiting for the master to arrive; we were playing with a ball against the gable-end of the school. I remember that when he arrived, he spoke to us in a very civil and measured way; there was something different about him however because he didn't usually talk to us in this tone of voice. He obviously knew what was in store for him. We were in the classroom just a short while when the parish priest arrived and he was in a big hurry. He didn't say hello to the master.

'Give me the school-key Power', he said, in an angry voice, 'you'll never teach another day in this school again'.

The priest told us all to go home and we all scurried out the door as quickly as we could. We were frightened and none of us hung around to see or hear what happened next. We knew that something very serious was up, but what it was, we had no idea. I suppose that we were glad to get a day's holiday from school, even if we didn't know what was going to happen to the master. By that evening, it was all over the parish that the parish priest had evicted Power and his wife from the school and everyone had their own 'take' on it and was trying to guess what might have happened to cause this. No-one knew what could have led to master being fired like that, especially since he had been teaching in the parish for more than twenty years by then. For years afterwards, people were surmising what might have caused him to be thrown out, and everyone had their own theory about it. The truth is that no-one knew the exact reason for his dismissal. Some people said that all that the priest wanted was for Power to apologize to him for something or other - but that Power wouldn't do this. I never did find out for sure why he lost his job or what he had done that was so awful.

I do know that Power was a very independent-minded and stubborn individual and wasn't the type to bend the knee to anyone too easily. He was a strict teacher and was hard on the pupils but that was the norm for all teachers then. He produced good pupils and many of them did very well in life afterwards. He was independent-minded and his own man, that's for sure; but that didn't mean that he should have lost his livelihood like that after twenty years working in the parish. No-one ever had anything but good things to say about Power's wife either but she too was dismissed from the school, the same as her husband. What happened to Power was as terrible as it was immoral and the laws of that era – be they church-made or state-made – should never have permitted such a thing to happen. I never heard anyone take the priest's side in relation to that whole incident with Power and his wife and yet the people of the local parish were a cowardly and craven lot weren't they? To think that there wasn't even one real man among the whole lot of them – someone who had the courage to go to the local parish priest and tell him that what he'd done to a husband and wife who had been teaching their children for more than twenty years was totally wrong.

Power and his wife and five children went to America and from what we heard about them afterwards, they got on very well in their new lives over there. One of their daughters visited this area just a few years ago and I spoke to her myself. She was a fine-looking woman and she only had a slight trace of an American accent. She was the youngest of the family. Although she was just six years of age when they left the area, she wanted to see the school where her father and mother had once taught.

The day that Power was fired was my last day at school in Baile an Droichid. I was fourteen years of age and there was plenty of work for me around the farm at home.

Lios na Faille

Our farm is situated at the bottom of the mountain. The few fields that are furthest away are fairly level but the one that is up highest on the mountainside has a big slope in it. The slope is so sharp here that it has to be ploughed with the gradient – i.e. by moving the plough and the horses downwards with the slope. It can't be ploughed upwards or against the hill at all. The farm is one hundred acres in total but thirty acres of this is just scrub that has never been tilled within living memory. It was definitely tilled once long ago however. Although it is overgrown with heather and gorse now, you can still see the ridges where someone ploughed it decades ago. The land that is tilled there is good land, especially the fields lower down and they say that the field known as Páirc na Naoi nAcra is the best field of all in An Gleann. The main slope lies to the south of the farm and Cnoc Dubh shelters this area from the east wind; for this reason, the crops here can be harvested more quickly than in other areas.

When I stopped going to school and the master was fired from his job, I began to help Seán Mac Craith on the farm. He had already made great improvements to it during the few short years that he had been with us. He had straightened up all the ditches and cut down all the hedges that had gone out of control. Needless to say, this work was all really badly-needed, as none of it had been done since my father died.

Our house had a slate roof and the same with the shed that burned down when I was a child. The other outhouses we had around the farm all had thatched roofs on them. Seán put galvanized roofs on these except the 'dairy' – this had a roof that was made of a mixture of metals including zinc and it was in a bit of a mess so Seán repaired it and strengthened it using a wood underlay on the inside. Sean-Risteard Ó Siadhaile used to help him now and then with jobs such as these but it was Seán who did most of the work.

We would get water for the house in Tobar na Foinse up on the flat field, about a quarter of a mile from the house. He constructed a long lathe or funnel extending down along the edge of the ditches from the well to the meadow. He constructed this in such a way that that the water emerged from a metal pipe at the end of its journey and this made a huge difference in terms of the irrigation of the fields. Before this we had to transfer barrels of water downhill from the well a couple of times a week and so this new system saved us a lot of work.

Of all the tasks around the farm, I preferred working with the horses the best of all and that first winter after I'd finished going to school, Seán had me ploughing the ridges and I felt really important in myself. Seán stayed with me the first few times I did this and then he let me do the ploughing by myself afterwards. Soon I was able to handle a plough and a ploughshare fairly well. Within a few years, I was reasonably good at ploughing and used to do most of this work around the farm. The only time Seán helped was when the going got tough on fallow or grass-land but I did most of it. Even when we were planting potatoes on the fallow land, I did the ridges because I could do a nice, neat job on them. That type of work is all in the past now; people don't plough the fallow ridges anymore here in An Gleann.

Whenever I wasn't following the horses, I did the milking with my aunt Máire and my mother, both morning and afternoon. I used to herd the cows in and out of the barn and I'd tether them and give them grass or hay whenever they were kept in for the night. By the time I finished school, we had ten milk-cows, although we'd only had six cows when Seán first arrived here. My aunt Máire would do the churning every Friday and she'd place the butter in a firkin and we'd bring it to Clonmel every second Saturday. They had a big butter-market in Clonmel every Saturday back then, in a place called the 'Weigh-house'. This was a large house with a great arch and large iron gates leading into it. That house is still there today. It looks the same as before although it's many years since anyone has bought any butter there. A man used to go round back then with a sort of a small cart in those days and he'd dip into the butter and taste it and smell it to test its quality. There were many butter firkins lined up there waiting for him to test them. Large numbers of women were lined up there with their baskets and different types of butter in them. Another different man tasted and smelt the butter in the different mixtures. There used to be a right ruckus while all this was going on, a right cacophony of sound. I think it was around ten pence a pound that you got for the butter then. I used to drive the horse for my aunt after I finished school and this was always my job every second Saturday in the summer and in the autumn. Seán Mac Craith only accompanied my aunt Máire to the town when he had particular business of his own to complete in Clonmel. He used to go there often in the spring when he had a load of potatoes to sell as he didn't have that much confidence in me to get a good deal on them when it came to selling them.

We had about twenty sheep. They were mainly mountain sheep that we kept out on the hills for most of the year. When I was old enough, I used to go up on the hill to check on them a few times a week. That was another skill that Seán Mac Craith taught me actually – how to work a shears – and within a couple of years of leaving school, I'd be helping him with the shearing. We used to sell the wool in Clonmel. Two or three families still wove linen and flannel in an An Gleann and although we didn't, I remember that there was a spinning wheel that had belonged to my grandmother hanging in the shed for years before it finally fell apart because of old age. There used to be weavers in Cloichín an Mhargaidh in those days whom people sent their thread to and they would make homespun cloth (tweed) or flannel from it. They made way more flannel than they did homespun cloth. Nearly everyone wore the flannel vests back then in An Gleann but only the odd elderly person wore a suit made of homespun cloth even in those days. No-one old or young has worn one of those white vests or anything made of homespun cloth in this area for years now.

Máiréad an tSiúinéara ('Margaret the Carpenter' – i.e. Margaret married to the carpenter) used to weave wool although she had to buy the thread as they only had a small patch of land and they had no sheep of their own. She used to get whatever wool she needed from us. There was no money exchanged; Sean-Risteard would do some work for us around the place in lieu of the wool. I often watched Máiréad at work. She'd have big rolls of thread next to her that were as big as footballs. I often watched her carding the wool also. The room where she worked would be crowded with the rolls before she began weaving. She would send the rolls of thread to the weaver to make flannel; she never made any homespun clothes from the materials she worked with. She made socks from some of the leftover thread and sold them in the shop at

Baile na hAbhann. She got ten pence a pair for them and they'd be sold in the shop then for a shilling a pair. People really prized woollen socks then, especially those made from the wool of the black-fleeced sheep. We also kept at least two or three of these black-fleeced sheep and Mairéad would normally get whatever wool they produced. We used mountain scraws that we gathered on the hills and bits of whitethorn and hawthorn bushes as fuel for the fire. The scraws would be harvested with a wide-angled spade known as the 'báisín' and they would be saved then in the same way that we saved turf on the bog. Once all the turf in Móin an Bhráca had been saved, the people of An Gleann relied on scraws from the mountain as fuel for the fire – everyone except Seán Mór Breathnach that is. The mountain scraws were transported downhill on a type of roller or cart. Once the heather on the scraws was withered and dried out, they would be used as kindling for the fire. All you had to do was to add them in with a few logs of wood and they made a fine fire. The Barons who were the landlords in Gleann Chárthainn never prevented their tenants from gathering scraws on the mountain as long as they didn't set the whole mountainside alight as part of this work. Langley, from Baile na hAbhann, wouldn't let anyone of his tenants cut scraws on the mountainside, however; he wouldn't even allow a bit of a gorse bush to be cut down. Consequently, it was very difficult for the poorer people to get any fuel for the fire back in those days.

In and around Baile na hAbhann, all the farmers burned coal. They bought most of this coal in Dungarvan. You could buy it straight from the ship at the quayside there for fifteen shillings a ton; it was about twice that price if you bought it in Clonmel. The farmers used to help one another transport the coal home. Every farmer would have a 'carriage-horse' – as they referred to it then – to transport his coal and five or six neighbours would travel together with their horses in a sort of a 'convoy' to get the coal. They would have 'cinders' boxes' on the back of each cart and each load weighed somewhere between one ton and 25 hundredweight. Only a really powerful horse was capable of pulling a ton-and-a-half. The bit that really killed the horses was the long journey against the hill for over three miles, from the 'Pike' to the top of Coilleagán. They'd leave home for Dungarvan at about eight o'clock on the previous evening and they'd reach the 'Halfway' sometime between eleven o'clock and midnight. The 'Halfway House' is a pub that is situated about halfway between Clonmel and Dungarvan. All the carters would stop there to let the horses have a rest and so that the men could have a drink. The carters would give a special 'bran' drink to the horses and they'd all stay there for a couple of hours. There would often be singing and raucousness there too, according to those who did the trip over the years. They'd all head off again then at a nice, steady pace and they'd reach Dungarvan at about six o'clock in the morning. Some of the men would sleep on the carts as they'd usually have a pile of straw that they could lie down on, on the back of the cart. Sometimes two or three men would go into the same cart just to have some company and they'd let the horses follow each other along. The first thing they always did on arrival in Dungarvan was to buy a few hake from the fishermen at that quay for their breakfast. Country people were very fond of fresh fish back then because they rarely ate fish that was freshly-caught if they lived inland or away from the sea. They'd cook the hake for them in one of the cafés along the quayside. You could buy a nice fresh hake for sixpence back then. After they'd eaten, they'd go to fill the loads of coal and when this job was done, they'd un-harness the horses and feed and water them. From then until about two o'clock in the afternoon, they'd hang around the town or go drinking until it was time to set off for home again.

They'd have another long break at the 'Halfway' on the way home again when they'd give water and corn to the horses and it was usually between 9 and 10pm in the evening by the time everyone was back home. The young lads loved those trips to Dungarvan nearly as much as they did going to the Races. They might have had just two or three shillings in their pockets but everything was cheap to buy that time. You could buy a half-gallon of porter back then for sixpence and you could get your breakfast for eight pence. The man who was buying the coal would pay the carters whatever money they needed for transporting it home. The most a carter got paid then was two or three shillings; it would be a generous man who was paid more than four shillings by them. Seán Mór Breathnach used to pay every man who drove a 'carriage-horse' for him to get coal one crown each. I know all this, because I often did the journey myself on the back of the 'coal-carriage' that the blacksmith had hired, this even though I was barely in my teens at that stage. Seán Mac Craith never went to Dungarvan for coal; I think that maybe he didn't want to run into anyone he knew down there.

We planted wheat some years in the two fields furthest away from the house. Seán Mac Craith cut the wheat using a scythe and my aunt Máire would bind the stooks. When I was bigger, I helped her with this work. Any year that we had extra corn for harvesting, we'd pay a couple of men to help us with the binding. Seán would thresh the corn with a flail inside in the barn and Peaid na Bríghí would often be with him if he had to get the work done quickly. We would 'scutch' some of the corn and feed the hay to the cows. 'Scutching' meant flailing the heads of all the sheaves of corn on a timber block or a barrel that was turned on its side. This 'scutching' wouldn't remove all the grains from the corn so there was still some grain left in the hay; this 'left-over' stuff made excellent fodder for the cattle. Seán Mór Breathnach got the first ever harvesting machine in our area and the first ever threshing machine in An Gleann. He'd rent out the machine to the other locals in An Gleann with Micil Ó Néill in charge. Over time, people abandoned the old-style flail and began to use this new machine for threshing their corn. We'd sell the corn in Clonmel. I often went there when we were selling a load of corn and there was nothing I liked better than to sit up on the back of the nine bags of corn – that was the load that a horse could normally pull – on the road to Clonmel one fine autumn morning.

We had a lot of fowl on the farm. I suppose we must have had more than one hundred hens never mind all the ducks and geese. We would eat all of the geese ourselves once they were fattened. We'd have a goose every Sunday from Michaelmas onwards. For as long as my grandfather was alive, we had goose with our dinner. This was a tradition that he wouldn't give up but after he died we didn't follow it anymore and we ate goose with our dinner. Another old custom that my grandfather followed was that a goose or a cockerel had to be killed on the evening of Saint Mártan and the shape of a cross was made with the bird's blood on the back of the door. My grandfather wouldn't let anyone do any work with anything round-shaped or any farm implement that had wheels on it when it was Saint Mártan's Day either. I don't remember any of these things too clearly now as they were so long ago and I was quite young when my grandfather died. I often heard my mother and my Aunt Máire talking about these customs, however.

We brought our stock to be sold to the fairs of Clonmel or Lismore, two places that are roughly equidistant from us. On those days that we were going to the fair, we left the house between two or three o'clock in the morning. I loved going to the fair in the company of Seán although I'd be very tired by the time that we reached our destination. We didn't have to walk home again however, not unless it turned out that we hadn't sold anything – because my aunt Máire used to follow us in with the horse and cart. We brought whatever sheep we had to sell on the back of the cart also, as it would have been too long a distance for them to walk.

Everyone in An Gleann planted their potatoes in ridges when I was young; they would be harvested using a spade but we used a shovel to spread the first layer of clay over them and then the second layer later. Nowadays, everyone makes 'drills' for their potatoes and the clay is worked with a plough. The neighbours used to make fun of us saying that the way that we did it was just a form of slavery. Times have changed a great deal now. No one today would use a spade to dig potatoes except when they'd be cleaning the clay off the new potatoes. Lios na Faille is a great place for growing potatoes. We always had a great crop and made good money on them each year. That said, you'd never get more than sixpence a stone-weight for them, and often less than that even. I remember one year when potatoes were sold for three-pence a stone-weight.

My aunt Máire was very dedicated about raising pigs, and we always kept some pigs. It was rare for us not to have a sow and seven or eight piglets and my Aunt Máire fattening them. Yellow meal was quite cheap back then and we had plenty of small potatoes so it wasn't expensive for us to raise them.

We'd slaughter a pig at the end of September each year. The day that we slaughtered the pig was always a sort of a holiday for us. Before Seán Mac Craith came to us, Risteard Ó Siadhaile the carpenter, used to slaughter the pig for us. He always came into the women in the kitchen and they gave him a big drink of whiskey before he began the work. The large kitchen table would be placed out in the yard and, Risteard would throw the pig up on the table after stunning it and striking it on the back of the head with an axe. Then he'd cut the pig's throat and let it bleed into a bucket. When the pig had been completely bled, Risteard would scour its flesh with boiling water and remove its body-hair using an extremely sharp knife that he had. Seán Mac Craith had a different technique. While sean-Risteard was always there to help him with the butchering, he didn't mind it when Seán took over this job, probably because he was getting older and his strength wasn't what it once was. I still remember well the first time Seán Mac Craith slaughtered a pig. He attached a pulley and set of castors to a point on the inside of the roof of the shed and then they drove the pig in. Then Seán tied the pig's two back feet. This part wasn't easily done because there was a huge ruckus beforehand with the pig screeching and all the rest of it – before they raised the pig high on the pulley. Then he stabbed the pig in the neck and it was dead within a half-a-minute. Seán didn't agree at all with striking the pig with the axe, the way that sean-Risteard did it, as he said that this affected the blood-flow because the pig's head was damaged. He didn't remove the pig's body-hair with a knife as sean-Risteard did either. Instead he used a blow-lamp that carpenter's used to remove old paint from timber and burned off the pig's fur using this. When he was finished, there wasn't a single hair left on that pig. My aunt and my mother used to stuff the puddings and they always had Peigí Bheag (small Peggy) in helping them with this work. For as long as Peggy and Risteard Ó Siadhaile were alive, I never remember us slaughtering a pig even once in Lios na Faille when they weren't both there helping out. In addition to her day's pay – a half-crown – she would also get a few puddings and some pork chops, as her wages. The night after we killed the pig, the pork was salted. Sean-Risteard would be there and once he had drunk a nice drop of whiskey, he would start the chat and the wit. The salt would already be scattered on the kitchen table and every piece of meat was rolled carefully in it so that it was well-salted. The meat was then canned and pickled. After three weeks in the cans, the meat was hung from hooks hanging from the beams on the kitchen ceiling. The meat would remain there after that until, over time, it was all eaten. The night that we salted the meat we'd always drink tea and have 'gríscíní' (chops) to eat, once all the work was done. My mother would always send me down with some puddings and chops to Mairéad, the carpenter's wife, the next day.

This was how our life was then in Lios na Faille when I was growing up. We weren't rich but we had enough to live on and we were happy with our lives in those days, because we didn't know anything different. Life has changed greatly since then. The younger generation today wouldn't have much respect for the things that made us happy. That said, I'm not sure that modern life is better now in many ways.

ANECDOTES RELATING TO POACHING

I'll always remember the day that we managed to re-route the river so that it flowed into the Burke's meadow down at Móin Buí. Dic Ó Siadhaile, Seán Baróid, Tomáisín and Séamus an Bhúrcaigh and I were there that day. Before this, the river had run sideways alongside the meadow, on the western end of it. The mud ditch here was reasonably wide and this space between the river and the field was covered in bushes and gorse. It was Dic Ó Siadhaile who had noticed that the field inside the ditch was at a slightly lower level than the river-bed. He used to say that if we made a hole in the bottom of the ditch it would be possible to re-direct the stream so that it flowed into the field and we'd catch a lot of trout there when the river-bed dried up. Eventually, after we'd discussed the pros and cons of this between ourselves quite often, we decided to give it a go one fair day in May. The fair fell on a Saturday that year; Aonach na Bealtaine (The Spring Fair) in Clonmel was one of the oldest fairs of all and it was always held on the fifth day of the month. This day was ideal for our work; we wouldn't have any school; Tomás de Búrc would be gone to the fair and there would be no-one to disturb us in our experiment.

We had a shovel and a spade with us as we set off across the fields; Séamus and Tomáisín had brought them with them from their houses. We arranged to meet after dinner and we decided where we wanted to dig the hole in the ditch fairly quickly. It was hard work making the hole in the ditch but we did it in the end and changed the flow of the water. We sat there for a while and had a rest, and watched the water's progress. It was only a small trickle or stream of water at first but, after a while, it flowed a bit more strongly. This was what Dic and Seán had decided and they knew more about this kind of work than I did.

This was the first time I had ever seen people changing the flow of water like this. Before long, we were excited to notice a few trout jumping here and there in the small pools that developed as the water spread out. We found water-pools in the middle of the stream that weren't dried up yet and we diverted the water from these too using the shovel and found more trout in all of them. We even spotted a few eels here and there but we didn't bother with them – apart from a large one that Dic Ó Siadhaile cut in two with his shovel. We spotted loach and other freshwater eels but we didn't bother with them either. Seán Baróid told us not to kill the smallest trout because they weren't worth killing, and they would make bigger fish one day. We followed the flow of the river downhill until we came to another pool that was a couple of feet deep. This pool was known as Poll Pheig Ailean. I never did find out who Peig Ailean was or why a water-pool in a river that ran through the fields was named after her. This pool was too deep for us to drain using a shovel so we sent Séamus de Búrc home to get a bucket. Then Dic took off his shoes and socks, bunched his trousers up over his knees, and stepped into the water. It took him about a half-an-hour to get all the water to drain out of it. When the water was nearly all gone, the last bit of it was teeming with trout. We got nineteen trout and that's not counting all the small ones that we didn't bother with. One of them was as big as a herring, I remember. It was the biggest trout I'd ever seen in my life. We finished with that pool and moved on to another pool that was further down from Peig Ailean and that was overflowing with water. It was as we turned back in the direction of the meadow that we got a right fright because there was about a half-an-acre of it under water! A pig pool had formed in the field and this had happened much more quickly than we could ever have envisaged. When Séamus saw this he started crying and said that his father would kill him. It was difficult for us to calm him down. With Tomáisín, it was different; he was so young that he didn't understand the damage he had done. He was more interested in the trout that Seán Baróid was affixing to the end of some sally-rods for him than he was in the flooded meadow. We shared the trout out between us; there were more than fifty of them. We gave the biggest trout to Séamus to try and mollify him. Then we closed up the hole in the ditch again and went home. We might have been happy about all the fish we'd caught but we were very worried about the way the meadow was half-underwater now.

Tomás na Mónach Buí went crazy when he saw the meadow and the big pool of water that was now in the middle of it. He questioned Séamus and Tomáisín about it and they told him the truth. Séamus got a few belts across the hands from him but nothing happened to Tomáisín. Tomás tried to meet up with the rest of us for about a week after that but we shunned him. Luckily, the water in the meadow drained away a few days later and Tomás' anger must have faded because when he spotted me and Dic Ó Siadhaile coming home from Mass a fortnight later, all he did was raise his fist in our direction and start laughing. The water didn't do any damage to the meadow in the end; in fact, I heard later that the grass grew better in the section that had been underwater than it did in the rest of it.

The people in An Gleann always liked fishing. This was no surprise I suppose seeing as the rivers and streams of the area were always full of fish, especially during the winter when the salmon and trout came downriver to spawn. The salmon used to come down as far as Poll an Easa but that was as far they got as the falls were too high here for them there to travel any further. There were often up to twenty salmon gathered in the Pool and many's the salmon that was taken from that pool using a gaff. There were always trout in the river on the north side of the falls and how they got in there was a question I often asked myself. When the flow of the river slowed and died during summer – because it was with the current that the trout and salmon travelled downriver – there was barely enough water left in the pools there for the salmon to survive. In fact, they could barely swim at all by then; they could only jump and slobber around really and the local lads used to catch them with sticks and rocks then. The really big salmon didn't come over an Tonnóg and they did their spawning in the fords and where there was gravel and a flow of water. At night, they were caught using a fish-spear and a torch. For a torch, the fishermen then used to use a long sheaf of wheat that they set afire. When people got used to oil-lamps, what the poachers did was dry out an old bag and then attach it to a stick that was six-feet long and dip it into the oil. These would give off a far better light than any sheaf of hay. It was against the law to catch trout or salmon when they were spawning, and anyone who did this and was caught found themselves in right trouble. That said, a lot of lads in this area took the chance and went poaching salmon when it was the right season. I don't think the lads were always that interested in the salmon to be honest; they just loved taking a chance and getting 'one over' on the 'peelers' and the bailiffs.

The blacksmith would make the fish-spears. They were shaped like a fork except that the prongs were straight and with barbs attached to the ends. There were seven prongs on each fork and a space of about two-and-half inches between each of them. The foot of this fish-spear was shaped like the end of a shovel. One person would carry the torch or 'sop' while the other carried the fish-spear or sometimes they might have two or three fish-spears with them. They would have spotted that there were salmon in the pool already earlier in the day when the water-levels fell in the river. And they would be on their alert then also in case the bailiffs or the 'peelers' were in the vicinity. Immediately darkness fell was the safest time to go out poaching as there was much less of a chance that your enemy would catch you out then. Another trick was that Tomás Dhonncha, the bailiff would be brought into 'Léan Mhairtí's pub and given plenty to drink while the other lads headed off to poach the salmon. It is difficult to believe that honest Tomás Dhonncha didn't know what was going on when he went drinking in the pub. He liked drinking too much, however, especially when he was getting it for free and wasn't too bothered about his duties as a bailiff on those occasions.

Séimín Céitinn (Keating) and his son Jim were the two best-known poachers in the area. Apparently, they had cans full of salted salmon that they used to sell to anyone who would buy them. Technically-speaking, the Keatings weren't native to this area as their house was on the river-bank about a quarter of a mile north of Baile an Droichid; nevertheless, I feel it is important to recount some of the stories about them that people in this parish still tell sometimes today. The 'peelers' knew well, of course, that the Keatings were out poaching salmon regularly and although they went out patrolling the rivers at night and did their best to catch them, they never managed to catch them in the act.

Séimín was going to bed one night when a knock came on the door. There was a dead salmon lying on his kitchen table.

'Who is it?' he says.

'Police', said the voice outside, 'open up quickly'.

'Wait a second while I put on my trousers', said Séimín, 'I'm just after waking up'. He already had his clothes on but he needed to think quickly of somewhere to hide the salmon. There was a small colander of newly-washed potatoes near the dresser, ready for breakfast the following morning. Séimín emptied the potatoes out of it and he placed the salmon in the colander and threw the potatoes back in on top of it again. The 'peelers' were hammering on the door outside but once he had this done, he opened the door for them. They searched the house from top to bottom but found nothing. The one place that they didn't search was the colander with the potatoes in it, although they were very suspicious that there was a pair of wet shoes just inside Séimín's door. It's not a crime to have wet shoes, however, and so they had to leave empty-handed in the end!

Another night, Jim was returning home having poached a salmon, when two of the 'peelers' spotted him. They followed him and he began running. He didn't make for his own house, however. One of the 'peelers' who was a fast runner was beginning to catch up on Jim and just as he was climbing over a high fence, the 'peeler' caught him by the leg. Jim turned around and whacked the 'peeler' across the head with the salmon and knocked him to the ground. He managed to escape them and to keep his salmon also! Whatever suspicions the 'peelers' had about him, they couldn't prove them in a legal sense, because it was too dark that night.

Jim was caught in the end, however. Apparently, there were five or six salmon spawning in Áth Pheaidí Jur (Pheaidí Jur's Ford) after the river-currents were high. This ford is situated close to a place that is just one field away from the Keating's house. The sergeant thought of a trick to try and catch him in the act. He and another policeman went to the ford before daybreak and they hid themselves in a fissure of rock behind some gorse bushes close to the river. They waited there all day and just before nightfall Séimín and Jim appeared at the ford. They lit a torch and out they went into the water. Jim had speared a salmon when the two policemen jumped out from their hiding place. The 'peeler' jumped straight out into the water and grabbed a hold of Jim but he sergeant didn't manage to catch Séimín because he immediately doused out the flames of his light beneath the water. Séimín disappeared beneath the water. He swam downstream with the current for a few hundred yards and then climbed up on the river-bank. The sergeant knew well that it was Séimín but he couldn't prove it as he'd only seen his face for a split second by the flickering light of the torch. The two men had also disguised themselves by tying scarves around their faces, so that only their eyes were visible.

The sergeant made for Séimín's house to try and catch him when he returned but Séimín was too clever for him. He guessed what the sergeant was likely to do so and he knew that he would be nabbed straight away if he returned home and his clothes were all soaking wet. The sergeant waited outside the house for a long time. He was soaked to the skin and shivering and as soon as Séimín walked in the gate, he went to arrest him. But Séimín's clothes were as dry as powder and the sergeant had no option but to let him go. Séimín had gone up to Jim a' Ghabha's (Jim the Blacksmith's) house in the meantime and got a dry set of clothes from him. Séimín was about the same size and shape as the blacksmith so the sergeant had no proof worth talking about to use against him. Jim got two months in prison and when he was released he left for America where he's been ever since. From that day to the day he died, Séimín never went poaching salmon again.

Donncha Pheigí used to engage in all sorts of poaching but he only ever went out alone. Salmon, trout, pheasants, hares, rabbits, grouse; he would poach any of them when the time was right and he had every trick in the book up his sleeve. Seán na Coille (John of the Woods) who worked as gamekeeper for Baron the landlord, was always trying to catch Donncha Pheigí because Donncha was regularly setting snares for rabbits and hares but he never did manage to catch him in the act of poaching. One day Donncha Pheigí was out on the mountain, dead hare in hand, when Seán spotted him coming in his direction. Donncha was about a half-a-mile away and coming around the shoulder of the mountain. Seán set off in hot pursuit but as Donncha made a run for it. He came to a crossing in the river where the water was quite deep and where the current was very strong. He hid the horse in beneath a rock and took off his shoes and socks. He put his shoes on again but without the socks, and off he went again. He held the socks in one hand, hanging there wet and dripping. Then he slowed to a walk and Seán na Coille caught up with him. When Seán noticed what Donncha was holding, he knew that he had been tricked straight away.

'What's the big hurry Seán?' said Donncha.

'Where's the hare you had earlier?' said Seán.

'What hare?' said Donncha. 'Your sight must be failing, I'm afraid. My shoe was pinching my little toe and I had to take off my sock. It must have been the sock that you spotted and thought was a hare?'

'The devil himself might help you, but I'll get you yet', said Seán turning on his heel.

He searched around the general area where he'd seen Donncha crossing the river but he didn't find anything. He didn't think of searching in the water, however. I heard both men's versions of this incident – both Donncha Pheigí's and Seán na Coille's; this is why I remember the details of this story even today.

Donncha played another trick on Seán na Coille after this also. There was a small white meadow between Seán's house and the woods and the hares used to go in there regularly to graze. Donncha knew this and decided to take advantage of it one day when he knew that Seán was away from home. He placed a snare on one of the hare's 'runs' near where the hares went in through the ditch and into the field. The following day, when Seán went out of the house, he saw a hare that had been choked, hanging over the edge of the ditch, less than one hundred yards away from the house. I don't need to tell you that Seán was angry when he saw this. He knew who was responsible and he knew what he had to do. The night that he told us this story down in Dic Ó Siadhaile's house, he swore blind that he would get Donncha Pheigí one way or the other. I had actually heard Donncha's version of this story already but I didn't let on this to Seán, of course. Despite his best efforts, Seán never did manage to catch Donncha in the act of poaching.

The sergeant who was in charge of the 'peelers' in Baile na hAbhann back then was out looking for salmon poachers morning, noon and night. This wasn't the same man who had caught Jim Céitinn red-handed a few years earlier. Because he was very interested in fishing himself, he was always ordering the police under his command to re-double their efforts in relation to poachers and poaching. He actually promised a promotion to any policeman who arrested one of the poachers at work. The best poachers in the county were in An Gleann and in and around Baile na hAbhann, in particular. It was no wonder then that the most senior officer in this region was always hassling the local sergeant about catching poachers and bringing them to justice. Despite this, they didn't manage to bring even one person to court on this charge. Once, they brought three schoolboys to court, three lads who were caught throwing stones from the timber bridge in Baile an Droichid at a salmon in the pool below. Nothing happened to them. They were let off with a warning and told not to do it again. When the 'peelers' opened the barracks the following morning, they saw three salmon's heads attached to the iron pillars of the gate outside their door. The people going to Mass saw them also and everyone was laughing about it for weeks. Of course, most people suspected that Donncha Pheigí was responsible for this prank but they couldn't prove it; he himself never admitted to anything, of course.

Donncha played a worse trick again on the sergeant another day and everyone knew about this one. It was a Sunday morning and during second Mass when the sergeant spotted Donncha walking along the edge of the river, salmon in hand – or so it seemed, anyway. Down went the sergeant in hot pursuit but Donncha left the river-bank and made for the road just as the congregation was coming out from Mass. Donncha stopped running and the sergeant came up to him where he had mingled with the crowd. He grabbed Donncha by the shoulders.

'I finally have you', he says.

'What the hell is up with you?' said Donncha, 'have you taken leave of your senses completely? This here is a hake that I bought from Seán after First Mass and my mother told me to go back to him with it because it wasn't fresh enough'.

Only then did the sergeant notice that Donncha had a hake in his hand and not a salmon.

Seán an Éisc (Seán the fish) and his wife Máire used to come from Dungarvan to Baile na hAbhann every now and then on a Sunday morning with a load of fish. There was always great demand for the fish they sold. They sold hake and herring and sprat and they'd sell everything that they brought with them. Donncha had been going home from the market that morning when he'd spotted the sergeant on the road and decided to make a fool of him. The whole thing about the hake not being fresh enough and all the rest of it – it was all a load of rubbish designed to make the sergeant look like a right idiot. It worked too, as the story of the hake was soon on everyone's lips. The sergeant's boss in the police even heard about it apparently because some time after this, the sergeant was transferred to another place in the north of the county. From what I heard, that sergeant was an honest man but he must have really hated those salmon poachers seeing as they saw to it that he ended up being transferred from Baile na hAbhann, a place where he was married and had his own house, to somewhere else completely.

Donncha Pheigí continued on with every type of poaching for as long as he lived in An Gleann and he was never caught. He rarely did any heavy work around the place, except maybe during the September harvest or the potato-picking season or other occasions when there was extra money to be earned. When his mother died, he emigrated to America. He joined the police over in Boston and worked his way up the ranks until he was a detective sergeant. It was one of life's strange twists that Donncha now ended up pursuing those who had broken the law rather than the other way around, especially when you think that he had spent his life up until then breaking the law himself. I suppose the robber is best-educated to chase other robbers. Donncha Pheigí was brighter and cleverer than most other people and it didn't surprise anyone that he did well over in America. He would have done well in any job that he put his mind to. Many of the people who emigrated to America from An Gleann went to Boston; that is one of the reasons why we were always aware of how Donncha Pheigí was doing over there.

GAMES AND ATHLETIC TRICKS

After Power was thrown out of his job, a man named Proinsias Ó Riain replaced him as schoolteacher here in Baile na Droichid. He was a small man of about thirty years of age. He was quite refined and was always well-dressed and spoke in a very correct and well-mannered way. Apparently, he had quite a job trying to keep control of the gang of wild blackguards that he had to teach in Baile na Droichid school here back then – this despite the fact that the biggest messer of the lot, Donncha Pheigí was no longer a pupil there by then, and neither was I. The new teacher used to lodge in Baile na hAbhann and he would walk the three miles to Baile an Droichid every morning and home again every afternoon. He wouldn't bother anyone but was quite happy to keep to himself. You'd always see him happily reading a book as he walked along the road. He spent nearly three years in Baile an Droichid before he got a job in a school nearer to his home place, back near Thurles. I'd say he wasn't sorry to leave this place as some of the messers here had the poor man tormented.

The man who came as teacher after him was a different character altogether His name was Liam Tóibín and it was his first job since finishing teacher-training college. He was in his early-twenties and was about six feet tall. Big and strong with a blonde head of hair, he was calm and gentle most of the time and although he rarely had to resort to the stick for punishment, the lads were afraid of him all the same. He lodged in the same house that master Ó Riain had in Baile na hAbhann for the first three months after his arrival but after this, he came to us here in An Gleann where he lodged with the Baróid family. He lived with this family for the rest of his life, in fact. He was originally from a village that was about five miles from Tullamore.

Tóibín was very interested in all forms of athletics and in football. Actually, he was the one who first set up the football team in Baile na hAbhann and taught the local lads how to play gaelic football in accordance with the new rules as established by the GAA. He raised money and bought playing gear and equipment that no-one had ever seen before. The club's new jerseys were red and blue and it was a wonderful sight to see 21 lads wearing the club singlets and walking out onto the playing field. Prior to this, the lads used to just wear their own everyday shirts when they were playing football. Within a few years Baile na hAbhann had one of the best football teams on this side of the county and they went a few years where they hardly lost a match. Seán Baróid was their captain and he was also their best player, although he was still just a teenager when the team was first set up. We had wanted to appoint Tóibín as a captain but he preferred someone other than him to perform this role. He preferred to give other lads a chance and only rarely played in the matches – and then only if the team were short of a few players. He was very interested in handball in addition to football. There was an old ball-alley near the school in Baile an Droichid but no-one had played any handball there for years. Tóibín encouraged the local lads to renovate this old ball-alley, level the floor of it, and plaster and secure the side-walls of the alley where holes had developed over the years. The local men spent a couple of months on this renovation-work. They worked in the evenings when they had finished their normal jobs. Once the job was completed, there was handball played there every Sunday and most afternoons during the summer. The older lads would play there whenever they got a break from school also. For years afterwards, competitions were held every summer between the handballers of Baile an Droichid and Cill Dhubh. The handballers from Baile an Droichid used to go to Cill Dhubh one Sunday and vice versa the following Sunday. Big crowds always came to watch the matches. Nearly every man, woman and child in An Gleann would be gathered down at the alley on those Sundays. Another group would travel eastwards from Baile an Droichid and everyone roared on their local players enthusiastically. It was the same any Sunday that the competitions were held in Baile an Droichid. Five games, as scored up to twenty-one were held and whichever team won three out of the five matches won the overall competition.

There was always very little between the teams at the end of the day. Usually, each team won in their home alley or on their home patch. There were very good handballers on both sides. Dic Ó Siadhaile and Seán Baróid were very good players but Micil Ó Néill would have beaten either of them. Micil did not play in the competitions very often, however. He preferred to watch the matches instead. Seán Ó Fógarta from the north side of Baile an Droichid was the best player in this locality although there was a man based here for four or five years – a 'peeler' from Kerry named McCarthy who was the best handball player anyone ever saw in this area. There was no-one here who could beat him. Not only was this Kerryman good at handball but he was brilliant at most sports. I remember one summer's afternoon when there were running and jumping competitions held down in Inse an Bhreathnaigh. Such competitions were frequent, particularly after Tóibín came to live here. McCarthy and another man came along to where three or four men were throwing a smoothing iron that was about four pounds in weight. McCarthy was asked to give it a go. Rather than standing up and throwing like everyone else, McCarthy sat down on the ground and threw the iron from a sitting position instead – and yet he still managed to throw it six feet further than any man had managed prior to then. The men asked him to throw it from a standing position then to see how he'd get on but he wasn't interested. No matter how much they went on at him to do it, he wouldn't do it. Micil Ó Néill told us about another day when he called into the Breathnach's hayloft when they were putting parts of the threshing machine together as they were due to start threshing the following day. There was an old giant cart-wheel there, one spoke of which the men were using to drive the stocks into the ground. These were the stocks that kept the threshing machine in the ground when it was working. McCarthy was there and he lifted up this spoke which was very heavy. He asked Micil to check if there was anyone on the other side of the shed. Then, when Micil said it was safe, he lifted up this spoke and swung it around a couple of times before flinging it right over the top of the shed. McCarthy was similar to Micil Ó Néill, however, in that he wasn't an attention-seeker or didn't look for adulation in relation to his sporting prowess. Similar to Micil, he never competed in any athletics or sporting competitions.

When Liam Tóibín first came to live in the Baróid's house we often went down to Inse Sheáin Mhóir where we did running and jumping. Seán Mór himself encouraged us to go there and he often joined us when we were doing these sports too. There weren't too many people around here who ever beat him when it came to throwing the (old) half-a-hundredweight. They'd throw it across the meadow when they were testing one another's strength and Micil Dhuinn the blacksmith put a ring into this weight so that people could catch hold of it for throwing. Dic Ó Siadhaile made posts and jumps so that we could practice our high-jumping and we got a larch tree that was suitable for the job from Seán na Coille that we cut into separate sections for the pole-vaulting. We also marked out a track around the field where we'd have running races.

Seán Baróid was the best of all of us when it came to running. He really developed as a runner and a jumper and he was soon good at weightlifting also. Liam Tóibín taught us the techniques of how to jump and how to throw weights without injuring yourself and Seán was the best of the lot of us when it came to adapting these new techniques.

Liam Tóibín used to bring him to any athletics competitions that were held anywhere within ten or twelve miles of us and they won many prizes. Although Seán Baróid was still in his teens when he began competing in the events, he was rarely beaten in the 100 yards or 220 yard races; anytime, he was beaten, it was because his competitors were given an advantage. He jumped 22 feet, twenty inches or so in the run-and-jump and once, down in the Island in Clonmel, he cleared six feet and one inch in the high jump. Tóibín mainly ran longer races such as milers or half-milers and he also won many prizes over the years. I often went along with Tóibín and Seán to the competitions; all I had to do was mind their clothes while they were competing.

Before finishing with this discussion of sports and athletic, I want to mention one other anecdote. One year there were competitions held in Cork on the Feast of the Assumption; this was the same day that the Pattern used to be held here in Baile na hAbhann at one time. The Pattern wasn't held in this particular year for a couple of years before this because the priest had banned it. Tóibín and Seán went to Cork for the competition. I didn't go with them that day at all although I can't remember now why I didn't. They travelled south to Cappoquin on Seán's horse-and-cart where they went to Mass. Then they took the train from there to Cork. They did well down there although they were up against some of the best athletes in Munster. The schoolmaster won the mile-race and he came second in the half-mile. Seán Baróid won the hundred yard dash, the run-and-jump and he came second in the half-mile. I know the results from these competitions very well because I kept the newspaper clippings relating to that day. I also kept the newspaper clippings relating to all the matches that Baile na hAbhann football team ever played. Now and then, when I'm reminiscing on times past, I take out these clippings and read over them again. To return to my story, however – it was between nine and ten o'clock when they arrived back in Cappoquin on their way home. They got the horse-and-cart ready again and hit the road. There was a pub about two miles on this side of Cappoquin called 'An Choirceog Bheach' (The Beehive) where they stopped and went in for a few drinks. Neither of them was ever very interested in drinking but they were very tired by then and needed a break. There were three men in the pub when they went in, one of whom was the local blacksmith, a man who was given to fighting and argument. This man was very fond of himself; he was big and rough and a bit of a 'hard man' apparently. The schoolmaster called a drink for the three men at the bar at the same time as he ordered a drink for Seán and himself. The blacksmith was rude to them however, and suspecting that he was itching for a fight – (they'd heard before what type of a man he was) – they just had one drink and went on their way again. Between 'An Choirceog Bheach' and the bottom of Ard na Circe was a big turn in the road. This road is more than a mile long and if you happened to go across the fields here instead of along the road, it would only take you a third of the time. Approaching the bottom of the hill here, Liam Tóibín jumped down off the horse-

and-cart while Seán stayed where he was, sitting on the
cart. Next thing three men jumped out on them – the
blacksmith and the two men who were with him in the
pub. The blacksmith wanted to fight Liam Tóibín and Seán
and taunted them while boasting of his fighting prowess.
He said that no-one had been born yet on the other side of
the mountain there that could stand up to him in a fight.
All the while, he was pushing in on Tóibín and telling him
how he was going to tear him and anyone else apart –
that's if any of them were man enough to step up and fight
him. The blacksmith's two friends were inciting him all the
while and urging him on with words of praise. Liam
Tóibín tried to calm him down but when the blacksmith
saw that Tóibín had no interest in fighting him, he became
twice as aggressive. 'Come on man … Have a go'. 'Take
me on …' he called out, removing his jacket. Just as the
blacksmith's arms were halfway out of his jacket, Liam
punched him just beneath the ear and knocked him
backwards into the ditch. The two others rushed Liam
then, but Seán Baróid jumped down off the cart and laid
into them. Tóibín and Seán gave those three men the worst
hiding they ever got.

The old days are just a memory now. Life has changed a
great deal since incidents such as the ones I described in
the previous few pages used to happen. There hasn't been
a ball-game played in the old alley at Cill Dhubh for many
years. The wall against which we once played is all
covered in ivy now. The floor of the old ball-alley that was
in Baile an Droichid is just a mass of nettles, thistles and
dock leaves. The side-walls are all gone now and it is many
years since the stones and bricks of those same walls were
broken-down and used for surfacing the road. No running
or jumping competitions have taken place in Inse an
Bhreathnaigh within the living memory of most people in
An Gleann today. All those strong and athletic lads who
once went running and jumping or playing ball are all

dead and gone now and buried on Irish or foreign soil. The only two people from that old crowd left now are me and Dic Ó Siadhaile and given that we are both a good age now, it'll hardly be too long now before we follow all of the others who are gone.

PASTIMES

The two most common past-times in An Gleann on winter evenings long ago were visiting people's houses and card-playing. The Ó Siadhaile's house was one of the best houses to visit. Storytelling of all kinds and competitions in eloquence and wit were the norm every night of the week, except on Sundays. People normally played twenty-five (cards) on Sunday nights. It was mainly the older people who gathered in Ó Siadhaile's house. The only youngsters there were Dic and I but I only went there the odd time. Most of the young lads used to meet down at Peigí Beag's house in Bóithrín na Cille where they played cards or did tricks every night of the week in winter-time. Apparently, it used to be a riot down there sometimes with all the games and pranks they got up to. Poor Peigí was too 'soft' to keep control of her son who was as big a prankster as anyone else there.

The biggest and best gamblers in the locality used to gather in the carpenter's house every Sunday. Anyone who had work for the carpenter and who loved cards and gambling would make it their business to call into him on the Sunday night with their requests for carpentry jobs – so that they could kill two birds with the one stone and get a game of cards in as well while they were at it. There were other people here in An Gleann, of course, who completely disapproved of card-playing and who wouldn't let a pack of cards in under their roof of their house, for love or money. Some of these people believed that card-playing had some connection with the 'old boy' (i.e. the devil).

Dic Ó Siadhaile was rated the best gambler and card-player in the locality. Seán Mór Breathnach was a big one for gambling also. The only night he called in was on Sundays, partly because he loved card-playing, but also because he had no interest in storytelling and chat unless it related to crops and stock, and farming matters generally. He was always very serious when it came to the cards and didn't like to lose. If he was playing a game in partnership with someone else and the other person played sloppily, he'd get very wound up and would give out stink to his partner. He loved to win but to give him his due, it wasn't for the money; it was just for the pleasure of winning. He often gave the 'rubber' (winnings) to his partner after a game especially if it was a labouring man who was playing with him. A few times each winter, the woman of the house would put a pair of chickens up as prizes. A game of 'nine' was always played for the chickens and the entrance-fee to the game was four-pence each. Seán Mór used to go all out to try and win the chickens. He was on such a 'high' going home any night that he won the pair of chickens and that you'd swear he had won a horse or something. It meant more to him to win a pair of chickens than to win a pound. Although it's in the distant past now, I still laugh when I think of that night when Donncha Pheigí called into us. I can't remember what brought him to Ó Siadhaile's house that night as none of the young crowd used ever call there or play cards there other than me. Dic never went anywhere outside his own house either.

They were short one player that night and Donncha was asked to join in the card-game. The prize on offer that night was a pair of chickens. When the cards were divided out, Dic Ó Siadhaile and Donncha were partnered with Seán Mór Breatnach. Donncha was a good card-player except that he often cheated if he could get away with it. He'd hide or disguise a card and pretend that he hadn't noticed what had happened sometimes, but he knew that he was only wasting his time trying a trick like that in the Ó Siadhaile's house as the other players there were too sharp and too smart to let anyone get caught out like that. As was normal, they played five games for the prize of the chickens. The games were very close with Seán Mór and his partners winning four games and the other two threesomes winning three games. Two fifteens and a twenty was the 'stake' and Seán Mór and his partners were on one of the fifteens. Donncha Pheigí dealt the cards and he turned over the king of hearts. Hearts was trumps and Seán Mór played the jack of hearts. No-one had the ace of hearts, at least not until it came to Donncha's turn to play. 'A gold ring be upon you, boy', said Seán Mór and you could hear the joy in his voice; he was sure that as no-one had played the ace yet that Donncha must have had it in his hand. As the other three hadn't the five of trumps and were only at twenty he was sure that he had the game won. 'Devil an ace have I, but I'm not sure who's that jack is – and so it's best I beat it'. And so he slammed the trump down on top of the jack. 'What kind of a bloody fool are you', Seán Mór roared, 'isn't the jack of hearts mine?'

He gave out stink to Donncha for a full minute, when he (Donncha) threw down the Queen of Hearts, the best card in the game. He knew all along who's the Jack of Hearts was and he knew the game was in his hands; so he beat the Jack with the trump deliberately just to get a rise out of Seán Mór. Seán didn't say one word for the rest of the game and worse for him, Donncha won the chickens even though Seán had been just a 'five' away from the chickens twice. Micil Dhuinn, the blacksmith here in An Gleann often played games also. Micil had a habit of slamming his fist down on the table when he made the 'five' or when he had the best card at the end of the game. One night, he hit the table so hard that he broke one of Dic Ó Siadhaile's fingers. The game was down to the last hand and Dic had a Queen of Clubs and if this had been the best card, he would have won the game – as he had already taken the other four 'fives' (hands).

'Who'll top this?' he said, laying the card on the table.

Before he had a chance to get his hand out of the way, Micil slammed down a King of Clubs on the table with incredible force and caught one of Dic's fingers in the process. Dic let out a cry of pain and I'm afraid to say that the rest of us were laughing more than we felt sorry for him. It was one of those freak accidents that you couldn't help but find amusing. Dic had to travel southwards to Cill Uachtar Maighe to a bone-setter who set his finger back together again.

After Mass every Sunday when the weather was fine and the day was long, a big crowd of people from An Gleann, both young and old, would gather together at Crosaire na Cille. People often came southwards over the hills or northwards from Baile an Droichid. They would have a big board for dancing on and Cruthúirín the Piper would play for the crowd sitting up on his perch, on top of the ditch – in beneath a bush. Others who weren't dancing would be playing ball up against the gable-end of the old church. Others were playing cards at the side of the ditch or playing pennies on the road.

The end of the old church was about twenty yards in off the side of the yard. The wall was plastered to a height of about fifteen feet up or so and two short side-walls were added, and the floor levelled. It was a reasonably good ball-alley except that the ivy grew thickly on the top of the end-wall and the ball often got stuck up there and was lost. They always played with a hard ball and the two teams were usually three-aside. The people made their own ball for the games back then and Dic Ó Siadhaile was the best person in An Gleann at making them. They would use pieces of cork that they had left in the fire for a while to burn the edges of them inside in the middle of the ball, and the rest of the ball was sewn together with a thread from an old pair of socks. There was a special skill to making a ball, to ensure that it was neither too soft nor too hard. The outside of the ball was made from horse-hide and this had to be carefully cut and shaped so that there were no splits at the seams later when it was all sewn together. At school, we often played with balls made threads of wool but they didn't have any cover or skin on them.

Most of the local girls and boys would be gathered around the giant board that served as a wooden dancing platform. There would be no let-up in the dancing, not until it was time for everyone to go home and milk the cows. Cruthúirín the piper would be sitting up on his rough seat in the bushes and playing for everyone with as much dexterity and speed as he could muster. Poor Cruthúirín was blind but he could walk through the entire parish without any guide and he could make his way to any house that he wanted to visit. He only needed to hear a person's voice once and he recognised that voice for ever more. There were few people in the area that he didn't know by their walk either and he would greet them and address them by their name before they had spoken to him at all. His only way of making a living was by playing the uilleann pipes. He and his sister Siobháinín lived in a thatched house near the Graveyard Bridge. In winter-time when there were no dances at the crossroads, he would have held smaller dances in his own house although the numbers of boys and girls who went to these wasn't very big. He would have a small pot near the wall inside the door as you went into the house, with the pot-cover placed back-to-front on it and everyone who came in to the dance had a to leave a penny – that was the fee – on the top of the pot. Cruthúirín lived to be a good age. The poor man died in the 'poor-house' but, when they heard that he was dead, the neighbours brought him home for burial in An Chill Dhubh. The set of pipes he played is in the Burkes house in Mónach Buí still, although it is a long time now since a tune was played on them. The phrase 'Ceol a' Chruthúirín' (little Conor's music) can still be heard in the people's speech around An Gleann to this day.

Every time I pass over the crossroads and the Graveyard Bridge, I always say 'Céad slán leis an sean-aimsir' (A hundred farewells to the old days) to myself quietly as I look at the ditch and the bush on which the piper once had his perch. And I think of the big crowds of people who were gathered around the wooden platform on those Sunday afternoons long ago. Those handsome boys and pretty girls were scattered to the four corners of the world in the intervening years, with many of them emigrating across the sea and very few of them ever returning to Ireland again. A good number of them died young also, but whether they went abroad and stayed at home, there are very few of them who aren't lying in graveyard soil now. And whatever the reason for it, the generation who came after them let the dances and the crossroads and the ball-games, and all the other old traditions we once followed, die out over time.

I called into the old ruin that is An Cill Dhubh the other day as I usually do whenever I pass by. I go in to say a prayer at the grave of my relatives and family, and especially for poor Sibéal, my wife. Walking around, I noticed the old tombs that are next to the wall on the southern side of the graveyard. I took particular note of two tombs that have headstones as big as kitchen tables, both of which are three feet high. The two tombs are next to each other and divided by a space of two feet between them. It was a kind of test of courage for An Gleann people to stand on the end of one tomb nearest the wall and jump over the next tomb. The space between the end of one tomb to another is about eight feet but you'd have to jump a distance of nine feet to clear that distance really; otherwise, you'd bang your hip off the top of one of the tombstones before you'd hit the ground. This jump was a dangerous one therefore, and not many people ever tried it. I only ever saw two people who gave it a go – Seán Baróid and Micil Ó Néill. From what I heard, Risteard Ó Siadhaile and Seán Mór Breathnach both jumped it when they were young. Micil Ó Néill only ever jumped it once and it was the rest of us who badgered him into it. He managed to jump it without much trouble. That jump was no bother for Seán Baróid and almost any time he was asked to do it, he would do so.

I still remember that Sunday long ago when Tomás Condún from Leacain Thuaidh got injured. There was a bit of the boaster in Tomás Condún and although he never took part in the official athletics competitions, he was always up for a challenge in terms of jumping or lifting heavy rocks. He was sure enough of himself to think that no-one would ever better him when it came to either of these tests. Once he heard about Seán Baróid's feat in jumping over the two high tombstones, he wanted to do the same. He came down to Cill Dhubh one Sunday and the crowd who normally went there dancing and playing ball all gathered around in the church ruins to see him in action. On the day of the jump, he was cocksure of himself and spent so much time stretching and getting ready that you'd swear people had put one-pound bets on him to complete the jump easily. Seán Baróid managed the jump no problem; all he had to do was fasten the buttons on his jacket. He took off his jacket and vest, blessed himself, and then took two stones in his hands, each of which were a couple of pounds weight. He was quite fussy about these two stones and spent a while foostering around before he was happy with the ones that he had picked. He stood on the edge of one of the tombs and swung his hands with the stones in them for a minute and then jumped, throwing the stones away from him at the same time. He nearly cleared the two tombs but struck his hip off the edge of the second tomb. He was badly-hurt and Seán Mór Breathnach sent Micil Ó Néill home with him stretched out on a horse and cart, a few piles of hay beneath him. He recovered from his injury but gave up any jumping, lifting or athletic challenges from then on.

Another thing that people who liked athletic challenges in those days did was jump from the pillar of one house-gate to another. Most pillars back then had a distance of about eight feet between them as the gates in front of big houses used to be quite narrow then; this meant that these were jumps were dangerous, especially if the gate was closed. I often heard the following about Risteard the Carpenter. He and Micil Ó Néill were returning from the fair in Clonmel when he was young. He was half-drunk and jumping from one pillar to the next all along the road between Droichead Áth na Scairbhí to Baile an Droichid. He'd jump up on each pillar and remove his shoes, then jump across from one pillar to the next, a shoe in each hand. While balancing on the next pillar, he would put his shoes back on again and then he'd go on up the road again until they came to another set of pillars and then repeat the trick again.

One of the Moores was living up in Ros an Aitinn a few miles south of Baile na hAbhann. He was a very independent individual and was reputed to be quite wealthy. I remember him when I was going to school. He was an elderly man, tall and well-scrubbed, and sporting a big grey moustache. When he went home from Mass on

Sundays, he'd get two or three shillings or a few pence from the sacristan and he'd throw the coins up amongst a group of kids who'd be waiting at the corner of the bakery for him. The children would be scrambling around on the ground trying to get the coins and he would be bursting his heart laughing at them. The day that his daughter was getting married, he threw two or three pounds up in the air, but there were more than schoolboys in the rush towards the money that day. The people of this parish only ever referred to him as 'Mister Willie'.

It was said that he was a great man for athletic tricks and challenges when he was young. He could leap over an entire plough-team. He was also extremely strong when he was a young man and there was no-one in the parish who could beat him when it came to weight-throwing. Sean-Risteard Ó Siadhaile used to say that he often heard it said that Liam Ó Mórdha (Moore) could write his name on a shed-door with a piece of chalk while holding a fifty-pound weight on his little finger. Another thing that Risteard said he could do was lie flat on the floor of the shed face-down and hands-down while the men placed a twenty-stone bag of corn across his shoulders. He could get up off the ground even while lifting this weight. Another strange custom he had for a man of his means and background was this. If there was a 'meitheal' gathered in the area harvesting potatoes or digging ditches or any similar type of work, he would join them with his shovel or spade and join in the work the same as the next man. He'd often spend a half-day working like this, and, now and then, when he was thinking of leaving to go home, he'd challenge the rest of the men in the 'meitheal' to let him finish the job by himself. When he was leaving, he'd often give, maybe, a crown to the captain to buy a drink for all the rest of the men in the 'meitheal'.

Peaid na Bríd played a trick on him once, a trick that cost him some money. Peaid was only eighteen years old at the time but he was a born trickster right down to the tips of his toes. One day Peaid was digging a ditch for his aunt; she owned a small piece of land near the Moore's house, in Ros an Aitinn. Liam Ó Mórdha saw him working and joined in the digging and they began to compete with one another. Peaid was too clever for him, however. He let on to be digging the ridges to their full depth but he was only pretending and wasn't doing the sides properly at all. Ó Mórdha who was working parallel with him in another part of the field was digging the ridges correctly but was killing himself to try and keep up with Peaid. Later on, when they were finished, he gave Peaid two shillings and told him that he was 'some man'. Of course, later on, when Ó Mórdha was gone home, Peaid had to go back and finish the ditches he hadn't done properly. Another quirk which Liam Ó Mórdha had was that he never put a spade or a shovel on his shoulder when he was walking as many others did; instead, he used to hold the spade or shovel with his two hands behind his back and drag it behind him as he walked. I never saw him doing this but I often heard the older people talk about it.

He followed the hunt and he was a very good rider. No jump was too challenging or dangerous for him and he always had a good horse on stand-by. He had an unusual strength and athleticism about him. He sometimes lined up six tins of mackerel in a row and he was able to jump from one to the next, without stopping. Another athletic feat he did once was to carry a half-a-hundredweight in either hand and to walk from the soldiers' barracks to the top of Baile Gaelach in Clonmel without letting the weights down at any stage. Afterwards, he promised ten pounds in money to anyone who could do the same thing. No-one else has ever tried this feat since.

On one occasion, Ó Mórdha met a man who refused to undertake one of his challenges. An army officer and a few members of the local gentry were in his house in Ros an Aitinn one afternoon after a day spent out hunting in the hills. They were standing out on the grassy lea opposite the hall-door of the house chatting. There was a big branch poking out of an oak tree that was growing there and the army officer gave a run and cleared the branch. He challenged anyone else to jump it and Ó Mórdha jumped it also without any difficulty. Ó Mórdha went into the barn and got a scythe. He took the handle off it and tied the blade, sharp side out, to the tree higher-up and challenged the others to jump it. He took a few steps back and ran up and cleared it fairly easily. He challenged the army officer but he declined and said that he was bested. Maybe he was right not to jump it. It was probably stupid to attempt a jump that was so dangerous.

Liam Ó Mórdha of Ros an Aitinn had just the one daughter. Her mother died when the girl was very young and Ó Mórdha did not get married again. Ó Mórdha didn't want his surname to die out in Ros an Aitinn, and therefore he wouldn't let his daughter marry anyone unless they were an Ó Mórdha (Moore). And he did find someone of this surname for her in the end. This man was from County Cork and he was a fine, handsome man. Everything went fairly well in the marriage for as long as the old man was still alive, but when he died, and the husband inherited everything, he went crazy drinking and carousing, card-playing and betting on horses – he spent all his time on these activities and went crazy with them. Within five years, he had blown the entire inheritance. He ruined the farm and even cut down all the ancient trees that were around the house, trees that Liam Ó Mórdha wouldn't have dreamed of cutting even one branch from. The farm was auctioned off, and once all the debts he had accumulated were paid off, there was very little money left. His wife became a housekeeper to the local parish priest and she spent the rest of her life in this job. Two years after the farm was sold off, her husband was found collapsed in a laneway in Cork city. He was brought to hospital but he only lived for another couple of days. He had just ten pence in his pocket when they found him. That was all that came of Liam Ó Mórdha's pride in his name and his determination to ensure that it remained in Ros an Aitinn; that was all it came to in the end. The story of Liam Ó Mórdha was well-known throughout An Gleann and still is to this day.

After I finished with school, I often went socializing to Ó Siadhaile's house on winter nights. Seán Mac Craith would go there every now and then although he usually spent most of his evenings reading. He had a good collection of books and he rarely visited town that he didn't return with a new book. His books are still here in Lios na Faille as are many numbers of the *Shamrock*; the volumes for each year are bound together. We used to get a copy of the *Weekly Freeman* and pass it onto Dic Ó Siadhaile when we were finished with it and then he'd pass it onto the blacksmith. No-one in An Gleann got a daily newspaper in those days and it was only the very odd person who bought a weekly paper. A local paper entitled *The Chronicle* was regularly published in Clonmel but only Seán Mór Breathnach ever bought it. That was three-pence a copy but the other newspapers were just one penny each. When I was a boy, the only bits of the newspaper that I found interesting were the coloured pictures in the *Weekly Freeman*. My mother would cut them out and stick them on the kitchen-walls.

The newspapers then used to include the text of long speeches as given by MPs in the English Parliament or at other meetings around the country. The people who read the papers then used to read every word of these long-winded speeches although I think no-one understood half of what was in them really. Any night I went socializing in the Ó Siadhaile's, I always sat in the corner. Sitting opposite me in the other corner was Sean-Risteard next to a machine for smoothing timber that he had invented himself. There was a hole in the hearth and it was filled with small twisted pieces of paper ready for lighting his pipe – the same as my grandfather had in our house once. All the others who gathered in Ó Siadhaile's house would light their pipes using a cinder from the fire but Risteard always used one of these home-made lighters of his. Sitting just outside of me in the corner, on those nights in Ó Siadhaile's was Seán na Coille. He always sat on a high stool close to the wall. Seán Mór used to prop himself in the centre of the hearth any night that he was there although he only rarely called in and then mainly on Sundays because he loved playing cards much more than he did storytelling or reminiscing about the past. Micil Mhártan and Micil Gabha were the two who went most often to Ó Siadhaile's house. The blacksmith used to visit almost every night, although it was often late when he arrived as he used to stay working in the forge until he had whatever urgent job that he was doing completed. Micil Mhártan wouldn't be there if the night was very dark as his sight wasn't good and he couldn't see very well in the dark. Tomás de Búrc of Mónach Buí would often be there also and two or three others who called in every now and then. Micil Ó Néill was one of this latter group. They used to discuss everything on those nights, every bit of local news and what was happening in the greater world outside. The Land Question was still a major and controversial issue in Ireland then and this would be discussed; they never dwelt too long on the more serious or 'difficult' questions. They were more given to humour and stories and witty talk. I need only close my eyes for a moment and I can see them all before my eyes again as clear as day. Sean-Risteard is there opposite me reddening his pipe with his home-made taper, his pipe and cover hanging down on its small bronze chain. Seán na Coille is to my right, dressed in his pigskin 'leggings' and Seán Mór propped importantly in the middle of us at the hearth as if he owned the house himself. The rest of us are perched in our own usual places around the small fire that was always burning.

Seán na Coille used to be in charge of the 'game' for the 'master' – as the landlord was then called. It was from him that Seán got an amazing pair of 'leggings' and footwear that he always wore when he went out fowling. These boots of his were buttoned up in the front and no-one else in the parish had anything like them. Consequently, Seán was held in awe by many people. I don't think I ever saw him anywhere – at Mass, in the city, or out on the mountains – that he wasn't wearing them. He had a single-barrelled shotgun that he used to kill hawks, magpies and other enemies of the grouse and the pheasants with. Seán didn't shoot many of these predatory birds however, as he was afraid of the gun; apparently, he used to close his eyes when he pulled the trigger. This didn't prevent him from carrying the gun with him everywhere he went; he nearly brought it to Mass with him once. And yet he rarely loaded it or shot it. I often saw him with the gun at Ó Siadhaile's house and he'd stand it in the corner inside me and he's give me a look as if to say 'don't touch that now, whatever you do'. He was very proud of the gun and any time he described where he was or what he was doing, he always dropped in the phrase 'And I had the gun with me' in the middle of the conversation. This phrase 'And I had the gun with me' was regularly used by the locals as a form of mockery. They would tease Seán about this whenever they got the chance. Seán might be describing something that he had seen at the fair maybe and some chancer would say 'And did you have the gun with you?'

'Ara, I did not, son', Seán would say, and you'd nearly swear that he didn't understand that they were mocking him really. I think myself that Seán knew well that they were teasing him but that he chose to ignore it – and that he let them tease him deliberately. Seán na Coille was no fool and he actually loved exaggeration, boasting, and mockery in his own way. He was an eccentric in ways I suppose. He always wore a two-peaked cap and the only two others who wore a cap similar to this locally were himself and Old-Leainglí (Langley) from Baile na hAbhann. And when it was cold in winter he'd have the two ear-flaps pulled down and tied beneath his chin; he'd have made the pigs laugh, he looked so strange!

Around here, everyone paid their rents twice a year – on the Saturday after the May Fair and after the November Fair. Although they already knew well when the rent was due, it was part of Seán's job to inform all of the tenants on the estate of rent-day in advance. The rent would be paid in the town where the 'agent' had an office. Seán na Coille would be very busy on those particular days calling each person in turn into the office. He would have shaved and be well scrubbed-up and wearing his 'Sunday best' on those days. He'd have his fancy brown 'leggings' on too, of course; he'd have polished them up so well that you could see your face in them. He wouldn't wear the two-peaked cap on rent-day, however; his head was bare and bald that day. Seán took his responsibilities very seriously whether on the mountain or in the woods and he'd be out in the countryside early in the morning and there till late at night. Despite this, there were very few people that he ever charged with poaching. When he caught someone out hunting illegally, he'd give them a right tongue-lashing. He'd tell them that he'd have them in court – as sure as he had his gun in his hand. That was as far as it went, however. He'd secretly let people have a day's hunting as long they gave him the 'nod' beforehand and he would make sure to be away that day. There was many a day that myself, Seán Baróid and Tóibín, the schoolmaster, spent out hunting hares on the mountain. Seán Baróid had a greyhound as did Tóibín and they used to have great fun competing with one another to see whose dog was best. We'd be out an An Maol at sunrise and we'd stay out there hunting until dinner-time and you had some appetite by the time you got home, I can tell you. There used to be many hares on the mountain in those days but there are not so many today. I remember spotting a particularly large hare on the slope of An Maol for a couple of years in a row; we'd spot him and get a run at it four or five times each season but we didn't have any greyhound that could get anywhere near him; he just shot straight off and left them trailing in his wake. He disappeared eventually and he may well have been caught in a snare because there were three or four people in An Gleann who were skilled at trapping hares and rabbits using snares. They'd get anything between a shilling and three four penny bits for a hare if they sold him down in the town (i.e. in Clonmel). Seán na Coille hated the people who set snares with a passion he always swore that he would bring the full rigors of the law down on them if he caught any of them setting snares. They were too clever for him, however, and I don't think he ever caught any one of the more experienced poachers and snares-men. Donncha Pheigí was the most skilled and the cleverest of all the poachers. Seán knew this but he never managed to catch him. To be honest about it, placing snares is a fairly mean or petty way to catch a hare because, out in the wild, the hare has only one way of escaping its predators and that is through running away. Using a snare gives the hare no chance; the hare gets choked in the snare straight away.

The twelfth of August was the most important day of the year as far as Seán na Coille was concerned. This was the first day of the season that people were allowed to shoot grouse. The master – i.e. Risteard Baron and two or three members of the gentry would be getting ready from the previous day for the shooting. They'd erect a small cabin on Réidh an Tobair next to the freshwater well there. Then they'd spend between a week and a fortnight out on the mountain shooting game. Seán would always have someone else with him to help him bring the trays of supplies up to the shooting party – lunch, dinner, bags of game etc. The hunters would drink plenty of whiskey as well and Seán would have a great time for that two weeks. 'Master Richard', as Seán called him, would often go out shooting between August and Christmas. Basically, he would continue with the shooting for as long as the weather permitted. He would shoot snipe in the Móin Ghallda and woodcock out in the woods depending on the season. Seán would receive a good fee for his services and this was only right considering that he always knew where they could find a good line of grouse, pheasant and woodcock and how they could go about bagging them.

I suppose the good number of wettings that Seán got over the years while out on the mountains must have affected him for the worst, as when he got older, he suffered badly from rheumatism and arthritis. In fact, for the last few years before he died, he suffered a great deal physically. Right to the end however, he never lost his interest in showing off and exaggeration. I remembering calling into him one day shortly before he died. He was sitting in the armchair in the corner of his room. He couldn't stand up at all and all his fingers were swollen and twisted with rheumatism.

'How are things Seán?' says I.

'Not great Séamus. Sure, all you have to do is look at me, I suppose'.

'Are you in pain?' I said.

'Pain', he said, 'by God, sometimes, it's so bad that I feel as if the marrow is bubbling inside in my bones. I was sitting here yesterday when a bout of pain struck me. It was so bad that I nearly jumped into the fire and went off up the chimney with it. Only for Siobhán caught a hold of me by the jacket, I was gone'.

Despite the enormous sympathy I felt for him at that moment, I couldn't help laughing.

'Oh, as sure as God, and I'm not telling you a word of a lie. Ask Siobhán there if you don't believe me'.

Siobhán was so used to his exaggerations by then that she just gave me a look as if to 'warn me off'. Poor Siobhán and Seán are both gone to Heaven years ago now, may God have mercy on them both. It's a sin that people like Seán na Coille have to die at all given how much they ease the worries of this life for everyone else and distract us from our own troubles. I'm afraid that I may have gone way off-course as regards my recounting of those evenings socializing in sean-Risteard Ó Siadhaile's house. I'll return to it now again.

Old-Risteard Ó Siadhaile was a wonderful storyteller. God knows how many stories and anecdotes he had in that head of his at any one point in time? He also had an incredible amount of old sayings, prayers, witticisms and riddles. I'm sorry now that I didn't note down any of them at the time; it was only years later that I came to realize how important and unique they were. Stories about ghosts and spirits were the ones Risteard preferred telling the most. He had tons of them and he'd spend half the night recounting the goings-on of 'Petticoat Loose' and the ghost of Scairt na Bhearnán and the ghost of Geata na Staighrí; or stories of the 'good people' or the 'sluagh sí' (fairies). I often returned home down the boreen in the dark after a night listening to Dic Ó Siadhaile's ghost stories and I'd be shaking with fear. Seán Mór used to dismiss these ghost stories as mere entertainment on the nights he was present, however. 'Tell me this, how is it that people always see the ghosts on their way home from the pub and they never see them on their way there. I think that it's a mixture of drunkenness and a lack of courage that has people seeing all these ghosts around the place'.

My aunt Máire often said the same thing.

'Sure, everyone knows that Micil Mhártan breaking his leg at Geata na Staighrí had nothing to do with a ghost'.

Micil didn't agree with this interpretation of events at all, needless to say. Geata na Staighrí was a place that was associated with the supernatural and I often heard people talking about the ghost that was supposed to live there. Micil Mhártan was returning from the fair a few years prior to this, his mule in tow. He had the side-rails up on the back of his cart as he had brought some sheep to the fair for sale. He was drunk of course, as anytime he went to town he used to 'go on the beer'. As he passed by Geata na Staighrí on the way home, he challenged the ghost to a fight. He was standing just inside the side-rail of his cart when he issued this challenge but then – according to him, anyway – he was flung against the side-rail of the cart with force and he and the side-rail crashed down onto the road. He broke his thigh-bone and he was lame for the rest of his days. And yet, most of the old people in An Gleann were absolutely convinced that it was the ghost that was responsible for what had happened to Micil Mhártan.

You'd hear them saying things like:

'I saw a ghost at Geata na Staighrí', said Seán na Coille once, 'and I was on my way to Clonmel and I hadn't drunk a drop. And another thing that I've never understood before or since is the strange supernatural feeling that I could feel there that night. But I'll tell you the full story now anyway. The events that I'm describing now happened more than twenty years ago now. I was young and strong then and I wasn't afraid of anyone or anything. I was walking to Clonmel to buy a pair of shoes; it was just two weeks before Christmas. Only the rare house had a clock in it back then and I got up that morning at cockcrow. I ate something and hit the road. As I was passing through Baile an Droichid, I saw a light in one of the houses at Mairtí's pub. I said to myself that I'd go to get a light for my pipe and I made for where the light was coming from. Old-Mairtí was still alive then and it was him who was up. He was watching over a sow that was sick and that was about to give birth to some bonhams. I lit my pipe from the candle he had. Mairtí asked me why I was on the road so early in the morning. I told him where I was going and just at that moment, the clock in the house sounded twice.

'It's only two o'clock', I said.

'That's all', said Mairtí.

I realized then that the cockerel had played a trick on me and woken me up far too early, but I had no choice other than to continue on. After a short while spent chatting with Mairtí, I went on with the journey, walking at a nice steady pace. As I passed over the big bridge at Baile na hAbhann, who were standing in the middle of the bridge but two 'peelers'? I said 'hello' to them and they said the same back to me. Then I paused for a moment and asked them for a match to light my pipe. All three of us lit our pipes and I chatted for a while with the sergeant, whom I knew quite well. He was a McCarthy from county Kerry, a man who spoke very good Irish. 'You don't mind me asking you where you're headed at this early hour of the morning?' he said to me finally. I told him where I was headed and asked him what time it was. He pulled his 'watch' out from the lining of his trousers and lit a match. 'It's two o'clock on the dot', he said. I got a fright when I heard this as you'd expect, but I didn't let on anything. I told them how the cockerel crowing so early in the morning had confused me. I said goodbye to them then and walked on again at a steady pace. There was no light in the sky yet but it wasn't too dark because there was a thin coating of frost on the ground and the sky was filled with stars. There is a path at the edge of the road going over Geata na Staighrí and I was making my way along this path, the wall on my left-hand side. As I approached the gate, I saw a man coming towards me from the opposite direction. He was about one hundred yards away from me at this point. As he came nearer, I moved in closer to the wall to let him pass by on the outside. I was practically touching the wall as he came up to me but instead of passing me on the outside as I expected him to do, he passed me on the inside, near the wall! I didn't feel anything as he passed me. He said nothing and neither did I. I looked over my shoulder a few seconds later but he was already one hundred yards away – this although he couldn't have taken more than three steps really within such a short space of time. Unsurprisingly, I got very frightened and broke out in a cold sweat. I knew that the creature I had seen was not a human being, whatever it was. I walked onwards, saying the Rosary to myself and I felt very frightened especially as I passed beneath the trees in the darkness on this side of Droichead Áth na Scairbhíghe. As I passed Tigh na dTrí Dhoras, I noticed that the main door of that house was open and that the lights were on in the windows on either side of it. I walked up to the door and went in. I spoke to two or three boys who were standing just inside the door. They were waking sean-Liam Andréis (old-Liam Andrews) and there were a good number of people gathered in the kitchen. I went to the door of the wake-room and said a prayer. I spotted one of the Ó Cinnéide (Kennedy) boys from Baile an Droichid who was working as a hireling for the O'Brien's of Cill na Mac and I went over to him. He made room for me on the stool and I sat down next to him. We knew one another well and he was surprised to see me there and asked me what had brought me to the wake. I told him where I was headed and how the cockerel had set me astray.

'What time is it now?' I said.

There was a clock in the kitchen but it had been stopped as soon as someone (i.e. sean-Liam Andréis) died, as was the custom.

Ó Cinnéide went over to a man who was sitting next to the fire and who was wearing a watch-chain. He asked him the time and the man pulled the 'watch' out of his pocket.

'It's exactly two o'clock', he said.

I was so shocked by now that I couldn't speak. I was trying to figure out whether I was suffering from some sort of dizziness or hallucination or whether I was under some sort of a magic spell. I stayed at the wake for a while and I had to drink some tea to try and calm down; then I began walking southwards again along Bóthar na Coille. This was a lonely road, as everyone knows. There was only one house on this road – for a distance of four miles along the entire road which passes through the woods. I was delighted when I reached 'Méar an Eolais' because I knew I was within a mile of the big town. I walked along at a steady pace until I was passing beneath An Geata Mór. There wasn't a soul to be seen anywhere and no sign of light in any house. I lit my pipe with one of the matches the sergeant had given me on the bridge at Baile na hAbhann and I passed the time smoking until it was daylight. About a half-an-hour later, I heard the 'Watchman' coming down along the street towards me and calling out at the top of his voice.

'Two o'clock and all is well.
That's my story for you and there is no word of a lie in it'.

Neither of us spoke for a moment but I could tell from the faces of everyone in the room that they believed every single word of Seán's story – everyone except Seán Mór Breathnach that is. He was the first to speak and his tone was mocking.

'By golly, Seán', he said, 'but you're the best liar I've ever heard in my life. Do you think that we're all a bunch of idiots here and that we'd be stupid enough to believe that these things really happened, and that they didn't actually come out of your imagination and you all alone?'

'Upon my soul', said Seán, 'there isn't a word of lie in anything I've just told you'.

'Many's the person who's experienced a bizarre experience like the one you've just described', said Tomás de Búrc then.

'I was in Clonmel one day with a load of corn and while they were unloading it and putting it into Grubb's store there, I went into Slattery's Pub on the corner and drank a half-glass of whiskey. When I came out of the pub I went into the office and got paid for the corn. Emerging out onto the street again, I sat up on the horse and cart to go down the street – (as I thought) to un-harness the horse that was in Graham's forge. I felt dizzy and disorientated however and I'm not sure how long I was going down the road when I felt my senses return to me all of a sudden. I noticed a man breaking rocks on the side of the road and this is exactly what he said to me:

'You're just a mile or so from Cill Chais', he said.

'You must have got a bad drop of whiskey', said old-Risteard.

'To hell with that', said Tomás.

'Surely, a half-glass of whiskey couldn't make anyone very dizzy – no matter how bad it might be?'

'Many people have gone astray as you describe', said Micil Mhártan, 'especially at night-time. Dath Mór was coming home from Baile na hAbhann one dark night on New Year's Eve and I suppose I had a few drinks in, as usual. Rather than following the boreen that goes in from the main road towards his house, he followed the short-cut. He only had to cross the length of one field but he went astray on the path, somehow. He ended up walking over and back for a while and he was totally confused about where he was in the end. Then he remembered often hearing that if a person turned their jacket inside-out on such occasions, they could get their bearings again. But whatever kind of foostering he did trying to turn the sleeves of his jacket around, didn't he let the jacket fall on the ground. He couldn't find it then because it was so dark, no matter how hard he tried. In the end and despite being completely exhausted from climbing walls and scrabbling over bushes and across branches, he just sat down on the ground in resignation. He was cold and miserable and he couldn't even have a smoke because his pipe was inside the pocket of the jacket that had gone missing. He found his jacket the next day behind a gorse bush about twenty feet from where he sat down that night'.

'Now I'm not saying that the stories Micil and Tomás told tonight aren't true', said Seán Mór then, 'but I'm absolutely certain that Seán made up his story and that there is no truth in it at all'.

Initially, I myself believed that Seán na Coille was telling the truth about what he'd seen that night on the road to Clonmel. He was so serious about it and related every aspect of the story in such minute detail that I felt his story jsut had to be true. Looking back on it now, however – and especially when I think of the many exaggerated stories and anecdotes he told us over the years – I'm inclined to think that Seán Mór's was probably right in his judgment of him.

Seán na Coille's father used to be in charge of the game for the landlord although I don't remember him at all and Seán himself was 'in service' with the O'Beirne's in Flemingstown, north of Baile na hAbhann. From what he used to tell us in Ó Siadhaile's house, there was no end to the number of amazing things he saw when he was in the 'Great House' with the O'Beirnes. He was actually worse than Seán Mac Craith when it came to idealizing the wonderful things that were 'south of us'. At least in the case of Seán Mac Craith, his stories *were* actually true; with Seán na Coille, however, some of the things he used to describe were just too incredible to believe. I only remember a few of these incredible anecdotes of his at this remove – it's been such a long time since I first heard them. One night, we were talking about good crop-yields and Seán said that Seán Beag O'Beirne had had a wheat-field with an incredible crop-yield one year that he had been 'in service' there. They had an incredibly rich yield of wheat that year and when they had it cut, it was so tightly stacked that they couldn't actually squeeze the horse into the field to collect the first load of it so as to pile it onto the back of the cart! – or, at least, so Seán claimed. Seán also described how they were harvesting turnips one year in Flemingstown and that one turnip was so big that he had a hell of a job trying to lift it off the ground and get it onto the horse and cart. Another day, he was gathering thistles in the ten-acre field and there were ten or twelve banbhs rooting in the ground there when they disturbed a rabbit that ran across the field towards the ditch. 'He was barely halfway across the field when the poor unfortunate creature was torn to pieces by them'. Another night he was telling us about the farm owned by Seán Beag's brother out in western Canada. It was so big that he had twenty ploughs working it at the same time, Seán claimed. They'd leave the house at six in the morning to start work and they'd come back at dinner-time with only the second sod turned, the fields were that large. Between this and nightfall, they might have only two more ridges done. When I think back on some of these outlandish and exaggerated stories now, it's no wonder that I had my doubts about Seán na Coille's story about the strange hallucinatory experience he had out on the road to Clonmel that night long ago. Micil Dhuinn, the blacksmith, was the next person to speak that night.

'There's no doubt that people see things sometimes that are not of this world', he said. Here's a story that my poor mother used often tell and she wasn't coming home from any pub when this incident took place. When she was about sixteen years of age, she was sent 'into service' with the Dalton family down in Sean-Phóna. One night a cow was sick while calving and she was hurriedly sent to Seánín Mhuiris, an animal-doctor who lived about a quarter of a mile from Baile na hAbhann in an easterly direction. It was the dead of night when she left the Dalton's farm although the sky was moonlit and clear. In fact, the night-sky was so clear and bright that night and she was in such a hurry that she didn't feel the slightest bit nervous, despite the lateness of the hour. About one hundred yards on the eastern side of the old graveyard, she spotted a priest walking steadily along the road and coming in her direction. He was reading a book and he did not look up at her at any stage. She noticed his three-cornered hat and his long black cassock that reached down as far the ground. She had already passed him by when it occurred to her that this priest was not an earthly being and she began running as quickly as she could. She was so frightened that she didn't dare look behind her until she reached Seánín Mhuiris' house. Seánín and she didn't see anything on their way back but until the day she died, she swore that she had seen that priest that night. 'There are things there', said old-Risteard, 'that are difficult to understand and that don't appear to relate to this world. You all know the O'Donnell's house in Móin Bhuí south, but did you ever hear why there is no lock or timber latch-stick put on the door of that house in the evenings? 'I heard why', said Micil Mhártan, 'although it's something that the O'Donnell's don't like to talk about much themselves'.

'It's true' said Risteard, that the door of the house is never locked and that the odd time, when the people of the house are sitting around the fire at night, they hear footsteps coming around to the door of the house and then onto the threshold. Then the latch on the door is raised but the door never opens fully – and that's all that happens. When the woman of the house who lives there now first married into that house twenty-five years ago, she was told the story but she just laughed it off and, against her husband's advice, she put the lock and the bolt on the door one night when they were going to bed. They weren't long in bed when they heard the steps come around the corner of the house to the front door and the latch being lifted. Then there came three knocks on the door, so loud that they resonated throughout the house. She never put the bolt on the door of the house again'. 'Although I've told you many ghost stories over the years', said sean-Risteard, 'I have to admit that I've never seen a ghost myself - and I only had one supernatural experience during the course of my entire life'. It's about forty years ago now but I was coming home across the mountains from Leacain north late one Sunday night. I was walking along the path across Réidh an Tobair when I heard an unusual sound coming from somewhere behind me. I stepped in off the path and crouched down behind a big furze bush. I didn't see anything but I heard a group of horsemen passing down the path past me. I heard the clatter of their horseshoes on the stones and the rattle of their harnesses and bridles and saddles as they roared past but I couldn't understand one word of the language the horsemen called out to one another in. It sounded like a great crowd of people humming in unison. I could have sworn that I heard the voice of an uncle of mine amongst the clamour, a man who was in America for years by then. They flew past me on the path and they were going at a frantic pace. A few months later, word came from America that my uncle had died and according to what we heard, he had died on the same Sunday that I heard the crowd racing past me. Another strange thing that happened at this same juncture was this; two mares belonging to Tomás de Búrc's father were in one of the fields facing the road and yet, on the following afternoon, they were found three miles away from where they were grazing originally. The place where they were found was about a mile south of Barra an Bhealaigh. If I was in some kind of a trance or hallucinating the night that I saw that strange magical crowd flying past me, what made the mares go so far away from where they were first grazing? Anyway, doesn't the whole world know that "Petticoat Loose" used to appear regularly up on the road near the mouth of the lake?'

'Oh!' said Seán, getting to his feet. 'If Risteard starts going on about "Petticoat Loose" we'll all be here till morning'. Seán Mac Craith happened to be in Ó Siadhaile's house that night, although he only went there very rarely; he joined the conversation now for the first time that evening. 'My own opinion', he said, 'is that the vast majority of these stories about ghosts and the like – as seen at night – are nonsense, and the product of nervousness and fear. I agree with Seán Breathnach here that drunkenness and cowardice are at the root of most of these apparent sightings'. Seán Mór sat down again; his walking stick propped beneath his chin. Seán Mac Craith continued talking – 'I wouldn't ever rule it out that God – a thousand praises be to him – might let a soul return if there was good reason for it – but not for something as innocuous as frightening drinkers coming home from the pub. And yet here's another story about something that happened south of here about ten years ago; there was a farmer's wife in the parish, a woman who was very devout and holy and she was quite elderly and, whatever happened, she fell out with the local parish priest. This was strange because they had been very good friends prior to this. Before they had a chance to make up with one another again, the woman died; it was a fairly sudden death because the curate barely made it to the house to prepare her for death before she passed away. One of the woman's goddaughters lived about five or six miles away from her and the old woman was always very fond of this girl. A week after the woman's death, this girl saw her godmother standing at the end of her bed when she awoke in the morning. It was a bright sunny summer's morning so there was no doubt about what she witnessed. Naturally, the girl became frightened and she couldn't actually speak for a few minutes, not until after this vision of her godmother had disappeared. Her godmother appeared to her three mornings in a row before the girl told her father and mother about it. They brought the girl to Mount Melleray where they asked the monks there for advice. One priest there advised the girl to speak to her godmother the next time she saw her. Apparently, the girl did see her again and spoke to her but whatever was said was kept secret and the only person told about the conversation was the parish priest. The following Sunday at Mass, he gave a sermon in which he outlined everything that I've described here. He didn't name anyone but most people in the congregation knew who he was referring to; he announced that he was offering the Mass he was then saying on behalf of someone whom the God of Glory had permitted to return to this world to complete a particular task and he asked the congregation to pray for this soul.

This isn't a story which was invented by someone as I was there myself and listening to the priest the day that he gave that sermon'.

'Incredible are God's miracles, praise and thanks be to Him', said sean-Risteard Ó Siadhaile. That was the end of the conversation and we all got up and went home.

OLD CUSTOMS

More older customs survive in an isolated place such as Gleann Chárthainn than they do in other parts of rural Ireland. There were a large number of customs and superstitions alive among the people of An Gleann here when I was young and although many of these have disappeared completely now, a good many of them continue to be practiced by the older generation.

When I was a child everyone believed that it was possible to 'take' the butter through the use of magico-religious beliefs and charms. There is still the odd elderly person here who believes this but when these people are gone, this belief will have disappeared with them also. Some of the inhabitants of An Gleann years ago wouldn't dream of giving anyone even a drop of milk to colour their tea with on a May Day evening. As a youth, I heard some amazing stories in Ó Siadhaile's house concerning the superstitions relating to milk. It is difficult to believe that some of these superstitions didn't have some basis to them. In the intervening years I've discovered that these superstitions are common throughout Ireland and not just to Gleann Chárthainn.

Risteard the carpenter was telling us a story one night about one of the Séarthaigh family from Leacain who was going to the fair at Ballyporeen one Mayday morning. At sunrise, he was walking the road parallel to the Tearra river and at Áth an Mhuilinn he saw a woman on her hunkers at the edge of the river holding a can and a skimmer. She was dipping the can in the river and filling it with water; then she was skimming the water from the top of the can as one would do the cream when churning butter. While doing this she was looking over at the cattle that were grazing on both sides of the river and chanting the following phrase: 'liom-sa bhfeicim', liomsa bhfeicim' (what I see is mine, what I see is mine'). 'Liomsa leath' ('Half is mine') called out Séarthaigh just for the hell of it and he continued on his way. Strangely enough, that summer Séarthaigh himself had huge amounts of butter back in his home place and his butter-yield was three times what it nornally was. Tomás de Búrc from Mónach Buí said that he often heard his father tell the story of how he had gone out into the fields where the milk-cows were grazing early one Mayday morning only to see a neighbouring woman – a woman who had a reputation for being involved in charms and the like. She had tied a cow-spancel to a stake at the side of the ditch and was 'milking it' (i.e. pretending to milk an imaginary cow) into a can there. He untied the cow-spancel from the stake, pulled the stake up out of the ground, and chased the woman away with it. Then he brought the cow-spancel home and threw it into an old empty barrel out in the shed. A few days later, when he went out to the shed to look for something or other, he looked into the barrel and, incredibly, it was half-full of cream or buttermilk.

Seán na Coille related a story about a man named O'Brien from Bóthar na Cille who went out one May morning, his greyhound at his side. When he went into the field where the milk-cows were grazing, he saw the biggest hare he had ever seen, suckling milk from a cow. The greyhound chased the hare but it made for a cabin a few hundred yards away next to the road, a cabin where an old woman lived alone. The hare got away from the greyhound and jumped in through the window of the cabin which was open. As it flew through the window, the hound managed to bite the hare on the leg but it still got away. When O'Brien caught up with the dog and looked in the window of the cabin, he saw the old woman lying on the floor, blood pumping from her leg. When I told Seán Mac Craith this story, he told me that he'd heard the same story previously about an old woman from his native parish.

I often heard people discussing others who's butter-churning had failed, this despite the fact they had spent the entire day engaged in this work. People were certain then that someone had performed a charm on them and 'taken' their butter. Anyone who entered a house when the churning was in progress was supposed to take hold of the churn-stick and strike the churn a couple of times while uttering 'God bless the work'.

Seán Mór Breathnach used to make little of these things any night he was in our company. I think sometimes that he was only doing this to be different from the rest of us, however, because various incidents occurred later on that indicated to us that he still believed in elements of these magico-religious charms himself. He said something very interesting one night that really set me thinking afterwards, I remember. They were discussing the 'taking' of butter by people who practiced magico-religious charms when Seán asked why didn't any of these charm-makers 'take' the butter from the new creamery that had been set up in Baile na hAbhann? It was strange that they didn't target a big creamery like that where there was huge amounts of cream; instead, they focused their attention on smaller and poorer farmers, he said.

Another old custom they had at one time was to shake the Easter (Holy) Water in the corners of every field on

May Eve. There were certain people who placed rowan branches in the shape of a Cross in each corner of the field on May Eve in addition to sprinkling these areas with Easter Water. The placing of these rowan sticks like this was undoubtedly a remnant of paganism, although the people who did this didn't realize this. When I was a boy, I remember a rowan tree that was growing on the corner of the boreen that goes from our house out onto the main road. Every Mayday morning, this tree was always bare and skeleton-like as so many of its branches had been cut down to make crosses for the fields. There is no-one in An Gleann now who places those rowan branches in the corner of the fields now on May Eve and only the odd person sprinkles Holy Water in the corner of the fields on that same feast-day anymore. I myself am one of the people who still do the latter. I think this is a custom that shouldn't be let die out – this request for God's blessing on the fertility of the land.

Some of the old people also believed that if you collected water and brought it into the house on May Eve, it would remain fresh all-year-round. Mayday was a big festival when paganism was still the main belief system in Ireland. This is probably the reason that there are so many old superstitions associated with Mayday even today. When I was still a teenager, there was an old man named Pól Dhomhnaill living up on the mountainside, on the south-eastern side of An Gleann. There were four fields surrounding the house owned by Pól and his wife Cáit. Their house was always carefully whitewashed and it was a lovely sight – the beautiful whitewashed cottage and the lovely green fields surrounded by heather. Any time I look up at the mountainside today, a picture comes into my mind of what that picturesque house looked like once. Unfortunately, there is no trace of it now and the fields nearby have all been reclaimed by the gorse and the ferns. Pól was a herbalist who also performed charms. He would cure horses that had 'farcy'. He also had Ortha na Fola ('The Blood Charm') and Ortha na gCnámh ('The Bone Charm') and he would collect various herbs out in the hills and make up 'bottles' or medicinal potions for people whose health was poor. He would go out to collect the herbs after sundown on May Eve and he wouldn't speak to anyone while he was engaged in this work. I met him one day when he was out gathering herbs on the riverbank, his hat in hand. They said that he could see people who were in the otherworld and that he could reveal them to other people also. I remember one Sunday afternoon when I was a boy and there were five or six of us gathered on the road close to Ó Siadhaile's house. Micil Ó Néill and Peaid na Brídighe were there. Pól Ó Domhnaill came down the road and he stood talking to Micil and Peaid.

'Pól', says Peaid. 'Is it true that you can show the otherworld to someone?'

'They' (i.e. the spirits from the otherworld) are all about us now', said Pól solemnly. 'The hills and meadows are black with them'.

'Show them to me so', said Peaid.

'Stand on the tips of my feet opposite me and look over my left shoulder', said Pól. 'But remember this; you're in danger of losing the sight in your eye or the power in your foot or in your hand, if you do so'.

'The devil I care', said Peaid, 'at least I'll be able to say that I saw the otherworld'.

'I couldn't have that on my conscience', (i.e. that Peaid would be injured physically), said Pól and he left, walking off up the road. It seems that Pól was only letting on that he could see the otherworld, even if there were plenty of people in An Gleann who believed that he could; many of these same people still believed this even after that encounter between Pól and Peaid na Bríde.

Pól Dhomhnaill was a seventh son of a seventh son, the old people said, and this was how he got his power. Many of the old people believed that he had such a power in him that he cut every type of worm or creepie-crawlie just by blowing on it. He used to say that he was obliged not to accept any money in payment for his healing work although he would accept tobacco or a half-pint of whiskey or something like that as a thank-you present. You'd only have been wasting your time if you'd tried to convince the people of An Gleann that Pól Dhomhnaill wasn't able to staunch blood using Ortha na Fola. The priests used to criticize him for his use of charms and the like, but it didn't do them any good because people trusted Pól healing abilities. I heard a story once about the young priest who was in this parish here and who was riding his horse on the road next to Baile an Droichid one day. He was crossing a ditch when some kind of a tack went into his horse's foot and the horse began to bleed heavily. The blacksmith and two or three others arrived on the scene and they were standing around the horse and trying to staunch the blood but without success. Who came along then but Pól Dhomhnaill and one of the men asked him to stop the bleeding. Pól looked over at the priest but the priest didn't say either 'do it' or 'don't do it'. Pól removed his hat and said the charm and the bleeding stopped immediately. I often heard this story told although I'm not saying that it was entirely true or not. I know that we all have a tendency to exaggerate a story or enhance it a bit, and I wouldn't be surprised if this story was added to a bit over time. Pól's wife Cáit, used to help people who had problems with 'splints' (i.e. cartilage problems). She died when I was a child and Pól lived alone for the rest of his life. He lived on for about twenty years after his wife died. People who had problems with the 'splints' were often lacking in energy and their health could be good or bad. One day, they might feel weak and the next day strong, one day good and the next day bad. The way that Cáit Phóil worked was to put the patient lying on their back on a table and undress them to reveal their chest. She'd get a half-pint glass or 'tumbler' as it is known and lay it upside-down on the 'lag' – that is just underneath the chest-bone; she'd place the stub of a candle about an inch in length beneath the glass. She would light the candle and after a while the person's skin/flesh would rise within the glass. When she was finished, it wasn't so easy to remove the glass because it was often stuck tight to the skin and difficult to pull off. I never saw her doing this but I often heard people speak about it. People used to consider the sight of the skin rising in the glass as a sort of a miracle. It's a long time now since I've heard of anyone who suffered from 'splints' in this locality, although I often heard of it when I was young. The doctors say that no such medical condition or ailment exists, and that it never really existed either – and I suppose that they are right. I came across Pól Dhomhnaill one day as a young lad when I was out on the mountain one Sunday during the summer. Pól was very old by then but he was still energetic and full of life. We sat down and began chatting as he was filling his pipe and taking an occasional puff from it. I asked him about the 'orthaí' (prayer-charms) at one stage and he explained to me that strictly-speaking, they were just simple prayers. Then he said the Blood Charm for me:

'The fellow who threw the javelin that pierced Christ's side, What came out? Blood, wine and pure water – Stop the blood from flowing too strongly'.

The person doing the healing had to say these words three times and also 'In the name of the Father, the Son and the Holy Spirit', both before and after uttering the words. I wrote these words down exactly as Pól said them. Afterwards, when I became more knowledgeable about these things, I realized that the words had become corrupted or 'obscured' over time. 'Loingín' should have been used instead of 'doinnín' and 'at-sléagh' instead of 'cleith'. Pól told me that there would be power in these words if I said them. A man had to learn the words of the charm from a woman and a woman from a man. If the charm was really a prayer, then what difference did it make how a person initially learned them, I asked him. Pól wasn't really able to answer this question. He said that all he had was what he'd learned from others and what had been passed onto him. Pól Dhomhnaill is dead and gone many years now, but people still mention him sometimes. If what they say about him is true, he had some kind of an unusual power. Sean-Risteard, the carpenter, was the man whom I heard talking about Pól the most. He told us how Pól was in Mairtí's pub in Baile and Droichid one day years ago and a man from Leacain known as Micil an Giolla (Michael the servant) was there and he began to make fun of Pól and his charms. Pól got angry and he told Micil to shut his mouth or he'd put a mark on him that would stay with him until the day he died. Micil made a right mockery of Pól, on hearing this from him. Next minute, Pól removed his hat and said something beneath his breath and then left the place. When he was gone Micil continued making fun of Pól, but before long he was singing a different tune. When he woke up the following morning every tooth in Micil's head had fallen out and they were was lying on the pillow next to him. Within a week, every rib of his hair had also fallen out. Risteard said that he often saw Micil an Giolla after this and he never grew another rib of hair, either on his head or on his face for as long as he lived. Here's another story Risteard told us about Peaid Dhomhnaill:

One of the Murphys from Flemingstown broke his shinbone sliding on the ice one day and he was brought to Pól Dhomhnaill. The boy was lying on a bed of feathers in the horse and cart and when they reached Risteard, the carpenter's house, they asked the people there for directions to Pól's house. It was evening and pitch-dark by then and the track leading up to Pól's house was quite rough so Risteard said he'd go with them. When they reached the house Pól told them to carry the boy into the kitchen and put him lying on the table. Then he went outside and collected a foot-and-half's length of a whitethorn branch or rod. He removed the thorns from this branch using his knife and then split the rod up the middle and used this as a splint, attaching it to where the bone was broken in the boy's leg. Within a month that boy was able to walk as well as ever. He became a priest later on in life. Cruthúr Garbh's wife Nóra used to cure thrush, a disease that usually affected young children. Anyone born after the death of their father was said to have this cure. He/She (i.e. the healer) – had to fast from the previous day before breathing air into the mouth of the child who had thrush – for three mornings in succession. I remember Nóra Chruthúir well; she was a big tough-looking woman who was very hunched-over. The poor woman didn't have a very easy life as her husband and their three sons were all very fond of drink. Long ago it was believed that anyone with the surname 'Caithil' (Cahill) was able to cure erysipelas or Saint Anthony's Fire. Some blood from one of the Cahill's needed to be applied to the inflammations on the patient's skin to cure this, it was said, and almost everyone, both young and old, agreed that this cure was effective. I remember having these inflammations on my side when I was about ten years of age. They were very sore and gave off a burning sensation. Liam Beilbhí brought me over to Páidín 'ac Caithil's in Leacain to get cured but I remember that my aunt Máire didn't believe that there was any greater efficacy in Cahill blood than there was in anyone else's. She was worried that the spots and inflammations which dotted my skin would remain as a permanent scar. Páidín wrapped a piece of twine around his finger and pricked it with a pin. Then he applied some of his blood to the inflammations that were all around my chest. The erysipelas was gone within three or four days, whatever cured it. My aunt Máire still wasn't convinced that it was 'Cahill blood' that had healed it however. She said that I would have recovered anyway, even if I hadn't gone to see Páidín 'ac Caithil at all.

The people had strange cures for whooping-cough, cures that you wouldn't hear about anymore today. 'A ferret's leavings' was one such cure. This involved feeding a ferret more milk than it was able to drink in a small bowl and giving whatever milk was leftover to the child that had whooping-cough. Another cure was to pass the child across the belly of the donkey three times or to ask a man who came by riding a white horse to give you the cure for whooping-cough. If you followed whatever cure the man prescribed – to drink boiled milk or to eat roast potatoes or to drink tea that didn't have sugar in it - then the cure was in that.

They used to tell a story in An Gleann long ago about a woman whose child had whooping-cough and who spotted a man going along the road on a white horse. 'Oh man of the white horse', she said, 'what would cure the whooping-cough?'

The man wasn't very nice at all because apparently he replied to her as follows: 'Dungarvan boiled in blood and the gripes on him as well as the whooping-cough'.

The old people had many different cures for lesser ailments also long ago. A spider's nest was normally applied to cuts. The leaves of the ribwort were also applied to cuts. The leaves would be chewed or boiled, or wrapped in a piece of cloth and placed between two rocks. Dock leaves or burdock was also used for cuts. Cití Currín, Micil Mhártan's wife had a cure for burns if someone got scalded by boiling water, for example. She would stir some kind of a herbal mixture (the sap from laurel leaves, maybe) in with goose-fat and this would be applied to the skin where it had been burned. Cití didn't make any secret of this cure but I can't remember the full details of it now. Apparently, it was very effective as people would come from all over the parish to her if they had a burn.

The people had various magico-religious cures for less-serious ailments such as warts. One of these was to collect tiny stones and to wrap them in paper, one wrapped stone for each wart, and to leave these wrappings out in the road. Whoever next picked these up from the ground got the warts and the warts would disappear from the person who'd originally had them. Another cure was to rub a snail against the wart and then to spear the snail on the end of a thorn-bush. As the snail weakened and died, so too did the warts disappear. Warts were also washed in the hole that was in a stone or a rock, or a person who fasted for the night would spit on the wart, nine mornings in a row.

There was a rock on the river-bank near Seán Mór's Inch that had three small holes in it. The holes were all located close to one another and they were as big as cups and about as deep also. There was normally some rain-water in these holes and the old people believed that there was a cure for sore eyes in this water. You had to go to this rock for nine mornings in succession before sunrise and apply the water to where your eye was sore. No-one has tried this cure for many years now. That rock is still there but the last time I passed, the holes in it were filled with clay and had grass growing from them.

A raw blister that appeared on a child's foot was known as a 'boinn-leach' (sole-flat) long ago; such blisters would appear because the children went around barefoot back then. If a boy stole a swallow's nest, people said that he would get one of these blisters on the sole of his foot as revenge for the bad thing he had done. A strange thing that I remember the people saying long ago was that they thought there was drop of the devil's blood in every swallow. A 'gearradh drúichtín' (literal 'little dew-cut'; athlete's foot) was what the small cuts or skin irritations that people got between their feet were called. Usually these happened in summer and were caused by great heat or perspiring heavily. Rubbing a few threads of lambs-wool or wool from the sheep was the cure for this. The people called any sickness that might strike someone very suddenly as a 'poc aosáin'. With this, the person's face got swollen, their temperature was very high and they perspired heavily. The sick person had to go to bed for a couple of days and drink hot drinks like heated punch or boiled milk with pepper in it.

The skin irritation that someone might get on the bottom of their foot was known as a 'míol ceardtán' (forge-mite) and the cure for this was that the sufferers had to go to the forge and dip their feet in the water-trough used to cool the forge-irons. Another condition, known as 'aos teannta', involved a rigidity in the bones of the feet of young children and was also cured by going to the forge. The child had to be brought to the forge for three consecutive mornings before sunrise. The blacksmith would place the child sitting on the anvil but I am not sure what else the cure involved; maybe it involved the blacksmith reciting a special prayer-charm. If I ever heard this prayer-charm, I can't remember it now. I remember Liam Beilbhí describing a cure for the 'big disease' (cancer) – God between us and all harm – a cure which was horrible. It involved taking the clay from the inside of a human skull that the graveyard-soil had thrown up and feeding some of this clay to the person who was sick, unknown to them. Another cure for this was to bring the patient to the priest who had originally baptized them so that they could get blessed again. Porter with boiled reeds in it was a cure for children who had measles; if you fed this mixture to the patient, it forced the infection and the spots to break out on the child.

The old people had great belief in purgatives as taken in Spring-time each year; another healthy practice was to drink fresh water each morning, having fasted from the previous evening.

Anyone who needed to build up their strength for a race or other athletics event was encouraged to eat corn-bread, particularly corn-bread dipped in 'cider'. It is a long time now since corn-bread was baked in this area however, although you can still see the old griddles in some houses today.

I mentioned earlier that Pól Dhomhnaill used to cure 'farcy' in horses. A man named Bil Phiarais who was a right trickster lived at the top of the boreen that led to Pól's house. One evening, just as darkness was falling, a stranger on a horse arrived into Bil Phiarais' yard and asked where Pól Dhomhnaill, the man who could heal 'farcy' lived.

'I am he', said Bil.

The man explained to him then about the horse he was riding and how the horse was suffering from farcy. He asked Bil whether he could do anything for him.

'That's no bother', said Bil and he proceeded to imitate some of the gestures that he'd seen Pól Dhomhnaill doing over the years, when healing farcy. He took off his hat and whispered to the horse and also wrapped a string around the horse's ear etc. When he was finished, the man asked him what recompense he should give him.

'Anything you like', said Bil.

The man gave him ten shillings as payment and – as Bil recounted later – he (Bil) found it very difficult not to burst out laughing at this. Bil had a great day down in 'Leán

Mháirtí's pub drinking that ten shillings-worth a few day's later, when he told all and sundry about the trick he'd played on the horseman. Bil actually ran into that same horseman about a month later down at Lismore Fair although Bil tried to avoid him – once he'd spotted him. The man followed him around the fairground however and he was full of gratitude towards Bil. He told Bil that his horse had never been better. As you can guess, Bil Phiarais was a right joker and loved playing tricks. Once, he played a similar trick to this one on Micil Mhártan. Micil was having problems swallowing and digesting his food at the time and for a few weeks he could only take drinks and was unable to swallow his food. He became weak and lost weight at an alarming rate so that he knew he had to do something about it quickly. There was a woman living out west in Gort an Chuilinn who was said to have the cure for this reflux problem. Micil and Bil were first cousins and Micil gave Bil ten shillings to go to this woman and get a herbal potion as a cure from her. On the way there, Bil met Peaid na Brídí and both of them went off drinking together. They spent the day in the pub in Baile an Droichid and they spent the entire ten shillings. They got an empty bottle then and made up some 'weird and wonderful' homemade syrup to bring back to poor Micil Mhártan. They put a mixture of juice, salt, red pepper, cowdung and leftover porter into this and mixed it all up with the water left over from boiling the potatoes. Bil gave this bottle to Micil and told him that the healing woman had instructed him to drink a half-glass of this mixture in the morning after fasting for the night, and then another half-glass before he went to bed again in the evening. Micil tasted the mixture and said that he'd never tasted anything as rotten in his life before. Micil saw this as a sign that it was a good medicine, however. Back then, the country people often thought that the more horrible a medicinal mixture, the more effective it must be. And believe it or not, this strange mixture did actually prove effective! By the time he'd finished the bottle Micil was healthy and eating like a horse again. Stories like this one and the one relating to the horse that had 'farcy' only confirm that that there are many things in this life that can't be fully explained or understood. And I can confirm here now that both of these incidents happened exactly as I have just described them.

Old Customs Relating to Death

There were many customs relating to death that were still followed when I was young. Most of these customs and traditions have died out now or have been forgotten, and the odd one still survives today. Everyone back then believed that the 'badhbh' (banshee/fairy woman) existed and that she followed particular families and keened their members when they were approaching eternity. It was always said that she could be heard keening anytime that one of the O'Neills, the O'Donnells or the Burkes were about to die. I remember Liam Beilbhí coming into our house one night and saying to my Aunt Máire:

'Micil's finished'.

'How do you know?' my aunt said.

'From once I left the main road, I heard the "badhb" keening, all across the fields and down towards the O'Donnell's house', he replied. Micil Ó Domhnaill (O'Donnell) from Mónach Buí was indeed on his deathbed and very weak. He died that night. I never heard the 'badhb' myself but that's not to say that there wasn't some truth in the many stories that were told about her. I remember Seán Mac Craith saying that the badhbs' were originally women who were paid for keening in times gone by and that they had to continue their keening work now in the next world until they had paid back all the money they owed. Who knows how much truth is in this? When the cockerels were calling out more frequently than usual, this was also a sign that someone in the locality was about to die. Many people believed this long ago and there are still people here who believe this even today. I remember one time when Cití Cuirrín, Micil Mhártan's wife was very sick. Everyone had given her up for dead and she had been anointed and given the Last Rites. The people were all around her bed each night, watching over her. Myself and Dic Ó Siadhaile and Seán Mac Craith went up one night to stay by her bedside until morning. About midnight, her breathing changed and everyone thought that she was about to die. Seán Mac Craith was reading the Litany over her and just as he finished reciting the Litany, the cockerel crowed out in the shed. It crowed again and then again once more. It was undoubtedly a strange and supernatural occurrence. This woman was dying and the cock crowing out in the shed and the rest of us standing there around her deathbed without a word from any of us. We were all startled and looked at one another in that moment.

'She's gone', said Micil.

We all thought the same thing although none of us said a word. Cití didn't die that night, however, and not for three years after this either. I've never had the same faith in the cockerel since that night.

The old people also believed that a corpse should not be prepared or moved, or keened over in any way until three-quarters of an hour after someone died. People believed that the devil's dogs were watching and would follow the soul when it left the body; therefore, it was better not to give these dogs any hint that someone had just died.

The water that was used to wash the corpse had to be thrown out on a ditch that bordered two fields. The razor that was used to shave a dead man was not to be kept in the house afterwards but should be given to someone else. If someone left a house where a wake was taking place, they should never turn back or return to the wake-house. If they did, then they might see something awful. If someone met a funeral on the road, they should wait for it to pass by and then take three steps after it. These were known as the 'three footsteps of mercy'.

I heard the old people say that they used to play many games and tricks, and sing songs at the wakes long ago. These traditions have declined greatly in recent years but the last remnants of them were still alive when I was young.

The clothes that people were wearing when they died were normally passed onto someone in the locality who needed them badly. The person who received the clothes was obliged to 'wear them to Mass' every now and then; they weren't ever allowed to pawn them either. If someone broke any of these unspoken 'rules', the consequences were terrible, the older generation believed, especially given that the person who'd first owned the clothes was now in the other life and helpless to do anything about it. The last person who'd been buried – i.e. the most recently deceased person – he or she was obliged to collect water for all the dead in the graveyard until the next person came in. 'Ní raibh tarraingt an uisce i bhfad air' (He didn't have to collect the water for long) was what they used to say about someone who'd died just a few days earlier but who had now been followed to the graveyard by someone else.

When the corpse was first brought into the graveyard, it was transported in a clockwise direction around the graveyard. They were also always very careful to lay the coffin very straight in the grave. I remember Micil Mhártan used to always have his stick with him at the head of the grave so that he could make sure that everything was straight when the coffin was placed in the grave. He was at every funeral and burial in Cill Dhubh and was always ready and waiting when the funeral arrived. The coffin would have to be moved an inch or two to the left or to the right (i.e. when it was placed in the grave) until Micil Mhártan was satisfied that it was straight. The screws in the coffin would be tightened a few times in an anti-clockwise direction before the soil was thrown in and the grave was filled in. This is rarely done nowadays and people who claim to be well-read and sophisticated make fun of such traditions. The person who thinks carefully about the symbolism associated with some of these traditions would realize that they frequently refer to the resurrection of the body in the after-life however. The old people believed that it wasn't right to dig a grave on a Monday. If a grave needed to be dug that day, they would make sure to do the initial clearing of the grave area – removing the surface soil and the first layer of sods – sometime before midnight on the Sunday night. It is difficult to know what the meaning of this custom was exactly but it is one of the few older customs that is still observed in this area today. In fact, I don't think there is anyone in An Gleann today who would even think of opening a new grave on a Monday. Long ago, no-one would ever get their hair cut or have a shave on a Monday.

If a grave was dug in an upside-down position, then it had to have a post or stake added to it before it was closed in. I remember long ago that Peaits Thomáisín committed suicide and that he was dug up again twice and re-buried again afterwards on both occasions. Long ago, they were very against burying someone who had committed suicide in consecrated ground. Initially Peaits was buried in Cill Dhubh with his own people but his coffin was dug up again and the following morning it had been left outside the cemetery wall. He was then buried within the yard or the surrounding the church in Baile na hAbhann but someone dug him up again. In the end, he had to be buried in the pauper's grave in Clogheen.

The priest in Baile na hAbhann spoke out very strongly from the altar, and came down very hard on those who had taken the body from the grave. I don't think they paid much attention to him however, and the same thing happened again when someone died by suicide. This was how deeply-embedded this old idea relating to suicide was in the minds of the people back then. When Pilib Ó Muirgheasa also died by suicide and drowned in An Poll Fada a number of years later, nobody objected to him being buried in Cill Dhubh graveyard with his own people. The older generation was gone and the older practice was gone with them. Children who died before they'd been baptized were buried on the southern side of the cemetery – an area where no-one else was buried long ago. This is another custom that has now died out. I often heard it said that unbaptized children were also buried in the corner of a field that bordered the northern side of the Séarthaigh family's land in Baile an Droichid. This burial ground, known as 'An Cillíneach' is still there and is covered in hedges and bushes. This part of the field was never touched or tilled at any stage. As soon as someone died long ago, everyone immediately downed tools and they wouldn't do any work again until the funeral had taken place. No funeral ever took the shortest route to the cemetery; instead, they travelled in a roundabout way towards it. It was often the case that one particular road was used for funerals and going to the cemetery but was not usually used by the people at any other time. Any tobacco or snuff handed out at the wake needed to be used by the time the wake was over; anything that was left over was considered worthless and was not used by anyone again. It was deemed unlucky to hitch a mare to a cart that was bringing a corpse to the graveyard, because if she had a foal afterwards, this foal would likely be still-born, it was believed.

'Pilib an Chleite' (Philip of the Quill) was the name of the man who had everyone ever born noted in his book and it is he who calls everyone from this life when their time comes. It was said of anyone who looked very pale or deathly-looking that 'Pilib an Chleite' had a 'decree' out on them – or that the raven had a 'decree' out on them. I often heard Risteard Ó Siadhaile say that each human being is made up of three elements, the soul, the body and the form. The form was essentially the shadow or the appearance of that person, when their substance had left them; sometimes this form would be seen in places other than where that person was at a particular time. It was usually a sign that this person was about to die. My aunt Máire often told the following story – (Bearing in mind that she wasn't someone who wasn't given to superstitions or belief in ghosts or the like): She was going to Baile na hAbhann one fine summer morning at around ten o'clock. When she left the boreen and went out onto the main road, she saw Billí Liam Bháin, the man who was responsible for the maintenance and repair of the local roads. He was sitting on a pile of rocks about twenty yards away from her. He had his back to her and she was positive that it was him. She greeted him but he didn't acknowledge her greeting. She turned on her heels and walked away – saying to herself – 'I wonder what's up with Billí?' She had walked about a half-a-mile down the road when who did she spot but Billí Liam Bháin walking down the road against her? He had a sledgehammer and a smaller hammer in his hand.

'By God, Billí, but one of us is going to die soon', she said to him.

Then she told him what she'd seen earlier.

'There's room enough for all of us in An Chill Dhubh', he said to her gruffly. A week-and-a-half later and Bill was buried in Cill Dhubh graveyard.

It often happened long ago that a corpse was carried a distance of three or four miles on men's shoulders to the cemetery. They used to say that the weight of a corpse (whether light or heavy) never matched the weight of that person when they were alive. When the corpse was light, it meant that the dead person wasn't carrying a big weight of sins. They used to tell stories about bad landlords and other horrible people whose corpses the horses were unable to pull, they were that heavy. Langley from Baile hAbhann and his wife and daughter are buried at gable-end of the old chapel in Baile na hAbhann. When his wife died, he took over a plot in the old cemetery there without asking anyone for permission and it was there that he buried his wife. He erected a big iron railing around it. I often heard that the horses that were pulling his hearse were bathed in sweat when they arrived to the graveyard, although they only had to travel about a half-a-mile of level road with the hearse.

CITÍ CUIRRÍN'S WAKE

I was about eight years of age when Cití Cuirrín died; she was the wife of Micil Mhártan. That's a custom that we have in An Gleann – i.e. that a married woman would keep her own surname. I went with Seán Mac Craith to the wake and now I'll describe some of the old customs and traditions that were practiced in the distant-past and which disappeared from the community's memory a long time ago. As I often heard it told by the old people, they sang songs and played tricks and games, and told stories – including the tales relating to Fionn and the Fianna at the wakes long ago. These older traditions were already on the wane by the time I was growing up however. None of these customs were practiced by then at the wakes of anyone who died suddenly or who was taken at a young age. There's no-one living in Gleann Chárthainn now who saw these customs being practiced other than myself and Dic Ó Siadhaile. I suppose that these older traditions were the remnants of the 'wake games' that were practiced as part of Gaelic culture in the distant past on the death of a chief or a king, traditional ritual games that survived almost down to our own time.

In the past, wakes were often held out in the barn so as to make room for everyone who was in attendance – as there used to be enormous crowds in attendance in times gone by. Micil Mhártan's wife was waked in the room where she had died; she was laid out on her own bed there. The women and girls were in that room and the men, both old and young, were in the kitchen.

When Seán Mac Craith and I arrived to the house, there were not many people there as it was still early in the evening. The crowd began to build up from then on and, by ten o'clock, the house was full. On arrival, each person went to the room where the corpse was laid out and said a prayer. The women would stay in the room but the men would come back into the kitchen again. Many people had to remain standing because, although there were benches and chairs there as borrowed from the neighbour's houses, there wasn't enough room for everyone to sit down there. There was a blazing fire there and everyone was crowded in around it; everyone was joking and laughing and being witty. In fact, there was so much fun going on that you would have thought there was a wedding going on rather than a funeral. About ten o'clock pipes full of tobacco were handed around – to both young and old – in the kitchen, and before long, we could hardly see one another anymore, there was so much smoke in the room. A plate of snuff was left on the table in the corpse-room for the women and they passed it around amongst themselves every now and then.

I remember one boy who was about my own age and who was sitting on the kitchen table close to me. A bunch of chancers were standing around him and they bet him that he wouldn't be able to take twenty puffs in a row from the pipe they'd handed him. He took them up on the bet and one of the lads sorted counted as he inhaled. The poor fool got to about sixteen puffs and then he keeled over, he fell onto his head on the floor. He was brought outside where he promptly got sick. When he came back in again, he looked as pale as death. I felt sorry for the poor lad as it reminded me of how awful I'd felt that time I'd smoked some tobacco at my grandfather's wake.

At about eleven o'clock, the women up in the room began saying the Rosary and we all knelt down on the floor and began to pray. Muiris na bPaidríní led the prayers and his voice was so loud, you'd have heard him out in the yard. He used to attend every wake in the two parishes and usually stayed in the room where the women were. Some of the jokers out in the kitchen would have tormented the life out of the poor man, if he'd stayed there with the men.

About midnight, the whiskey was handed out. Two men did this job, Seán Mac Craith and Dic Ó Siadhaile. Seán poured out the whiskey while Dic held the candle for him so that he had enough light to do the job properly. As usual, everyone said a prayer for the soul of the deceased before knocking back the whiskey. The whiskey kicked in fairly quickly and some of the men got more lively; Peaid na Brídhe began humming a tune in the corner.

'Louder there Peaid', someone called out.

'No. Don't!' said Sean-Risteard Ó Siadhaile, 'Micil wouldn't like it'.

Peaid did as he said. This was the very last time I ever heard a song sung at a wake.

They began to prepare tea at this point. My aunt Máire and some local girls were in charge of the tea. The people who were crowded in near the fire had to move out of the way so that they could put the kettles over the fire and brew the tea. They drank the tea at the kitchen table and everyone got plenty of soda bread and butter to eat and as many cups of tea as they wanted. Micil Mhártan didn't have much in the world; he owned a small patch of land that was poor enough ground. He had three daughters, all of whom were living in America for many years. I only remember the last girl who went abroad, and she left

Ireland at least ten years before her mother's death. They were very good to the old couple and when they got news that their mother was in danger of death, they sent twenty-five pounds home to Micil so that he could lay her to rest in a fancy grave, if she died. The reason that I know about this is because my aunt Máire used to write his letters to his daughters on Micil's behalf.

The local carpenter usually made the coffins for most people at this juncture, but in Cití Cuirrín's, Micil wanted to have a 'hearse' there to bring her to the graveyard, although the cemetery was only a half-a-mile or so from their house. Seán Mac Craith and Séamus na Mónach Buí told Micil that this was ridiculous and that it would do Cití a greater honour to be transported to the cemetery on the shoulder of her neighbours than by 'hearse'. Micil agreed with them on this although he was initially reluctant to do so apparently. Cití Cuirrín was carried to Cill Dubh cemetery after two Masses had been read over her in her own house. I attended both of those Masses. Seán Mac Craith was the person who prepared the house on both occasions and who served at the two Masses. My aunt Máire prepared breakfast for the priests.

When they were finished drinking tea the night of the wake and when the women who were staying on had returned again to the room where Cití was laid out, the young people began to play games in the kitchen. It was Donncha Pheigí, needless to say, who began the trickery. The first game they played was called 'Bróg about' and this involved about eight or nine boys sitting on the floor in a circle, their knees tucked beneath their chins. One boy was placed in a circle in the centre of the floor and on his hunkers. Then the other lads passed an old shoe around from one to the next, hiding the shoe behind their backs as they did so. The boy who was in the centre of the circle had to try and guess which of the other lads had the shoe and grab him. It wasn't easy to guess correctly each time and sometimes when the boy in the middle made a lunge for someone, he would get a whack down on the back of the shoulders from whoever had the shoe behind him. No sooner had he twisted around, but the shoe would be out of sight again and the lads were passing it on around the circle behind their backs again. The lads had great fun with this and they were all in stitches laughing – but eventually they got bored and moved onto another game. This next game was called 'An Chorcóg Beach' (The Beehive). Maitiú Liam was put sitting in a chair in the middle of the floor where he was 'king of the bees'. He removed his hat; Maitiú was as bald as a coot and this is probably the reason he was chosen as 'king'. The other lads (i.e the 'bees') all walked in a circle around him, their mouths closed – as they hummed in unison – uhhhm, uhhhm etc. as if imitating bees. Then they all went out the door one after the other to 'collect the honey'. They returned again after a while, their mouths closed and still humming. Then they all walked in a circle around the 'king' again, Maitiú Liam breaking his heart laughing at them all the while. Then, suddenly all the lads opened their mouths – that were full of water – and emptied them out onto Maitiú's bald head – as if gathering in the 'honey' that they'd gone outside to gather. Maitiú jumped up out of the chair with a roar and everyone fell around the kitchen laughing!

Maitiú Liam was a very soft-spoken and gentle man; no-one every saw him get angry. He took this trick in the spirit which it was intended. All he said was: 'The devil wouldn't be in it with you lot' as he dried himself off with a big red handkerchief he always had inside the rim of his hat. He roared with laughter himself. Donncha Pheigí from Baile an Droichid was the next to play a trick and on this occasion, it was Séainín Ó Deá who was the victim. He told Séainín to stand outside the door for a minute and to wait until he was called. Donncha told Séanín that if the flue of the chimney wasn't chock-full of pig puddings when he came back into the room that he (i.e. Seáinín) was free to choke him with the tongs.

When Seáinín went out of the room, Donncha placed the legs of the tongs in the fire and heated them up. He made sure that they weren't red-hot however and that they looked the same as before. Then Seánín was called in and he looked up the chimney. Needless to say, there weren't any pig's puddings up there and neither was there anything else either. 'Huh … you blackguard', he said to Donncha and grabbed the legs of the tongs to give him a good 'choking'. He dropped the tongs as quickly as he had picked it up however, and let out a roar. Then he rubbed his fingers furiously against his trousers and in his hair to try and ease the burning sensation. Everyone burst out laughing. Seáinín ran out the door cursing Donncha furiously all the while. He ran home without even saying the prayer in the wake-room before he left. It was the custom then to say a prayer when you came into the wakehouse first and then another one before you left. Despite sean-Risteard's cleverness, Peaid na Brídí caught him out with a trick once. Peaid placed a clay pipe on the edge of the hearth and then he challenged sean-Risteard. I'll place a stick – straight between your hands – but I'll bet you four pence you won't be able to break the pipe with it.

'Why wouldn't I be able to break it?' asked Risteard.

'Put down your four pence'.

'And you'll put the stick straight into my two hands?' said Risteard.

'I'll put it straight into your hands', repeated Peaid.

'It's a bet so', said Risteard and he handed four pence to Micil Ó Néill who was sitting in the corner. Peaid handed Micil his four pence also.

'Where's the stick?' said Risteard

Peaid brought him over to the door of the room and placed Risteard's two hands around the door-jamb.

'There you go now. There's a stick placed between both your hands. Now, go and smash the pipe with it!'

Everyone started laughing. Even Risteard laughed after a minute. 'Give him the shilling Micil', he said. 'Even the devil himself couldn't be up to him. And I was a right old fool to take him on in the first place. Some of the boys who were sitting around the fire began to play a trick called 'Ceanna Briain'. This is how you play this: You placed a small stick in the fire until the tip of it was red-hot and burning. Then you twirled the stick around in the air so that it was a small circle of flame moving above your head.

Ceanna, ceanna, Briain
Dén sórt fear é Briain?
Fear fada caol árd, is mhair sé daichead bliain.

(Head, head, Briain,
What sort of a man is Briain?
He's long and thin and tall and he lived for forty years).

Then the first person handed the small stick to the person closest to them, who twirled it above their head, and so on around the room. Whoever had the stick in their hand when the fire in it went out, would get a slap on the head. When they tired of this game they would begin playing riddles and try to solve different types of problems and conundrums. Many of these riddles and puzzles have been documented in other books and were the same in other parts of Ireland as they were here in An Gleann. I won't go into detail about them here, therefore.

About two o'clock in the morning, who should call into the wake but Séan na Coille? Seán used to attend every wake in An Gleann but he had a particular habit of calling into a wake in the early hours of the morning, as he did in this case. On the evening of a wake, he would go to bed at his usual time and have a good sleep. He would wake up then in the early hours after midnight and go the wake, where he would stay until morning. He said that there were always too many people at a wake in the early-evening and that only a few people ever stayed until the morning. He was right about this of course. Once people began to go home, having said their individual prayers at the door of the wake-room, the crowd got much smaller. Whiskey was doled out to those who remained and they brewed more tea. Only Muiris na bPaidríní and four or five women would remain in the wake-room and there might be eight or nine men and boys around the fire in the kitchen listening to Risteard Ó Siadhaile telling ghost stories. As usual, I used to sit in the opposite corner of the kitchen to Risteard and the stories he related would have made the hairs stand on your head, they were so frightening. These included stories about 'the headless coach' and the 'Slua Mhá Deilge' and the like. By the time Seán Mac Craith and I went home at about four am, I would probably have died of fright if he hadn't been with me walking along the dark boreen; I used to imagine that every bush and shape in the ditch was a ghost.

I don't remember seeing any games or tricks being played at any wakes in An Gleann after Cití Cuirrín's wake. Storytelling still went on, of course, although I never heard anyone since Risteard Ó Siadhaile who could spice up or enhance a story as much as he could. He is buried in the graveyard clay for many years now – may the Light of Heaven be upon him. Life has changed a great deal in this locality since that night long ago when Cití Cuirrín was waked. I was still a young boy back then with my life stretched out before me.

Now that I am old, I am waiting for the day when I get the call home myself. The night when the people of An Gleann will gather for my own wake here in Lios na Faille can't be too far off now. All I ask of God is that he takes me at the most appropriate time.

REFLECTING ON THE OLD WAY OF LIFE

Gleann Chárthainn has declined a great deal in recent years; the population has fallen a lot since I was a boy attending school in Baile an Droichid. I realize that the population of Ireland as a whole has declined since the Famine but it seems to me that the population decline in Gleann Chárthainn has been particularly high when compared to anywhere else on this side of the county.

I was thinking about this the other night and comparing how many families were here in Gleann Chárthainn when I was young as compared with today. There are 23 families in An Gleann today but when I was young, I remember 41 families living here. This is a major decline, of course. You can't walk for half-a-mile anywhere around here that you won't see the ruins of an old house, a place where people once lived. The remains of an old wall or the pillars of an old gate, or a ditch where there was once a farmyard. The single tree that marks a once-tilled field, or the old remnants of a gable-wall; all of these reminders are around here. Seeing these traces of the past always reminds me of what must have been – a warm hearth, friendship, love, laughter, talk and song, weddings, baptisms and funerals. Emotions such as happiness and strife, success and hardship; every aspect of the human experience was once played out here – in the same place that there is now just a trace of rock or a wall. They were all here once but now, nothing remains of them except these lonely traces and reminders. And – says he – where are all the people who once lived here now? Most of them are gone into eternity, I suppose, the blessings of grace be upon them. Their children and their children's children are scattered to the four corners of the earth and no-one here remembers them anymore. This human life of ours is sad and strange.

About halfway between Baile an Droichid and Bearna an Mhadra, on the east side, stand the pillars of two old gate-posts. Where the gate once stretched, a lonely stone-wall now stands. In the corner, inside the ditch there, a rowan tree grows. This tree is beautiful and in early summer or late autumn, when the blossoms are in full-bloom or the tree is covered in bright-red berries, you won't see a more incredible sight than this one. One of the nicest small houses you have ever seen stood next to that rowan tree at one time. It was a thatched cottage with lovely ornamentation in its thatching. It was kept immaculately all-year round. The door and the gate were painted red, the window-frames a pristine white. The walls were always perfectly whitewashed as was the chimney. There was a black line of tar forming a neat line around the bottom wall of the house, about a foot from the ground. A similar line – this time a red one – encircled the dresser in the kitchen. The kitchen table was always as scoured as 'freestone' and perfectly-clean. The plates always shone bright on the dresser including the three pewter dishes that gleamed and polished in the light of the fire. I remember too the old clock with its chains and weights that hung on the wall opposite the kitchen-door and the omnipresent tick-tock of the clock's great 'hand'. Peaidí Condún and his wife Ailí lived in that house at one time. Peaidí was a roofer by trade. In fact, he was the best roofer in the two parishes. He was always booked up for work and people often waited six months or more for him to come and do a job for them, he was such a good tradesman. A talented timber-worker, he could do all types of work. He made screens that were used for picking potatoes and beehives and the platforms on which they were set. He crafted these beehives from straw and the odd person who kept bees in this locality always went to him for their equipment. He used to collect wattles and tie hundreds of them together with a sally-withe.

He used to work on the platforms and the withes and the other parts of the beehives during the long winter nights and on days when it was too wet to work outside on the roof of a house. The garden was adjacent to the house and a bush skirting around it that was always kept neatly-trimmed. There was an apple-tree and a plum-tree in the two eastern corners of the garden and rows of gooseberry bushes and currant bushes on two sides of the paved path going down through the middle. At the northern end of the garden were four or five beehives. Ailí was in charge of the bees and whenever a comb was removed from one of the hives, you'd hear Ailí tapping a tin can with a spoon and calling out 'go chraobh!', 'go chraobh' ('Up top' 'Up top' – (i.e. 'To the top branch of the tree') in a loud voice. She'd place the comb back into the hive again without any protection on her hands and face – not even a handkerchief covering her head. And even with the bees mixing in her hair and humming loudly, she never got stung. I watched her a few times preparing a new hive for the swarm. She would rub some milk or fresh cream around the inside of the hive first using a fistful of sally-leaves, then place four wattles in through the beehive from the sides forming two cross-like shapes – like two crosses lying one on top of the other. Three or four of these beehives were sold each autumn. The first thing Ailí did then was 'quench' or clear the hive. This is how I saw her doing this: Firstly she put a poisonous liquid mixture within the hive on an old small skillet and then placed long thin pieces of cloth in the melted mixture. Then she wrapped each of these threads of cloth around the wattles and left them aside until the mixture was hard. She dug a hole in the garden for each beehive that was to be removed. These holes were about a foot deep and their mouths measured no wider than the entrance to the hive. Once darkness fell and the bees had all returned to their hives, Ailí would place two candles made of the same poison at the bottom of each hole. Then she placed the hives over each of these holes. The smoke emerging from the candles would kill the bees and they would fall down into the hole. When all the bees were dead, she removed the beehives and replaced the clay back in the hole. When I saw Ailí Condún doing this, I thought to myself that this was a cruel end for these hard-working bees that had spent the summer out busily collecting honey. That said, I suppose that this pattern as relating to the bees was no different really from killing a lamb for food at the end of the season.

On our way home from school, as children, we would look into this garden at the gooseberries and the currants to see when they were ripe. Although there wasn't anyone at home, and no matter how tempted we were by them, we were too afraid of the bees to go into the garden and pick the berries.

Ailí often gave me a piece of a honeycomb to eat but I'm afraid that I used to be thinking too much about the poor bees that had been killed to enjoy the honey properly. I remember one afternoon that Dic Ó Siadhaile tried to get into where the beehives were. Five or six of us waited at the gate out on the road for him. He was hardly in over the wall but he was back out again twice as quick, a stream of bees chasing him.

The bees followed us up the road but the only person who got stung was Dic. He was stung just below the eye and his eye swelled up within a matter of minutes. He had a black eye for more than a week afterwards. In addition to her work around the house, Ailí used to collect eggs and sell them at the market in the town. She'd pay other housewives in An Gleann two or three pounds for a batch of eggs and every Friday she'd travel to Clonmel with her mule and cart and many boxes of eggs which she would sell at the big market there. Ailí was non-literate but she had her own way of keeping account when buying and selling. She would place a mark with chalk on the side of the dresser in each house that she collected eggs from – a long stroke equalled one penny; a short stroke was a half-penny; a small circle meant a shilling while a big circle with a cross on it was equal to a crown. She always carried a big knob of chalk with her as she went from house to house although I noticed that this chalk was different from the chalk that our schoolmaster used. When she was counting the eggs, I remember that she used to take three eggs in each hand and although she would count – one, two etc. – quietly, beneath her breath – she never faltered in her conversation with my Mam or my Aunt Máire all the while.

She always had a fine load of eggs for sale whenever she went to Clonmel and when it came to the bargaining at the market there, I heard that she would have the prices worked out in her head before the clerk did, even though he was using a pen and paper. It happened more than once that the figure Ailí had come to in her head didn't match the price the dealer was offering but when the clerk double-checked and totted up again on paper, Ailí's final total proved the correct one. Ailí also made quilts. She had a frame in her kitchen that she made them on; it was like a big kitchen table without a cover on it. She made the quilts from flannel, white flannel underneath and red or blue flannel on top. She placed wool in between both sections of the flannel and then quilt everything together using two huge sewing needles, one for regular sewing and one for sewing wool –mixing the red and the blue colours, as appropriate. Her sewing was very polished and she would incorporate circles, diagonals and other lines and patterns in her work. She would draw out these decorations beforehand on the flannel using a piece of chalk.

Any housewife who needed a new quilt made would give the flannel, the wool and the thread to Ailí and she looked after the rest. We had a few of the quilts she made in the house here for years. We'd still have them only that the youngsters didn't like the quilts so much because - even if they lasted forever - they were very heavy. Even one of her quilts was enough to keep you warm on a freezing, frosty night.

The blessings of grace be upon poor Ailí. I can still see her in my mind's eye, a small, thin woman, as lively as a bee, energetically going about her work. She wore a white cap on her head as tied beneath her chin in a big ribbon-knot, the cap embroidered with lace indentations on the front. She didn't give a hoot for what anyone else thought of her dress-sense and wore a set of elastic-type shoes or slippers all year round, shoes that were always finely gleaming with polish. Her check apron and blue coat were always spotless also.

I often watched her embroidering a lace cap. She used an iron bar/jam about the thickness of your finger for this work, a device she referred to as a 'Teailí Iron' (tally-iron), even when she was speaking Irish - which was nearly always. Although she had reasonably good English she almost always spoke Irish. I have never seen another woman who dressed as neatly and as stylishly as Ailí did; she was always stylish and not just on Sundays. She wore a long navy cloak that reached to the ground when she went to Mass or to town but she always wore a black shawl when she was collecting the eggs.

Peaidí Condún was a great fisherman and only ever did rod-fishing. He hated the poachers who used traps and gaffs to catch salmon and was always giving out about them. He made his own fishing rods and flies and he made flies for all the rod-fishermen around here; his flies were said to be far more effective than those you could buy in a shop, in the town. He always let the nails on his two thumbs and his two index fingers grow very long so that he could tie the flies better when he was making them. He also made wooden tobacco pipes that he ornamented using a cover and a thin brass chain.

Peaidí and his wife Ailí were the most comfortably-off couple financially in the entire parish but while they lacked for nothing, there was nothing miserly about them at all. No sooner were you in the door of their house but the kettle was on the hob over the fire and you had to drink a cup of tea. Ailí used to make lovely apple cakes, I remember; I often stuffed myself with them. She made the tea far too strong, however. 'What good is water?' she'd say by way of explanation.

Peaidí and Ailí were already elderly when I knew them as a youngster. They had a son and a daughter living in America but I don't ever remember seeing either of them. They had already emigrated before I went to school for the first time in Baile an Droichid. The local people here in Lios na Faille were always very fond of this old couple. When Peaidí died, the family in America asked Ailí to join them and she went over to live with them there, this despite the fact that she was seventy years of age by then. I often heard the neighbours saying that five years before Ailí emigrated from An Gleann a 'bean feasa' (wise woman/healer) had passed through the area and she'd told Ailí that she would journey across the sea and die in a foreign country.

The house became dilapidated fairly soon after Ailí left. Without a fire in its grate, most houses don't stay intact for very long. The roof fell in eventually. The walls and the ditches in the garden fell apart and the apple and plum trees were cut down. The gooseberry and currant bushes were dug up and the place is just a bare field now. There is nothing to remind you of that family now, a family that were well-known and well-liked in their day. The only trace of their passing is the big rowan tree that still grows in the corner of the field, next to the road. And now here is a description of another and different type of family that I remember from long ago also:

Within one hundred yards or so of the crossroads at Cill (Crosaire na Cille) the remains of an old wall can be seen at the side of the road. There was a cabin there when I was a child and an old man known as Bil Learaí lived there. I don't remember his surname now but I do remember the man himself; he was tall and thin and slightly hunched. He always wore trousers to the knee made of king's cord, trousers which had three brass buttons on the side of each knee. He sported long woollen socks, low-sized shoes and a tweed jacket that also reached down to his knees. To top it off, he always wore a half-caroline hat which had been the fashion when he was young. In fact, he and Liam Buithléar were the only two men left in the area who still wore that type of hat and who stuck with that fashion until they died. Bil Learaí had no-one belonging to him still living. His wife and children were all dead and buried years earlier, long before I was born. People said that Bil Learaí had some money but I don't know whether there is any truth to this or not. He certainly didn't look like he was that well-off. He had owned about twenty acres but when his last remaining son died, he sold this land and just kept the garden where he grew potatoes, cabbages and onions. The only stock he owned was two goats and a dozen hens that were always sitting on the mantle above the door when you went into the house. Originally, the house had consisted of two bedrooms and a kitchen but I only remember the kitchen having a roof over it and the other two rooms being broken down and dilapidated. He slept on an old king-sized bed in the kitchen facing the hearth.

I never met anyone as cranky and hot-tempered in my life as Bil Learaí and because this was his nature, all the blackguards of the village used to constantly torment him and play tricks on him. I remember that they placed an old bag over the top of the chimney one day and he nearly choked with the smoke before he realized what had happened. Other local boys used to play ball against the gable-end of his house that faced the road but then Tomás Bhrídí convinced Bil that the lads banging the ball against the wall was affecting the hens and their egg-laying. Bil used to hunt the boys away then when they came around to play ball. Next thing, the boys would hide behind the ditch and throw stones at the wall just to drive Bil crazy. When Bil ran out of the house cursing, he wouldn't see anyone outside but no sooner was he back inside again than the wall would get another few rattles.

Siobhán Thomáisín, the sewing-woman was visiting the Burkes in Móin Bhuídhe one summer's evening. Sometime around nightfall, she was passing by Bil Learaí's house. Siobhán had just gone about twenty yards past the house when some blackguard threw a stone at Bil's wall. Bil had just gone to bed and he burst out of the house wearing only his nightshirt, shovel in hand. He always kept this old shovel just behind the door. The only person he spotted outside was Siobhán. He began cursing and chased her up the road with the shovel threatening to split her head open. Siobhán said later that she was lucky to get away from him; only that he was in his bare feet, she mightn't have got away from him at all. The local lads, young and old, gathered at the crossroads on Sunday afternoons playing ball in the alley. Some of them played cards at the side of the ditch while others tossed pennies on the road.

Tomás Bhrídí went into Bil's one Sunday – but before he went in, he picked up two or three stones and stuck them in his pocket. Bil was boiling something in a skillet that was hanging over the fire. When Bil wasn't looking, Tomás quickly threw a stone up the chimney and it fell into the skillet with a clatter. 'They're some blackguards, aren't they, to be throwing stones down the chimney like that?' he said. A few minutes later when he got another chance, Tomás did the same thing again. This time the stone fell down and hit the cover of the skillet. Bil cursed and ran over to grab the shovel. Tomás followed Bil as he ran outside shovel in hand; he was afraid that he might kill someone with it. Dic Ó Siadhaile was standing near the ditch hunched over and tossing a penny at the 'bab' when, without any warning, he got a heavy blow of the shovel down on the shoulders. Bil knocked him right over and he fell on the road. He was lucky that Bil didn't get him with the sharp edge of the shovel or it could have been a lot worse. The other lads playing there wanted to grab Bil and fling him into the river and they would have done it too if Tomás Bhrídí hadn't protected him and prevented them from doing so. Bil used to go up to the rock-ledges in An Choiminis to collect ferns that he'd then lay on the ground outside in his yard. Some of the pathways up to these rock-ledges were so steep that a path made of stone-steps had been cut into the rock on the way up. One day when Bil had gone up to collect a batch of ferns, Donncha Pheigí hewed out a hole in one of the stone steps and covered it with sticks and dried leaves so that it was disguised – like a hidden trap. Bil was returning down the path carrying a big batch of ferns when he unwittingly stepped into this hole. He flew head-first into the ground and both he and the bundle of ferns flew forward and rolled for about twenty feet across the ground. Later Donncha Pheigí said that Bil exploded with rage when he fell and that he nearly set the furze around him on fire with the ferocity of his curses. It was a rotten trick to play on someone but it wasn't even the worst trick that Donncha Pheigí ever played on Bil, to be honest. Once or twice a week Bil would head down to the Burkes of Móna Buí to collect a small gallon-can of milk to feed his calves with; this was in winter-time when his goats were dry and had no milk. Usually, he would stay and visit for a while with the Burkes – until about ten pm in the evening. It was frosting hard that night and while Bil was inside talking to the Burkes, Donncha Pheigí and a few other lads threw four or five buckets of water on the boreen outside the gate of the house where there was a slope leading down to the main road. As you'd expect, the surface of the road was coated with ice by the time Bil was leaving the Burkes. He fell on the road and the gallon-can of milk spilled all over the road. Needless to say Bil went crazy and turned the air blue with his curses; all the while, the messers who caused him to fall were listening to his every word from behind a ditch and having a good laugh at the same time. Bil died in the poorhouse in Cloichín and a group of local men – including some of the lads who were always rising him, you can be sure – brought him back and buried him here in Cill Dhubh. May God have mercy on the poor misfortunate man and may he forgive everyone who tormented him down through the years.

About a quarter of a mile from the crossroads in Bóithrín na Cille, you will see two old gate-posts or pillars on your left as you walk in a southerly direction. As usual, an old stone-wall has been built between two old gates here. An old boreen – about the length of a field in terms of distance – leads inwards from these pillars, a boreen that is now covered in weeds and briars. This boreen hasn't been used for years but I remember a fine thatched cottage at the top of it at one time, a house that had a half-acre of an orchard behind it. This house was once circled by a beautiful and carefully-tended hedge, a hedge that had carefully-ornamented shapes cut into it at intervals of every ten yards or so. These ornamentations included the shapes of cockerels, dogs, beehives and so forth. As a child I was fascinated by how these shapes could be cut into the hedge. The people who lived there long ago were named O'Donnell. I remember the old couple and their three sons who were all fine, handsome men and their daughter who was one of the prettiest women that the sun ever shone down upon. One of the three sons, Liam, was a little bit odd at times, especially when it was a full moon. As children, we were all afraid of him and ran away when we saw him coming. In fact, I was never as afraid of anyone else in my life as I was of him. One night Dic Ó Siadhaile and I went into the orchard behind the house to steal some apples. This quick foray into the orchard was only a bit of messing really as everyone already had apples anyway. Dic Ó Siadhaile was high up in one of the trees wearing a straw hat when the dog spotted him in the moonlight and began barking up at him. We all did a runner. I ran into the field beyond the orchard where the corn was collected in stooks and hid myself under one of them. The other three lads ran up that same field towards the ditch. Next minute, Liam Ó Domhnaill appeared in the corn-field holding a hay-pike and cursing profusely. He was barely five yards away from me and I nearly died of fright. Luckily for me, however, the dog followed the other three lads. If Liam had spotted me, I'm sure that he would have gone for me with the hay-pike, he was that angry.

The O'Donnell family experienced great tragedy a few years later and it certainly wasn't that they had ever done anything immoral that drew this bad luck on them. They were the kindest and most honest people you've ever met. They would never have dreamed of being involved in anything immoral or dishonest and were very devout and hard-working. Any Travelling man or woman that passed their way always received alms and many of them got a comfortable bed for the night out in the O'Donnell's barn. That said, they say that God only gives his Cross to those who can bear it and maybe this was what happened in the case of the O'Donnells. It was that tragic disease known as tuberculosis or what people around here called the 'decay' that brought great suffering to the younger O'Donnells. They seem to have contracted it from relatives on the mother's side of the family and it was the eldest lad, Seán who was first struck down with the disease. He was very sick for about a year before he died and in the following four years, there were four more funerals from that house to Cill Dhubh. Eibhlín, one of the most beautiful girls in An Gleann, was the last of the children to die and the poor parents were left bereft and heartbroken, and alone.

I was standing close to her mother on the day that Eibhlín was buried and I'll never forget the haunted look on her face. She was beyond weeping, her face the colour of marble; she was like someone who was in an unconscious state almost, as if she could no longer see what was in front of her or feel anything anymore. I suppose that when someone has suffered a great deal of sorrow, as she had done – that they can barely weep anymore. Their Cross is so heavy that they no longer even experience the release of weeping or crying. She died only a short while after her daughter Eibhlín. She didn't contract the tuberculosis; it looks as if she died from a broken heart. Within the year, she too was in Cill Dhubh graveyard in the company of her four children – that was five funerals within five years, and all from the same house. The father sold the house and the land that went with it to the Lonergans who lived nearby and he moved into the town. He took lodgings near the Brother's church there and it was in this church that he spent most of his time from then on. He only lived for three-and-a-half years longer than his wife did. He too is buried in Cill Dhubh alongside his wife and family, his life's troubles finally behind him.

If I was to tell the story that lies behind every ruin and relic from the old life that dot the landscape around here, I would be here for quite some time.

BACAIGH[1] AND TRAVELLERS IN THE OLD DAYS

When I was young, Travellers and people who begged from place to place didn't go around in groups as they do today. The most common sight travelling the roads in this area long ago was that of old men or women travelling alone from place to place, begging. They all had their own circuits that they travelled and they had particular houses that they always called to where they got lodgings for the night. And people welcomed them then as they had all the local news and could do a great job of telling a story. Intermittently, you'd get groups of tinkers coming this way – usually with a significant period of time between the rounds of each group. Back then, they didn't have the wagons that they have today. When the weather was dry, they'd sleep at the side of the ditch on a pile of straw as placed beneath their carts; when the weather was bad, they would look for lodgings in a farmer's shed or barn somewhere. Another thing – these tinkers long ago were 'true' tinkers; they fixed pint cans and gallons and strainers and other metal items for the country housewives; some of them also moulded metal implements and made any metal parts that the farmers needed for their machines. I often saw them on my way to school or coming home from school when they would have a big coal fire by the side of the road and a bellows working so as to run the metal. They would have moulded shapes out of the sand and dirt on the side of the road and they would pour the molten metal into these as easily as water. I found their craftsmanship and work amazing and I often spent up to an hour watching them running the metal.

The tinkers who travel the roads now are just beggars. Most of them don't have any trade or anything and just look for alms, especially when the only person at home is the woman of the house. They steal sometimes and also fight among one another. The McCarthys used to practice the tinsmith trade in this area when I was young. They often fought one other at the pattern of Baile na hAbhann. I saw them two or three times when I was a child. Domhnall Mór (Big Domhnall/Big Daniel) was their leader. He was a big, tall, handsome man with curly dark-red hair. He was very strong and looked more athletic than most people. I remember him well, kneeling in front of me at Mass in Baile na hAbhann, his head shaved tight to the bone and his skull marked with the grooves that were the legacy of old fights. Domhnall Mór might have been considered to be just a travelling tinker but people had respect for him. He was never involved in stealing or any sort of crookedness like that and anytime there was a fight or an argument, his family kept it amongst themselves; they never interfered with anyone else and Domhnall wouldn't allow them to either. I'd say that hardly a year passed that he didn't spend some time in prison. Back then, when English justices were in charge of the law in Ireland, they had very little sympathy or mercy for tinkers or other travelling people. Even the smallest dispute or fight at a fair or a market and a fine of 'forty shillings' or a month in prison was the least punishment that they got. And since most tinkers were loath to pay any fine, they'd normally end up going off to prison. They'd ask for some time to get the money together in order to pay the fine but, in reality, they'd be stalling the judge so that they could put in their prison sentence during the winter when the weather was bad.

Domhnall Mór had a month's prison sentence imposed on him at one juncture. One day, he was walking along the road that went from An Gleann to Baile an Droichid and just as he was going around the corner at Bearna an Mhadra he saw the 'peelers' coming towards him in the opposite direction. They were about twenty yards away and Domhnall jumped over a ditch. He ran as fast as he could, and even flung off his shoes and his jacket at one point so that he could sprint even faster. The 'peelers' followed him for about a mile across the fields until he reached Seán Mór Breathnach's 'Páirc na Naoí nAcra' (Nine-Acre Field). This field was recently-ploughed and the 'peelers' gave up the chase at this point. Domhnall Mór got some old clothes and shoes from Séamus na Mónach Buí and he was ready to hit the road again. Afterwards, people said that it was only for fun that the 'peelers' followed him as they knew well that Domhnall Mór would give himself up a the Barracks when it next suited him.

Another day, he was at the Pattern in Baile na hAbhann when there was a summons out for him. A young 'peeler' who hadn't been stationed in the area very long went to arrest him but Domhnall gave him a shove and threw him a couple of feet across the ground. Domhnall Mór disappeared in the direction of Droichead Mór then while the peeler went down to the barracks to report him. Apparently, the local sergeant, who was getting on in years, wasn't too happy about this younger member of the force reporting Domhnall Mór because there was supposed to be a sort of a 'ceasefire' as relating to this type of thing when the Pattern was being held. The sergeant went out to look for him and he wasn't long finding him as Domhnall made no effort to run away from him. The sergeant told him that it was best if Domhnall gave himself up there and then and came into the police station as he would receive an extra month in prison for assaulting the peeler if he didn't do so. If he voluntarily came down to the barracks right then, he would only have to serve the original prison term that he'd received. Domhnall said he'd do as the sergeant requested on one condition – 'I'll go with you as long as you don't lay a hand on me'. Then he accompanied the sergeant up through the crowd and down to the barracks. He was sent to Waterford Prison the following day.

There were a group of tinkers at the fair in Cahir one day and they were fighting and planking one another at the corner of the Square there, Domhnall Mór amongst them. There was a manager in the local bank there who had the same surname as Domhnall Mór – i.e. McCarthy – and he sent one of his sons, a lad who of about twelve years of age, outside with a message. He had to pass right by the corner where the fight was going on and when he got there he stopped, because he was afraid to go any further. Domhnall Mór noticed him there in the middle of the mayhem and shouted out to everyone:

'Stop men for a moment and let this lad pass. He's one of ourselves – of course'. The fight stopped until the young lad had passed by and then it recommenced again as soon as he was gone. There was a farmer living near Baile na hAbhann when I was growing up and his name was Éamonn Paor (Éamonn Power) although he was more frequently referred to as 'An Bully' because he was so given to arguments and fighting. He was super-confident of himself when it came to fighting and he'd travel twenty miles to challenge another man to a wrestling match or a fist-fight; he didn't mind which. On his way home from Clonmel Fair one day, he went into a pub at the top of Baile Ghaelaigh to have his last drink of the day. Mící Baróid, a man who specialized in 'breaking' horses was with him. In the pub, Power heard that Domhnall Mór and his tribe were camped down near Tobar na Fuinse, about a half-a-mile down the road. Éamonn Paor was always saying that he wanted to 'have a go' (i.e. challenge) Domhnall Mór and now this was his chance. He brought Mící Baróid with him and they went over to the tinker's camp where he challenged Domhnall. They decided to have a fist-fight and so they threw off their jackets and shirts and began boxing. They were both such good fighters and the fight went on so long with no sign of a clear winner that they had to give it up in the end. When the fight was over and both men had sung one another's praises, Power went back to the pub and bought a half-barrel of porter and returned to the tinker's camp with it. He and Mící Baróid stayed around the fire with the tinkers until they had drunk the half-barrel. The 'Bully' came to an unlucky end, however. With all the drinking and wandering from place to place, and challenging people, he fell into arrears on the business side of things and he couldn't pay the rent anymore. Langley evicted him. Power had once owned the finest farm on the entire estate, in behind Baile na hAbhann; according to the older people, the land there was some of the best land in the entire county. Éamonn de Paor emigrated to America but according to the reports sent home, he didn't do that well over there. I remember the surnames of very few of the travellers who wandered alone from place to place, long ago. The people had different nicknames for all of them and, after all of these years, I can only remember their nicknames now. Here is a description of some of the people I remember. I alluded previously to Nóra na Ceirte ('Rags Nóra') or Nóra Mór, and the cure that she had to staunch the flow of blood. She wandered around this area for years and given the fact that she had a lame foot and poor breathing, it would take her an hour to walk just half-a-mile. She had a walking stick that was as thick as a spade and a lumbering gait when she walked because she was lame. She also wore a big pair of heavy men's boots that she never tied and that never had any laces in them. The local people were good to her, and to give her due, she was always very polite and well-spoken until she had too much drink taken.

I remember her calling to the school in Baile an Droichid regularly and she and Power, the schoolteacher, would have a good chat together. I saw him giving her sixpence a few times also. 'Haitín' was the most contrary of all the travellers who called around here when I was a boy. To be fair to him, he wasn't actually a beggar at all – as he never looked for any alms but just got a bite to eat every now and then; also, he would get work here and there on his travels. If any local blackguards began annoying him or teasing him he would just leave the job right there and then, however. It didn't matter how urgently he was required for the work or who had hired him. On these occasions, he never even waited to receive whatever few pence he had earned; he just left immediately. Whatever the reason, he hated being called 'Haitín' and if anyone called him this he would chase them up along the road as quickly as he could, cursing and swearing at his tormentor as he went. Because of this, the local blackguards used to try and make a fool of him as often as they could. When we were going to school, I remember us teasing him and calling him 'Haitín' but we always made sure to keep in close to the ditch when we did so. He would reach down and throw whatever sods or anything else that he could find on the road at us. Then he'd kneel down on the road, remove his hat and frighten us with the terrible oaths he would fling in our direction. He would ask God to break our hands and legs and to blind us and to make our tongues stop dead in our mouths; and failing this, that God would carry us down to the furthest and hottest recesses of hell. It was terrible to listen to him and when I think back on it now, it was truly sinful the way that we tormented him and made him so angry. Of course, youngsters don't think of these things when they are at that age; they like nothing better than teasing people and getting a rise out of them if they can.

In the end, all you had to do was whistle in such a way that it sounded like the word 'haitín' and the poor man would go crazy. They had a story that one day he was passing the church in Baile na hAbhann and there was a thrush singing high in the one of the trees that was in churchyard. The poor fool thought that the thrush was actually whistling out the word 'Haitín'. 'By your red heart, you high-up devil you', he said waving his fist at the thrush; 'aren't you out singing early in the morning anyway?'

Another man who used to travel around this area long ago called himself 'High King'. He used to claim that he was the real 'High King' of Ireland although the poor man had very little that was regal about him. He was already very old when I first saw him and that was when I was first going to school; I saw him once then but I did hear people talking about him on various occasions after that. He had a long white beard and long hair down to his shoulders. He held himself tall and erect and he had an angelic-looking face, like the face of a saint that you'd see in a picture. He never wore socks or shoes at any time during the year. Pairs of 'trousers' I should say as he used to always wear two sets of clothes – two trousers, two jackets, two vests and two shirts – irrespective of whether the weather was hot or cold. He used to wear an old-caroline hat also but it was just barely perched on his head, given that he had so much hair. The local jokers used to bow and courtesy to him when they came across him as if to acknowledge his regal status. He would remove his old-caroline and bow as if acknowledging his royal subjects.

All of this was done without a word being uttered by anyone. He never accepted alms and would only accept some food or old clothes no matter where he went. He only ever came around here to An Gleann once or twice a year and he always went to Seán Mór's house for lodgings. He'd only stay the one night and he'd leave again the following morning. From what I heard, he used to walk everywhere throughout Munster. Whenever he said goodbye to Seán Mór, he'd promise him that he'd pay him well for his kindness as soon as he acceded to his throne. In fact, I heard Seán Mór say that 'High King' offered him money on more than one occasion but that he refused to take it from him.

Micilín Dhomhnaill was a small, neat man who only circuited around the parish here and who went from one house to the next in An Gleann. Every now and then, he'd do a few weeks work here and there picking potatoes or studding around September. He was a great conversationalist and had a very poetic streak about him. He loved tobacco. He preferred to smoke some tobacco more than eating his dinner. He always had this verse:

'No need to pity Micilín Dhomhnaill because he has neither cow nor sheep,
No need to pity Micilín Dhomhnaill because he has no woman in the night,
But Micilín Dhomhnaill is to be pitied that he has no smoke in his tobacco'.

A person said to him once:

'Micilín Dhomhnaill, you're a very sophisticated person'.

Said Micilín in reply:

'I'd want to be son; I was made many years ago'.

Pádraig Ó Domhnaill bested him in wit and repartee one day. They met one another one Sunday at Droichead na Cille and they were chatting for a while. Said Micilín to Pádraig after a while:

'Oh kind watcher, from the best breed of men,

Seeing as I've come your way today, you might give me a
tobacco-pipe to smoke'.

Said Pádraig in reply:

Oh you who does not understand the ways of this world,
You won't mind me explaining to you how this world works,
That is – that everyone has to light their own pipe'.

All the travelling people and wanderers I mentioned above
went to Heaven many long years ago. They left this mortal
coil one after another. Most of them ended up in the
'Poorhouse'. They had no option but to go there when they
were old and feeble and lost the use of their legs, despite
the fact that they hated having to go there at all. One or
two of them died while still in this parish, whereas two or
three others left here and never returned, and no-one is too
sure where they ended up in the end. As with everything
that relates to one's youth, there was a type of romanticism
associated with these 'bacaigh' back then and this probably
explains the fact that I can still picture them so clearly in
my mind all these years later. It is an old saying that God
creates all types and although many of the poor
unfortunates I have just described must have suffered
from hunger and hardship in their day, they surely had the
same desire to live life to its fullest and the same fear of
death as even the richest man does. At its core, all human
nature is the same; this is the way that God created us.

While we used to tease these wanderers and make fun
of them, there is a good chance that the God of Glory had
more regard for these people than He had for any of the
rest of us. These wanderers were putting in their
Purgatory on this earth and long before anyone of us ever
did so. I think that the 'bacaigh' and the travellers of today
are very different from those of long ago. There are
'bacaigh' and beggars and tinkers travelling the road today
just as when I was a boy – and I suppose that there always

will be – but they aren't the same as the 'old crowd' who once travelled the same roads. Slyness, crookedness, stealing and trickery; these are the traits one associates with the 'bacaigh' today. It is a rare to find any fools amongst them – whether men or women – and I can tell you that none of them would let any blackguard mock them or make little of them now. A hundred farewells to the old crowd. May the God of Glory be good to them because they made our lives more rewarding and happy when I was a child; their like won't ever be seen again.

THE OLD WORLD

When I reminisce now on life as it was many years ago – when I was going to school – and compare it with life as lived today, it is amazing how much things have changed. In an isolated place such as here in An Gleann, you always get older customs and traditions that survive for longer than in less-rural parts of the country. While this is true to a certain extent about An Gleann, there have nevertheless been profound changes in the lifestyles of the people. Take food and drink, for example. Tea was the beverage of choice when I was a child here and yet I remember my grandfather and Liam Beilbhí describing the time when tea was only available in the odd house around here. Risteard Ó Siadhaile used to say the same thing – i.e. that tea was only drunk in most houses on Christmas Day at one time and that the people would even ask one another on their way to Mass on Christmas morning – 'how many cups did you drink?' in the same way that they asked one another on Easter Sunday – 'how many eggs did you eat?'

They had funny stories about people who drank tea for the first time. Women used to make tea and drink it unknown to their husbands and four or five women might gather in the house of another to have a 'tea' party. They used to say that when people drank tea for the first time, it made them drunk. Apparently, they used to make the tea very strong – 'so strong that a hen could walk on it' and they would put a lot of sugar into it. As the old saying goes: 'The sugar *is* the tea'. A sign of a woman's generosity when visiting her house was if 'she filled the saucer with tea as well as the cup'.

There was one housewife here in An Gleann back then and when she first heard of tea, she bought a half-pound of it so as to have it for the priest when he came for the 'stations'. Because she didn't understand how to make tea, she put the entire half-pound's worth of tea into a saucepan to boil and then she strained it so that only the leaves were left and placed this mixture on a saucer with sugar and cream on top of it. Then she presented this to the priest. His response to this strange mixture hasn't been recorded.

There was a married couple here in An Gleann back then also and their son was suffering from madness. As with most houses then, they didn't have a clock and they were reliant on the cockerel crowing to wake them up in the morning. Usually, the hens would be resting on the lintel just inside of the door. One Christmas Eve, this lad was looking forward to the tea so much that he tied a piece of twine to the cockerel's foot and brought the other end of the twine into the 'settle-bed' with him. After they'd been in bed for a few hours he gave the twine a tug and the cockerel began to crow. Everyone in the house got up because they thought it was morning and I suppose the poor lad got the blame for waking everyone up so early. 'God with you forever, oh holy little cockerel', the boy said, when the cock crowed for the first time that night.

They used to boil up a skillet-full of eggs in every house on Easter Sunday morning and every adult would eat about a half-dozen of them. I remember eating five eggs in one sitting when I was about twelve years of age. I suppose that I was testing myself to see could I eat that many in one go but I paid dearly for it afterwards. For the next three or four days, my stomach felt sick and my digestion was in a mess. It was a few months later before I could even think about eating another egg. People said that Cruthúr Garbh once ate 29 eggs one Easter and that one of these eggs was a goose-egg. I'm not sure whether this story is true or not, but I can say with certainty that if there was any man in this parish who could eat that many eggs in one sitting, it was Cruthúr Garbh. He had an incredible appetite by all accounts and anytime he finished eating a half-a-pig's head, there was nothing left but the skull-bone.

People had given up eating corn-bread and rye-bread when I was young although I often heard the old people mention these two types of bread. My grandfather and Liam Beilbhí and everyone else who belonged to that generation ate these breads when they were young. Many's the kitchen locally in which I saw the griddle on which this bread was once baked. The people used to have two different types of griddle in Lios na Faille – a large one and a small one. In the end, when these two griddles were no longer used anymore, they were left in at the back of the hearth where, over time, they burned away or disintegrated. Apparently these two types of bread – the corn-bread and the rye-bread – were as hard as a rock and you needed to have good teeth to be able to chew them at all. No wonder the people who ate this bread had good teeth. Personally, I think that one of the reasons people have such bad teeth today is because the food that they eat is too soft. Anytime a skull is unearthed down in the graveyard nowadays, there are nearly always at least a couple of teeth that are still intact. Contrast this with many of the younger generation today; you'd be hard-pressed to find five out of every hundred who have a full set of healthy teeth – even by the time they reach twenty years of age. When the white bread – or the 'flour bread' as it is known first made its appearance, people only ate it on special occasions – similar to the 'bairín breac' (barm brack) today. It was a great treat for a youngster to have a piece of this new-fangled bread.

They had another type of food long ago also which they called 'gráinseachán' (gruel). This was wheat that was boiled in a pot until the grains were very soft and which was eaten with milk, similar to the way porridge is made today. I never ate 'gráinseachán' myself but I believe that it was very tasty. When I was growing up, there was still the odd household here that ate potatoes for breakfast, washed down with tea. Everyone ate potatoes with their other main meals of the day, of course. In the poorest houses here, they had no meat except on Sundays, and then it was always salted meat they ate. Only the odd person ever bought fresh meat and then only at Christmas-time. Most people ate steak (beef) with their breakfast on Christmas morning. They used to buy salted fish back then, big bunches or strips of them, and they'd hang them in the chimney to smoke them. They'd also hang salted herrings in the chimney. These fish, especially the salted herrings, gave their meals a great flavour even if they were incredibly salty. Any farmer who was reasonably well-off would kill a pig at the end of autumn. The bacon would be hung from hooks in the kitchen. You'll still see those hooks in the kitchens of many houses today although you'd hardly ever see any meat hanging from them now; the younger generation today have very little interest in fatted bacon. I remember the old people saying that they wouldn't eat a bite of meat for the entirety of Lent long ago. They would have meat with their meal on Advent Eve and whatever was left over was placed on a scallop in the roof of the kitchen. This meat was known as the 'Little Fatty Advent Spool' and, on lighting the fire on Easter Sunday morning, the woman of the house would place the 'little spool' over the fire.

Once the 'old potatoes' were all used up, they ate porridge until the 'new potatoes' were harvested. They normally drank buttermilk with the porridge, although the people often had to eat the porridge dry or maybe just with a drop of sugar or coffee sprinkled over it as a kind of sweetener. The poorer people mainly ate Indian meal. Also, when making porridge people often mixed Indian meal and oatmeal, half and half. Long ago, the old people considered July the 'hungriest' month as their food supplies for the year were getting scarce as they waited for the 'new food' to arrive in. 'July an Ghabáiste' (July of the Cabbage) is how they referred to this month.

Spalpeens and labourers from this part of the country used to travel westwards towards Cahir and Ballyporeen picking potatoes when it was harvest-season. They would get four or five weeks work and would earn between twelve and fifteen shillings a week for their work. They considered this very good pay at the time, because their normal pay at home would have been about one shilling a day – or even less than this in winter. The potatoes were all dug then using spades and although the pay was fairly good, it was very hard work and the food they got was terrible. In most of the houses, they would only get potatoes and buttermilk three times a day for their meals. Any house where they got pickled herrings or any other bit of salted fish for their dinner was deemed a very good house to work in. The poor men used to work from dawn till dusk and they were often out standing at the potato-ridges again once more just as dawn was about to break again the following day. Every farmhouse had a boy who worked as a helper or 'yard-boy' and it was his job to lead the line and supervise the 'meitheal' as they worked. The only break they got was when they walked across the field again having harvested all the potatoes in one of the ridges. And the 'man of the house' was usually standing watching the spalpeens during the day and checking to make sure that they had definitely dug up all of the potatoes. And from what I heard, the places where the spalpeens slept were as bad as the food.

In wide ridges, the width of three potato sets, was how all the potatoes were planted in times gone by, and almost all of the work was done using just a spade and a shovel. Potatoes were normally planted in a fallow field back then and when the seed was all sown, the ridges were 'arranged' using a hoe. The potatoes-sets were planted in holes as dug out of the earth with a spade. These sets were usually in a type of bag that the sower carried over his shoulder. Usually it was someone low-sized or small like a young girl, for example, who did the actual sowing because you had to be small and lithe to plant the sets within the holes correctly. The holes would be closed then and raked over with a 'toothless' rake. Usually it was a boy who did this part of the work. I often spent a day out raking the soil like this myself. Fertilizer would be spread across the ridges then, the furrows smoothed with a board-less plough, and the bigger lumps of clay broken and flattened by a horse pulling a flat stone slab across the soil. Each furrow would be ploughed about four times depending on the softness or otherwise of the soil. The clay would be piled up on the side of the ridges with a shovel; and when the 'trees' (plants) were about six inches high, the soil would be filled in on them again; this was called the 'first soil' and the 'new soil' and this job was known as 'ag caitheamh clas' (rising furrows). People who didn't have any cattle of their own dug their own furrows using a spade but the person who had land rented from a farmer didn't have to do this work himself. The farmer he rented from did this work for him, normally using a horse. Long ago, people even planted wheat using the spade and the shovel. They would make big wide beds of new-dug soil and then cover the seed with soil from the furrows.

All of this work was done for years around here using a horse but that way life is changing now; the time will probably soon come when the horses won't be needed anymore either and everything will be done with a machine. I remember the first man around here who began to harvest potatoes using a plough. All the neighbours were critical of him saying that this was only a lazy way of doing it but over time, they all followed his lead. Now, no-one digs potatoes anymore using a spade, not unless they were digging new early-season potatoes and even then, it's usually a fork that they use for this.

Long ago, the spalpeens would give anything to have a good spade or scythe or sickle. There was a blacksmith whose surname was Ó hAllaidhe living in Ros an Aitinn on the east side of Baile na hAbhann who was well-known for the quality of the spades he made. Every spade that he made had the letter 'H' inscribed on the front of it and you wouldn't have seen anyone using a spade in this area when I was young that didn't have this 'H' cut into it. Ó hAllaidhe would visit Baile na hAbhann every year a few Sundays before the potato harvesting season. He'd have a load of new spades on his donkey and cart and he'd start selling them when Mass was over. Ten pence a spade was how much they cost and he rarely had any left over by the time he was finished selling them. Anyone who intended buying a spade would usually have cut branches from a young 'larch' tree to use as handles for the spades, and have been seasoning them for three months before his arrival. Then, once they had bought the spade-heads from Ó hAllaidhe, they would go to the blacksmith who would put the handles on the spades for them. The usual pay they gave the blacksmith for this job was two ounces of tobacco although it has to be said that neither Dic Ó Siadhaile nor his father before him ever accepted any payment from a labourer for doing this job. The spalpeens long ago were experts on everything to do with the digging work, whether with spades or shovels and how to approach the different soils and terrains. And it wasn't always the strongest or the most powerful men who were the best when it came to this type of work either. At one time, the best diggers were known and spoken-about far and wide in the same way as sporting heroes and brilliant athletes are today. There was a man living on this side of Bearna an Mhadra long ago and his work as a spades-man or when using the scythe was known far and wide. His name was Daithí Beag Condún and although he only weighed about ten stone and was just an inch or two above five feet in height, there was no-one in the two parishes here who could best him when it came to digging or scything.

There was many a 'meitheal' captain who was trying to show off and whom Daithí put in his place. One year he was digging potatoes for a farmer out near An Chúirt Dóite. There was a 'yard-boy' in the house who fancied himself as the best worker and, as you'd expect from such a boy, he began to show off one Monday morning after they had begun the digging. They were going at such a cracking pace that the lad working next to Daithí was struggling to keep up with this lad who was the 'meitheal' captain. Daithí, who was working just behind them with the other men, went up to the captain a few times and asked him to take it easy. On being asked to slow down, this lad increased his pace, as if to 'show off' and told the men to work harder. Daithí decided to show him what was what and in addition to digging his own furrow, he also dug two other furrows next to the boy he was working beside and who had been struggling. When they finished that field, Daithí and the lad who had been falling behind earlier were five yards ahead of the 'captain'. To 'rub it in' as regards the 'show-off's' strength and ability to work, Daithí didn't remove his homespun great-coat the whole time that he was working – (he had been wearing it at the start of work that morning, because it was early-dawn and quite cold). Not only did Daithí hammer the 'yard-boy' when it came to the digging, but he also gave him a right tongue-lashing too, a tongue-lashing that this lad wouldn't forget for a long time afterwards. The 'meitheal' were half-idle for the rest of the week, because Daithí had done so much work that first day.

I also remember three elderly men who lived in this parish when I was a child and I often heard a story about how they had been working on the railway track between Clonmel and Cahir at one point. They used to walk to work every morning and back home again every night and that was fourteen miles each day in total. They earned three-and-sixpence a week for their work and that was without any food. From what I heard from the old people, they were so desperate to earn some money that time that men who had no work would stand watching the men who were working in the hope that someone would drop out and that they could take their place or replace them on the job. And, apparently, men used to drop out every now and then too because they hadn't the strength to keep going anymore. They were weak because of hunger, no doubt. It was a harsh life then when men were so poor that they had to wait and see would someone else weaken; and then try and get that work themselves, and all of this, just to survive. When I was a young lad, there used to be spalpeens here in An Gleann who worked gathering hay for the day and who would then work half of the night out in Móin an Bhráca cutting turf. You had to be seriously tough to be able to work as hard as these men did.

Spalpeens used to travel up from Kerry at one time and go into the countryside around about here working. It often happened that two or three of these men would return to the same house for work year after year, helping with the harvest and the potato-picking. They may have come to An Gleann at one time, but that practice had stopped by the time I was young. These spalpeens were great workers apparently and they were very clever and fond of witticisms. They weren't easily fooled by anyone. The people had many stories about them.

A Kerryman was working for a farmer in Leacain one time and he had no shoes. The farmer was at the midweek fair one day and he bought a pair of shoes for the spalpeen. That evening, the spalpeen was walking up and down the kitchen floor trying out the new shoes. The Kerryman kept raising the shoes and looking at the heels.

'I might go backwards (i.e. workwise) wearing these', he said.

'Arrah, not at all', said the farmer. 'That's a great pair of shoes you have'.

'I'm not sure', said the Kerryman. 'I think these will set me back a bit'.

It was true for him. Come the next morning, there was no sign of the Kerryman. He had gone back (back west) in the shoes and he hadn't earned enough by then to pay even half of what those shoes were worth! I remember Risteard Ó Siadhaile telling me that he once saw sixty men harvesting wheat in a field belonging to the Daltons, up north of the old-pound. They were cutting the wheat using reaping-hooks and their pay was thirteen pence a day and their dinner. Normally, a woman followed behind every two reapers and bound the wheat. 'Gaoth is thirteen' (i.e. 'The wind and thirteen') was a phrase used by the reapers long ago. This was a reference to the fact that a windy day when the corn was ripe was the perfect day for reaping because the farmer would be afraid that the corn would be flattened. The Dalton man who had the sixty reapers working for him at one point was harvesting on another occasion. A group of men were cutting corn out in the field again using the same reaping-hooks that they always used. A spalpeen called to the field where they were working, a man who had one of the 'newer' implements – i.e. the scythe. He asked Dalton for work and Dalton asked him to use the scythe on a small section of wheat to see how good it was. He had only swung the scythe for the second time when Dalton let out a shout:

'Stop! Stop!' he said. 'You'll cut half of the corn away with that'. It was the first time he'd ever seen anyone cutting wheat with a scythe and he seemed to think that it was a crazy way of cutting it. How things have changed over the years? Now the reaping-hook, the scythe and flail are a thing of the past so that many people would not even recognize one of them if they saw one. You'd only see a scythe used now the odd time and that just to clean and straighten the rougher edges of the ditch before the machine sets to work, or to cut an area where the ground is too steep for a machine to operate on it. The horse-powered machine will probably be relegated to the past soon also as other modern devices and machines come in from America, machines that will cut and pound the corn right there and then for you, in the field. There was a blacksmith living south of An Geata Dearg who was very famous for making reaping-hooks. Anyone living within twenty miles of him used to go to him to get a new reaping-hook; back then, a well-made reaping-hook such as his could last you a lifetime. I never actually saw anyone using a reaping-hook myself and I don't think anyone was still using any of them here in An Gleann when I was young, although I did hear the older people talking about this type of work. I also remember seeing two old rusted reaping-hooks jammed beneath the rafters of the potato-shed when I was young.

Working with a flail is another skill that has disappeared from this area completely now, although this was still done by some people when I was young. For a few years prior to the Great War, there was a demand for dry-grass stalks and seeds; they were worth between three shillings and seven-and-six a stone at this juncture and it was a great way for poorer people to make some extra money. The local farmers never had any objections to people picking these grass-stalks on their land. They would cut them with a small reaping hook, one that was much smaller than the normal reaping-hook people once used for cutting corn. Then they'd pound them with the flail. In fact, the last time I ever saw a flail being used was by someone flaying these grass-stalks. The bits of the flail that were used for pounding grass and corn were usually cut down and shaped about six months in advance of the harvest season. They were then placed up in the chimney to harden and season. The withe or strap on the flail was made of horse-skin and it wasn't everyone who was able to tie this correctly and affix it to the main part of the flail.

At one time, they used to make the withe out of a sally-rod but that was many, many years ago and I never saw one of these. Two people used to thresh the corn together and it was a joy to watch them working in unison. The two would be threshing with the flails in equal time with one another and they never disturbed the other's rhythm. They were so practiced at this work that they were even able to transfer the flail from one hand to the next as they shifted their weight from one calf to another without breaking their rhythm or stride. There was a time when three people worked in unison and it wasn't every three who were skilled enough to work together like this either. I remember seeing women sifting the wheat from the chaff using sieves outside in the breeze. Once again, this was another skill to be learned and it wasn't everyone who was proficient at it. It caused a great stir around here when Seán Mór bought the first ever threshing machine in An Gleann. Four horses were needed to turn the wheels on this thresher and the first day he used it, most of the local men came to have a look at it working. For a long time, the only person who knew how to service this machine around here was Micil Ó Néill. Seán Mór used to rent the machine out to the other farmers in the locality and Micil was in charge of it. The horses that turned the wheels would work in tandem. Every farmer would have half a barrel of porter in for the threshing and all the local boys and girls would be dancing for the night. No-one uses the horses and the machine for the threshing anymore. That practice too has also gone by the wayside, as have the use of the flail, the reaping-hook, and the sieve.

A half-mile down from Baile an Droichid is the ruins of an old house. It is on the right-hand side at the corner of the road as you are going down that way. A man named Peaidí Séibhín used to live there long ago. A carpenter by trade, he specialized in making winnowing machines for corn. Another device that he also made from timber was a bellows as used for the fire. He made these machines for the entire area around about here. We had an old winnowing machine of his out in our barn for years and many's the happy hour I spent turning the handle on it as a child when we were doing the winnowing years ago.

It was Peaidí Séibhín who made this new winnowing machine for us when the older one got burned. That happened when my aunt Máire set fire to the barn by accident. Those old rollers and sieves are all forgotten and in the past now. You're as likely now to find an old piece of metal from one of those machines thrown in the nettles or the ditch somewhere near the old haggard. The machines they have now can do the threshing and the winnowing simultaneously and while it is true that the world is developing and improving each day, it seems to me that in other ways, our lives were simpler and less stressed in many ways when I was a youngster and before all these new machines for farm-work were invented.

The ruins of three old kilns can still be seen here in An Gleann, kilns where they used to burn lime to be used as fertilizer at one time, this despite the fact that there is no limestone rock anywhere within four miles of Gleann Chárthainn. It is all sandstone that is in the ground around here and they used to bring the limestone over from a quarry that was about a mile-and-a-half north of Baile an Droichid. They used to spread quite a bit of lime as fertilizer on the fields here in times past, especially when they were growing corn. Another practice they had back then that isn't followed anymore was as follows: they used to plough the ground in the ditch at the top-end of the field and then burn the bushes there and the scraws that were around the field. Then they'd spread the ashes from these scraws over the field, using it as a fertilizer. 'Béiteáil' (soil-burning) is what they called this in Irish and it was always done when preparing to grow a new crop of wheat. We own a field here in Lios na Faille and it is still known as 'An Bhéiteáil' to this day. The Burkes in Monarch Buí also have a field called by the same name.

POTS OF GOLD

At one time, they had an incredible number of stories about people who had found a pot of gold under the ground. When I was young, I heard Liam Beilbhí tell many stories like this at our own hearth. According to the old stories, it was never easy to discover a pot of gold. Firstly, you had to dream about it for three nights in succession; then, when you went to the place that you thought the gold was buried in, the chances were that there was a spirit guarding it. The person who had hidden the gold there initially was likely to have appointed a spirit or ghost to guard the location from both the living and the dead. That's what the old people always said. The other difficulty associated with trying to find a hidden pot of gold was that you had to search for it once night fell; you couldn't do it during the day. Seán Mór Breathnach owns a field that has a 'lios' (fairy-fort/ring-fort) in the corner of it. It is known as Lios an Óir (The Fairy-fort of Gold) and it was said that there was gold hidden there; there are still some old people here today who believe that this story is true. Liam Beilbhí and some of the other older people long ago had a story that three men went to this fairy-fort one night searching for gold. They brought a defrocked priest who was then living in An Gleann with them. This priest was reading out from a holy book. Shortly after they arrived there, they heard what sounded like the loud bellowing of a bull coming towards them across the field. Next thing, a huge pack of wild, black snarling dogs came towards them as if to surround them, their eyes ablaze with light. The men ran for their lives. The priest asked them to stand their ground and that they would be safe, but they didn't pay any attention to him. No-one ever went back since to search for that gold.

I often heard long ago that there was a lot of gold hidden in An Cnoc Dubh. The 'Danes' had hidden it there apparently prior to going into war. None of them ever returned alive to search for it and the gold is still there to this day. The gold was buried beneath a big rock up there, according to the old people. When I went out hunting rabbits or searching for sheep on the hills, I always kept my eyes peeled for this black rock. Alas! I never did discover it. Stories about rapparees or 'Highway-men' hiding gold are common throughout Ireland. There were plenty of these stories in An Gleann also. The stories always had the same theme – the rapparee on the gallows hinting at where the gold they had stolen was buried.

A highway-man was being executed in Cork city and before he was hanged, he asked the people assembled there whether anyone was from the Waterford area. The only person from Waterford there was the hangman and the highway-man didn't want to tell him where the gold was buried and so he said: 'There is a boot full of gold in Réidh na nGabhar (The Plain of Goats) and a box of gold ornaments and silver is buried in Gleann na Faille'. Gleann na Faille is near us here and there is a smooth plain there that is still known as Réidh na nGabhar. Liam Beilbhí was certain that the two places that the rapparee was referring to were both in our locality, but even if they were, more accurate information would have been necessary to locate these hiding places. I think that Liam was hoping that where the gold and ornaments were buried might reveal itself sometime to him in a dream. My aunt Máire used to joke with him about this and say that gold wasn't that widely-available long ago that people would be burying pots of it all around the countryside. I was only a boy when I heard Liam Beilbhí telling these stories. His favourite stories were ones about hidden pots of gold while Risteard Ó Siadhaile preferred telling ghost stories. Liam was always hoping too that sometime he would catch a 'clutharacán' (leprechaun) and that he would force the leprechaun to give him the 'sparán na scillinge' (the shilling-purse). This was a magic purse that always had a shilling in it every time you opened it. Poor Liam never did find this purse, however. Neither did he ever manage to catch a clutharachán. Any shilling that Liam ever earned throughout his life, he earned it the hard way.

There was a bush growing in the flat area that was An Gabhar at one time. Apparently, it had been there for years and years. I remember one day when Seán Mac Craith and I went out onto the flat there to gather in some timber beams we noticed that the ground had all been ploughed up around the bush on either side and within a couple of yards of it. The ground had been dug up but then all the soil and sods flattened back down again. Whatever had happened there earlier, a very deep hole had been dug, a hole that could only have been dug by a number of people working together.

We never did find out who had been digging there or what they had found there, but it obvious that they were looking for the gold near this bush. I didn't notice that anyone in the neighbourhood had got any richer however, so it looks as if their digging was in vain.

One night when a few of us were visiting the Ó Siadhaile's house, Old-Richard told a story about the O'Donnell's from Crosaire na Cille. He said that he'd heard this story from his father years earlier. The

O'Donnells were originally living in Leaca na Raithiní, up on the side of the mountain there. The land around there was only fair as regards crop-growing because it was too high up on the side of the hill. They kept a good number of sheep on the mountain there however and it was from them that they made their living.

The people heard at one time that another outlaw who was about to be hanged down in Waterford city had spoken from the gallows to the assembled crowd and told them that there was a big pile of gold hidden in the mountains in Sliabh gCua. It was buried next to a rock that had the shape of a horseshoe carved into it. A young boy was in service with the O'Donnells and he was watching over the sheep on the mountain every day. One day, as he was eating dinner, he happened to mention that he was sitting on a rock out on the mountainside when he noticed that there was a horseshoe shape carved into its side. None of the O'Donnells present let on anything apparently as this young lad had never heard the story about the gold that was supposedly hidden out on the mountain there somewhere. The next day when the boy was out tending to the sheep on the mountainside as usual, the man of the house came out to him and they were chatting for a while. Then the man asked the boy, as if nonchalantly, where he had spotted the rock with the horseshoe shape on it. The boy showed him the rock. Six months later O'Donnell gave the boy a sum of money, enough to pay his passage to America, and shortly after that again, O'Donnell bought the farm at Crosaire na Cille. Whether there is any truth to this whole story, who knows? If it is true and that young lad did well out of it, the O'Donnells certainly didn't have much luck themselves as the farm they bought didn't remain in their hands for a long time. They vanished like the foam on the river and no-one of that family or surname has been living in An Gleann for many years now.

There used to be 'Highwaymen' robbing people on the lonely roads that pass through the mountains on the southern side of Barra an Bhealaigh long ago also. This is why the barracks was built for the 'peelers' at the bottom of An Bhealach originally. Cruthúr Garbh ('Rough Conor') and his wife were living in that old barracks when I was young and the old ruined shell of it is still there today. I often heard this story told about an unusual incident that happened in that area long ago. A man named O'Grady was living down near the Old Pound there. He had a small bit of a farm there but he was only just barely surviving on it. He was subject to a 'decree' forbidding him from selling this small strip of land. One day he got wind of the fact that the sheriff was coming to take away whatever he could get in terms of animals or produce in lieu of what money was owed to him. All that O'Grady had was a cow and an old horse. He transferred the cow into a field belonging to one of his neighbours and he headed out to Móin an Bhráca with his horse and cart to gather in a load of turf. Móin an Bhráca is situated on the eastern side of the road in Barra an Bhealaigh. He had saved the turf and footed it previously but when he arrived on the bog, he saw that the stacks of turf had been knocked over and the sods scattered all over the place. Just two of the turf-stacks he had made were still standing. 'I suppose', he said to himself, 'the person who has bad luck in the morning, has similar bad luck in the afternoon also'.

He couldn't understand why anyone would knock over his stacks of turf like that, because he hadn't fallen out with anyone, and he couldn't think of anyone who had something against him. There had been a heavy rain on the previous night and the scattered turf was all heavy and wet. He began to fill the cart from the two stacks that were still standing. He had only started putting the turf into the cart when he came across a woman's old stocking and something heavy inside it. Inside the stocking were eighty gold sovereigns. He didn't have a day's hardship from that day on. It must have been a robber or highway-man who had hidden the sock in the stack of turf originally but when he'd returned to collect his gold in the darkness of night, he couldn't remember which turf-stack he'd left it in. He mustn't have noticed the two turf-stacks that he had left standing as he flailed around in the dark.

I remember Micil Mhártan telling us another story about pots of gold and the like when we were all down in Ó Siadhaile's one night. He was knocking an old wall down in the garden one night years earlier when he came across an iron skillet full of snail-shells in the middle of the wall, down at the bottom of it. He threw out the snail-shells and threw the old skillet sideways across the grass. Because it was all rusty, he thought that it was no use for anything. But when he went out to work the next day, there was no sign of the skillet or the snail-shells anywhere. Risteard told Micil that he had lost his chance then, because that skillet was actually filled with magic gold that was in the form of the snail-shells. If he had brought it into the house originally, those snail-shells would have transformed themselves into real pieces of gold.

The year that I got married I was ploughing in Páirc an Leasa when I turned over a sod and found two small rings. I brought the horses to a stop and picked up the rings. The two rings were about three-quarters of an inch in diameter and as thick as the end of a pen. The ends of each ring were not closed entirely on top of one another; there was a space about the width of a fingernail left between each where they should have been fused together. When I first rubbed the soil off them, I thought that they were probably just made of brass but when I showed them to Seán Mac Craith, he said that they were probably gold, given how heavy they were. Shortly after this, he was going into town to get his watch fixed and he brought the two rings with him and showed them to the jeweller. He checked them and said that they were both made of solid gold and that the two of them were probably worth about five pounds each. I was telling Liam Tóibín, the old schoolmaster, about this shortly afterwards and he said that the experts of the day were of the opinion that rings like the ones I'd found were used as a form of money in Ireland as far back as three thousand years before Christ. He said that the chances were that there were probably more of these rings to be found in the same place that I had found those two as there had been small piles of such rings found in different places throughout Ireland over the years. If there is a small hidden store of these rings in the field at an Lios, I certainly never came across it, and I kept a close eye out when I was ploughing in that area over the years. I gave one of the rings to Liam Tóibín and the jeweller put a pin into the other one so that it made a brooch I gave that to Sibéal. I still have it in the box down in the room.

The Drowning of Seán de Barra

We were down in Inse an Bhreathnaigh (Walsh's Inch) one beautiful Sunday in June. There were a group of lads from the village there, five or six of whom were playing on the northern side of the village bridge. The schoolmaster Tobin was with us and he was making us compete against one another with races and other athletic games. Eventually, we all sat down for a rest, we were so exhausted from all the running and jumping. One person suggested that we should go for a swim in Poll Fada (the Long Pool). Three or four boys stayed behind and practiced their jumping over the stakes and posts while the rest of us went upriver to Poll Fada, up beyond the second of Walsh's Inches. The older lads nearly always went swimming either in Poll Fada or in Poll na Culmhónach. The younger lads who were still in national school would swim in Poll an Easa not far from our house here, partly because they liked to stand beneath the falls I suppose – but also because the water wasn't too deep there. Even in the deepest part of the pool there, you wouldn't have got more than four foot of water at the most. Poll Fada is around sixty yards long. At the upper end of it, the bank is about six foot above the level of the water, below the surface of which there is a sheer drop. The further you go downstream towards the other end of the pool, the shallower the pool becomes until, at the very bottom of the pool, the bank is just a couple of feet above the water. In the deepest end of the pool, the water is more than ten feet deep whereas at the shallowest end, you can stand up in the water without any difficulty. There is a good flow to the water and anyone who'd jump in at the deepest end would be carried downstream to the shallower end very quickly. That said, this was a great place for someone learning how to swim. You'd just need to have courage enough to jump out into the water, that's all. You didn't need to have a safety ring around you or to have someone helping you out into the water. The older lads would be exhorting the younger lads to jump out into the water. Some lads would jump in and others were too afraid to do so. I'm still thankful to the Long Pool as it is there that I learned how to swim so well the first day ever. You had no choice other than to learn how to swim when you were in the Long Pool whereas you could have been in the Waterfall Pool forever without ever learning how to swim at all – since you could stand up anywhere in that pool. Most of the local lads could swim quite well and Seán Tóibín and Seán Baróid were very good swimmers indeed. Swimming was one of the few things that I was good at although I wasn't a patch on either of those two lads. We made our way along the riverbank until we came to the Long Pool where we sat down and got undressed. None of us had swimming trunks in those days. We just jumped into the water in the nip and ran around the river-bank to dry ourselves off as we didn't have towels either. Two or three lads had already jumped into the water and I was stripped down to my trousers. On the river-bank, Seán de Barra was sitting next to me and when he was undressed he made the Sign of the Cross and dived into the water. I watched him dive out into the deep. He seemed to take ages coming back up to the surface of the water but I didn't take any notice of this for a few seconds. Then I began to get worried and I said this to Seán Tóibín who was sitting to one side of me. I threw off my clothes and jumped in. I found Seán de Barra prone beneath the water and next thing, Seán Tóibín was beside me. Between the two of us, we managed to pull him out of the water and carry him over to where the water was shallower. Everyone gathered around to see what they could do to help. Seán had been in the water for less than three minutes altogether but he was stretched out now without any sign of life from him. The poor boy looked as if he was dead. The schoolmaster Tóibín knew a bit about mouth-to-mouth resuscitation and he did his best to try and revive Seán. He spent about an hour trying to revive him, but without success. We had already sent for the priest and the doctor, and for Seán's father. The doctor was the first to arrive on the scene and no sooner had he looked at Seán but he said that it would have made no difference even if he had been on the spot when it happened. Seán hadn't drowned really. Instead, he'd suffered a heart attack when he'd jumped into the water; his body had suffered a shock when his body temperature changed so suddenly – jumping from the heat into the freezing cold. When the priest arrived he anointed Seán with the Last Oils and we were all filled with a great sympathy for Seán's father when he arrived on the scene to find his son stretched out stone-cold on the ground. Seán's body was carried on a door up to Seán Mór's shed. That was a custom that was common to this area then. You never brought a dead person back to their own house to be waked. We held a sort of 'commission of enquiry' the following day with Seán Mór Breathnach as chair when we all discussed what had happened. The committee decided that the tragedy was an unavoidable accident and no-one was to blame for what had happened. Both Liam Tóibín and I were praised for the efforts we had made to save Seán. Seán de Barra was a fine, handsome lad, someone whom we all had nothing but good things to say about. He was barely twenty years of age when he drowned, just a few years older than me. What made matters even sadder than they were already was the fact that he was his father's only son, although he did have five daughters. From what I'd heard people say, Seán had been interested in becoming a priest, albeit his father wouldn't have been happy with this, given that he had no other sons except Seán. His father had always said that he couldn't have managed without Seán but now, tragically, he would have no choice other than to manage without him.

Seán de Barra's death haunted me for a long time afterwards. I was still young when it happened and had little experience of the tragedies that define our lives here on this earth. It was the first time I'd ever seen someone die as suddenly as that, and it shocked me greatly. It was very difficult to understand. There he was – a fine, lively lad, full of life one moment – and then everything being taken away from him in one fell swoop. One moment, he was brimming with life, the next he was a corpse stretched out cold and still on the ground. And he one of the happiest and most pleasant of all of us gathered at the swimming pool that day. There is no doubt about it; our lease on this life is very insecure at the best of times.

Of the eight people gathered at the Long Pool that afternoon, I am the only one who is still living. Seán de Barra was the first of us whom God called home. The others passed away one by one down through the years, and when you think about it, our lives are so fleeting that our sojourn here on earth and the time that passes between the first of us going and the last of us seems like just the briefest of moments. I don't think anyone ever went swimming in the Long Pool since, because another tragedy occurred there just a few years after Seán de Barra was drowned when Pilib Ó Muirgheasa drowned in the exact same place. You can understand why no-one would ever want to go swimming there again after all of that.

Peaid na Brídí (Pat the Maiden)

I suppose that there must be people who are a bit odd living everywhere. There were a few people who were a bit odd or eccentric living in An Gleann when I was young and there still are today. I suppose that will be the way of the world forever. And even then, everyone isn't eccentric in the same way. Everyone has their own strange quirks and oddities, as Peaid na Brídí used to say. But Pat himself was the funniest and most eccentric of the lot. Indeed, he was the funniest person who ever lived in An Gleann, even if I say so myself. If I could remember all of the funny incidents, Peaid was involved in and all the funny things he said over the years, I could write another book. Poor Peaid had no house or family; there was no-one belonging to him. A big man, strong and handsome, he was already getting old, when I remember him. As straight as a whip, his walk was so graceful and light that he wouldn't break eggs beneath his feet. When he was in the mood for it, he could do a day's work with the shovel or spade as good as any man in the parish. But he had no real ambition in life. He was happy as long as he earned enough to eat from day to day. He didn't care about tomorrow. Above all, he liked to have fun and to enjoy himself at gatherings and amusements. That was his thing. Anywhere within a ten mile radius that there were people gathered for a bit of crack, Peaid would be there. He'd walk five miles no bother just to attend a dance or a wake.

Long ago, when people were leaving for America, they'd normally have a dance in the house that would last all night long, the night before leaving. There'd be a half-barrel of porter and tea and other refreshments for everyone gathered – even if the people of the house were hard-up, they'd still have it. An 'American Wake' is what the English-speakers called it and, in truth, it was often a sadder occasion than a wake itself, especially when the emigrant was saying goodbye to everyone in the morning. Because, more often than not, there was no going back; they never saw that person again. Peaid na Brídí was at every American Wake in the two parishes. He wouldn't miss it for the world. There was always a great welcome for him from everyone. He was a great man for dancing and for singing songs in both Irish and English. He often played music for the dancers also as he was an excellent fiddler and piper to boot. The only musical instrument he owned himself was a long whistle and he could make sweet music with it – he never had enough money to buy a set of pipes or a fiddle. They said that he used to invent new dance steps and that he'd sometimes tie bells, similar to what would be attached to a horse beneath a carriage, to his heels – one bell on each heel. He did this for a bit of fun and to act the fool when he danced.

I remember one morning that I was going to school when I came out at the head of the road and Peaid na Brídí was walking ahead of me on the road and he was playing 'Ó Domhnall Abú' on the whistle – at nine o'clock in the morning!

One year, he was gathering potatoes for Dómhnall Ó Lonnargáin of An Mónach Buí, he and two or three others. Dómhnall was a very devout man and once dinner was eaten on the Monday night everyone in the house, including those working as part of the 'meitheal', had to go on their knees to say the Holy Rosary. The following day when dinner was over Peaid said: 'Dómhnall, seeing as we're all here together, we might as well say the 'Rosary' now so that we don't have to stay behind too late tonight'. But Dómhnall wasn't happy about this arrangement as he felt that it would interfere with the potato-gathering. Peaid didn't stay behind for the Holy Rosary any other night. Peaid visited America three times. It was easy for him to visit America in those days because the passage was very cheap. It only cost a couple of pounds to visit America back then. He'd never tell anyone that he was going but just disappear unknown to anyone else. He'd just drop everything and go. And it was the same when he returned. There was no big fanfare or anything. He'd just arrive back again, looking the same as usual. He never looked like he had made any money or that things had improved for him while he was over there. According to the stories that filtered back to us, he never killed himself working when he was over in America and just enjoyed the crack and played music the same as he did at home. The last time he went to America, someone sent a message home saying that Peaid had died and we said prayers for him in Baile na hAbhann church even though he wasn't dead at all!

Himself and Micil Ó Néill were very good friends. Micil lived in Seán Mór Breathnach's house where he slept up on the loft out in shed. Peaid often stayed with Micil there when he was working in the area. A few weeks after the report of Peaid's death came from America, Micil Ó Néill was returning to his bed in the loft after midnight one night. That day was a holiday and he had stayed late at Mairtí's pub in Baile an Droichid. As he arrived back to the farm, he heard whistle-music coming from up high on the loft. He recognised the tune and knew by the way it was being played that it was Peaid na Brídí playing it. Micil was a courageous man, a man who was afraid of nobody, whether living or dead. He climbed half-way up the ladder towards the loft and spoke:

'Is that Peaid who's there?' he says.

'Whey-hey, it certainly is!' replied the man from the inside.

'You alive or dead Peaid?' said Micil.

'Whey-hey! I'm alive as I'll ever be, son', replied Peaid.

Even when he got old, Peaid liked to dress in clothes that were a bit different from everyone else. Liam Tóibín, the schoolmaster, used to always give Peaid his hand-me-downs, his short pants and long stockings and low-heeled shoes. Both men were similar in height and the clothes suited Peaid very well. Where he got them from I don't know, but he always wore navy-style vests that were red, green or some other unusual colour, vests that were buttoned. I never saw him without a peacock's tail-feather in the rim of his hat. I was in Waterford city once selling some fattened pigs when I spotted a pile of old hats for sale in the window of a shop by the quayside. They were sixpence apiece. I bought a grey-coloured half-caroline and brought it home for Peaid; I knew he'd really love it, especially when he was going to Mass every Sunday. A man used to come to Baile na hAbhann regularly selling fish, himself and his wife together. I never heard them mentioned by any name other than Seán an Éisc and Máire an Éisc (i.e. John the fish-man and Mary the fish-woman). I can't remember what their surname was. They'd travel from Dungarvan with the fish and arrive in Baile na hAbhann while Sunday morning Mass was on. Seán was a cantankerous and ill-tempered individual and he was very jealous of his wife. He hated it if he saw her speaking to any man other than him. One Sunday, they were in Baile na hAbhann selling fish and there was a crowd gathered around them, Peaid na Brídí among them. Peaid began blathering away to Máire and giving her the eye. He did this deliberately to rise her husband. Seán restrained himself for a while but eventually he exploded. He lashed out with the board that they used to sit on, when they were on the cart, and before Paid had a chance to protect himself, he caught him straight across the face and knocked him backwards on the ground. Peaid's nose was broken and knocked out of shape. On his return from Mass, Peaid called into the carpenter's house where there was a mirror on the kitchen wall. He stood in front of the mirror trying to straighten his nose. 'Is it straight now Risteard?' he asked Risteard a few times and every time Risteard told him that it wasn't, Paid went back to the mirror again and tried to straighten it. Whatever he did, it didn't really work however, as from that day until the end of his life, Peaid's nose was always slightly bent.

Peaid used tobacco pipes that were unusual from other people's for smoking. While most people used clay pipes back then for smoking, Peaid made his own pipes made of wood, pipes that he decorated with all sorts of small knick-knacks and to which he would have a small chain attached. Peaidí Condún would often make one of these pipes for him. I remember one day when I was still going to school and I met Peaid at the small road out near Cill Dhubh Domhnach. That day he was holding the funniest tobacco pipe you've ever seen. I haven't seen anything like it either before or since. You'd often have seen a twist in the foot of a pipe back then but generally the bend in the pipe would be going downwards. In the case of this pipe however, it was bent to the side so that the head of the pipe would be directly beneath his ear when he smoked it. I remember that Micil Mhártan asked Peaid why he had such an unusually-shaped pipe and Peaid explained it in the following way. He said that he was suffering from pain in that ear on a regular basis and that the doctor had advised him to get a pipe shaped like this so that he would have a regular source of heat placed next to the ear that was causing him pain. Peaid said that this was one of only two pipes of this type in Ireland and that the other one was owned by the lord of Lismore. I think Micil actually believed him. I heard later that Peaid had made that unusual leg for the pipe from a broken piece of umbrella that he'd picked up in the Breathnach's house.

There was an elderly pensioner, 'a peeler', living by himself in a small house on the side of Baile na hAbhann nearest to us. It was in Baile na hAbhann, in fact, that he had completed his last years working as a 'peeler' a few years previous to this. Langley, the landlord, had given him this house to live in when he'd retired. Born and reared in England, (George) Crump was a very honest and straight-laced individual. Peaid was going down to Baile na hAbhann one Pattern Day when he met Crump and asked him for a match so that he could light his pipe. Crump gave him a lecture about people who wandered through life without goals or aims. He told Peaid that when he was buying tobacco, he should also buy a packet of matches and not to be going around bumming off other people all the time. Then he handed Peaid one match. Peaid took the match and said thanks very much to Crump and off he went. It was after midnight that same day when Peaid and Micil Ó Néill were walking up town and the pair of them were 'well-oiled'. As they passed Crump's house, Peaid skipped over and kicked the door. He kicked it again and again until Crump appeared and opened the door in his nightshirt.

'Who's that and what do you want at this time of the night?' Crump asked angrily.

'It's me', said Peaid. 'I came to give you back your match. I wouldn't want to keep it from you for too long. I'd be afraid that if I died, it'd be on my conscience. Here you go now and I'm really grateful to you'. Crump took the match from him without a word. I suppose the poor man was probably too stunned to say anything. It was a right bit of blackguardry of course, to wake a man up and get him out of bed at that hour of the night for something as small and insignificant as this. But I suppose that Peaid was keen to get revenge on Crump for the lecture he'd given him earlier in the day.

When people first began to get bicycles in this area, Peaid was getting on in years but was obsessed with owning a bike. He never did manage to save enough money to buy one, however. There was a baker working for Seán an Bhácúis (Seán the Bakery) in Baile na hAbhann who had his own bicycle and when he got a new one, he gave the old one to Peaid because he was always very friendly with him. The old bicycle was fairly battered-looking; it was heavy and had those big old-fashioned tyres, both of which were punctured. This didn't bother Peaid, however; he finally had his own 'iron horse'. But try as he might Peaid could never cycle this contraption although he kept trying to learn how for a few months. Every afternoon down in Inse an Bhreathnaigh, he would try and cycle this yoke, all the local lads helping him onto the bike and trying to get him rolling along the road. He expended a great deal of energy trying to learn how to cycle this broken-down thing and I don't know how many times he fell off it also but he was loath to give up. He said that nothing would have made him happier than if he had been able to sneak up behind Micil Ó Néill on the bike and ring the bell loudly behind him and then pass him right out on the road on his 'iron horse' – that's how he always referred to his bike. Poor Peaid never did get this satisfaction, however. Peaid received the pension from when it was first introduced in Ireland and all the other elderly people in the area applied for it. The regular pension payments gave him some independence and although he was still quite strong and energetic for his age, he never worked regularly after that except during the autumn when he went picking potatoes. He had a bed for the night anytime he needed it with Micil Ó Néill and he'd get food in Seán Mór's house whether he was working there or not. When the Great War broke out, Peaid had Seáinín Ó Deá – another elderly pensioner – convinced that all the pensioners would be rounded up and sent out in front of the soldiers on the battlefield to take the first wave of bullets. Poor Seáinín was frightened out of his life that this was true and didn't Peaid bring him out onto Cnoc Dubh one Sunday where the two of them spent the entire day looking for a hole or a cave that they might hide themselves in for when the army came looking for them! Seáinín died shortly after the war began and I don't think that all the ridiculous scaremongering that Peaid indulged in did much for his health when he was dying.

Peaid had a cage-like contraption that he used to catch otters in down on An Tonnóg. That was the only form of poaching that he indulged in. He earned somewhere between a crown and ten shillings for every otter-skin he sold to someone down in Clonmel. He usually set his trap in the water just where Tobar na Carraige flowed straight into An Tonnóg. The cage was hidden behind a pillar of stone there so that you couldn't see it. After dinner, one Sunday, Micil Mhártan walked down along the riverbank. When he reached where the water flowed into An Tonnóg, he went down flat on the ground and put his hand out into the current to get a drink of fresh water. He dipped his hand in but the trap closed over his hand and he couldn't get it open again, it was that strong. The poor man had to walk up as far as Droichead na Cille with this contraption on his hand. Micil was lame in one leg anyway so he had to hobble along until he got as far as the boys up there. They helped release him from the trap but poor Micil had a sore hand for quite a few weeks afterwards. When Peaid heard what had happened, he was more critical of Micil Mhártan than he was sympathetic towards him. He brought Micil Ó Néill down to the stream to show him where he had placed the cage. 'Look Micil', he said, 'he could have drank from the water here, and there, and in any of twenty other places, but nothing would satisfy the fool than to put his hand into the water just where I had the trap placed'. Although Peaid used to attend Mass on Sundays, he didn't take his religious duties too seriously at the best of times. He usually slept up on top of the loft with Micil Ó Néill for company but even here Micil used to quiz Peaid as to why he never said his prayers before going to sleep. Peaid's response to this was to say that God knew that he had all his prayers in his mind and that it would only be a waste of time saying them aloud.

And yet at the end of a life of fun and frolics, poor Peaid had to prepare himself to leave the stage, the same as anyone else. As Peaid himself used to say about anyone who was dying, 'Pilib had issued his 'decree' in relation to him or her'. Pilib an Chleite (Philip of the Feather/Quill) was the person who in charge of the roll-call of humanity and he calls everyone home when their time is up. Peaid was eventually called home. He got sick while he was in Breathnach's house and he was sent to the hospital in An Cloichín. He recovered and improved slightly while he was in the hospital. When the priest visited him to prepare him for death, he didn't have it easy. When he told Peaid to recite his sins, Peaid told him that he didn't have any worth talking about. He hadn't ever done anything wrong – he hadn't struck anyone a blow, he hadn't killed anyone; nor had he ever stolen a farthing from anyone; he had spent his life in search of fun and laughter. He and the priest sorted out their differences in the end and the priest prepared him spiritually for the journey to the other side. Peaid told everyone who came to see him, even the nuns, about the discussions he'd had with the priest and everyone was in the fits laughing at some of the funny things he said.

One day, the nun who was nursing him said to him:

'Now Pádraig. When you go up to Heaven, won't you promise me that you'll say a prayer on my behalf?'

'Reverend Mother', Peaid replied. 'you'll have to excuse me if I don't do that for the first week at least. I have to visit all my relations first and I won't have much time for prayer in that first week. But I promise you that I won't forget you after that!'

He only lasted two months in the hospital. The man in the bed next to him was dying also and they used to be reciting the Litany over him. When they were finished saying the Litany for this man, Peaid said to one of the nuns that they might as well make the 'one job' of it and include him in their recitation of the Litany because he wasn't going to last much longer. It was true for him. He was dead before the following morning and no doubt, God wasn't too hard on the poor joker because whatever faults he had, he always had a soft and kind heart. The blessings of Grace be upon his soul because he was an amazing son-of-a-gun really when all was said and done. It's awful but the likes of him have to die like everyone else in the end.

An Gealt – 'The Crazy One'

The person we knew as 'An Gealt' (the Crazy One') was odd or eccentric in a completely different way from Peaid na Brídí. He was totally obsessed with religion and religious 'devotions'. Muiris Ó Gormáin was his name but he was never known by his real name. People always referred to him as Muiris na Mácaí or Muiris na bPaidiríní (Muiris of the Rosaries), or just as 'An Gealt' (The Crazy One). The most common name by which people in An Gleann knew him was 'An Gealt' (The Crazy One). Muiris wasn't actually a native of An Gleann but he was so many years wandering around the area that he might as well have been. He was such a strange person that this book wouldn't be complete without reference to him. Whenever he was in this parish here, he always attended the Masses in Baile na hAbhann. He always received Holy Communion on Sundays and holy days. He would fast until after second Mass was over when he would go to the house of one of the locals to get his breakfast.

He had no formal education but any money that he ever had, he spent on religious books. He'd ask someone to read out of the book for him and he memorized anything that was read out for him; any excerpt from the Gospels that he heard, he would have it off-by-heart forever after that. Pádraig Ó Domhnaill used to read a good number of the books for him and he'd leave them in his house when he hit the road again. I heard that there were more than twenty books belonging to him in Ó Domhnaill's house when Muiris died.

Whenever there was a mission in any parish near ours, Muiris would be in the church every morning and afternoon for as long as the mission was taking place. Afterwards, he could give you a blow-by-blow account of everything the missioners had said, whether it was their criticisms of dancing or drinking or of boys and girls courting; Muiris was very strict in relation to that sort of thing. 'The Crazy One' arrived into this area a long time before I was born. His father was a travelling man and he accompanied him everywhere when they first came to An Gleann, his father begging from place to place. When his father died Muiris continued the tradition of wandering from one farm to another. Unlike other travellers here, he never carried a bag. He spent his life coming and going and travelling around An Gleann here. A tall, thin, round-shouldered man, he wore a straggly beard. He was bandy-legged and lame which gave him an unusual gait. He swayed from side to side as he walked, his arms swinging to the rhythm with his long strides. You'd have recognised him from his walk even if he was a half-a-mile from you. Neither before nor since have I seen anyone who wore such enormous shoes. Tadhg Ó Dúbhlainn, the shoemaker in Baile na hAbhann made the shoes for him and any time that Muiris needed new shoes Seán Mór Breathnach always paid the shoemaker on Muiris' behalf. Seán Mór Breathnach was very punctual with his payments and always paid the bill straight away.

Muiris was a bit slow, even when he was a young lad. They used to tell a story about his father and him walking along the road one summer's afternoon, Muiris following slightly behind his father. 'You have a horse-fly on your back, Dad', he said.

'Kill it son', said his father. Muiris whacked his father across the shoulders with his walking stick; he hit him so hard that he knocked him over on the road. No-one could tell whether he killed the horse-fly or not. Muiris would be at every wake that was held in the parish and he always recited the Rosary in a voice so loud that you would hear him a half-a-mile away. You'd always find him in the room where the corpse was laid out alongside the women. He had a giant Rosary beads, with beads as big as gooseberries on it. He also always carried three or four sets of smaller Rosary beads. He wore a half-dozen or so scapulars which he wore outside his shirt and he was always discussing the prophecies of Colmcille. He interpreted from them that England's rule in Ireland was coming to an end. It was also his opinion that George the Seventh would be the last ever King of England. There was a schoolmaster in Baile na hAbhann at that time whom Langley, the landlord, had employed to teach his children, who were members of the Church of England. This schoolmaster was able to read and write Irish and was able to speak the language also. He used to debate religious matters with Muiris but Muiris was too knowledgeable for him and regularly got the better of him. Eventually, this schoolmaster used to avoid Muiris whenever he saw him coming. Muiris used to say to this schoolmaster that he had only learned Irish because he was a 'Souper' and that he was trying to proselytize the Irish Catholics up in the west of Ireland. For his part, the schoolmaster would say to Muiris that the Catholic religion was too demanding and too strict. In his view, people shouldn't have been required to walk three miles to the church while fasting on the mornings that they intended receiving Holy Communion; he didn't agree either with the practice of Confession and the fact that people had to tell another person (i.e. the priest) their sins; nor did he agree with the ban on eating meat on Fridays.

'Oh', Muiris would respond to him; 'if we could make up our own rules as part of our religion as you did, it wouldn't be long before it just became an easy, unchallenging religion and a soft option to follow. I can guarantee you that'.

Muiris' reply was a good one, especially for someone who did not have any formal education. He only ever ate meat once a year – on Christmas Day – and he never drank alcohol. Apparently, he also mortified himself using a small rope every Friday during Lent as reparation for his sins, just as the Saints did long ago.

One story about Muiris that I often heard the local people tell was that he had been seen down in Burke's quarry wearing only his trousers and scourging himself with a rope, when Peaid na Brídí had come upon him by mistake. 'Lay into it!' 'Lay into it!' Give me the rope and I'll give you a good scourging. You can't give yourself a right lashing that way' Peaid said to him apparently. Muiris didn't let Peaid wind him up, however. That said, it wouldn't have surprised me if it was Peaid himself who spread this story around as he would always wind up 'An Gealt' whenever he got the chance. Muiris was at Seán Chaitlín's wake in Bun an Bhealaigh and there was a group of chancers or blackguards there as you'd expect on such occasions. They were playing different games at the wake and Muiris was in the kitchen drinking tea. What tricks they were playing, I'm not sure, but at one stage, Peaid told Muiris that he had supernatural powers, similar to a priest. This startled Muiris because he would never let anyone insult the clergy without challenging them. He told Peaid that his claims to have powers similar to a priest were just bare-faced lies.

'Right so; it's easy to sort this one out', said Peaid. 'I'll prove it to you. I'll bet you any money that I can stick you to the floor here and you won't be able to get up, no matter how hard you try'. They persuaded Muiris to sit down and stretch out in the middle of the floor, and Peaid pulled a prayer-book from his pocket and began to read a load of gibberish as if out of the prayer-book over him – letting on that it was Latin he was reading. The lads had planned this prank beforehand and when Muiris was stretched out on the dark and Peaid had him distracted reading out these supposed prayers, the lads were quietly tacking his long jacket-coat to the clay floor. After a few minutes, Peaid told Muiris to get up if he could. Muiris tried to get up but he couldn't move. All the lads burst out laughing. Muiris went ballistic and made a huge effort to raise himself off the ground. His jacket-coat ripped however and there were bits of it left stuck to the ground. He chased the lads who had made a fool of him out of the house. He was absolutely raging and would have killed someone if he had got his hands on them.

There was nothing holy about the threats he shouted at his tormentors that night! Muiris normally wore a long jacket-coat which differed from the shorter-length jackets that most men wore in those days and he always wore black. Even the hat he wore was black. It was as if he was implying that he was a member of the clergy. In fact, the clergy always gave him these clothes as hand-me-downs, although they rarely fitted him properly. These clothes were usually too long or too wide in the waist. Muiris was a funny shape, tall and thin, so it would have been unusual if these clothes had fitted him really. Muiris was very disapproving of the new types of dance that were coming in from abroad at the time. 'Dirty cornering (smooching) is how he referred to the 'sets' for example. He'd say that it was the devil had invented these dances and that it was very sinful to practice them. He was very opposed to alcohol and drinking also and regularly criticized the 'peelers' for not controlling the drinking in the pubs better. Needless to say, Muiris was just wasting his time, the poor fellow. They used to just make a fool of the poor man. Muiris was scandalized when women began wearing short skirts and this style became fashionable. He'd tell the priest that he wasn't fulfilling his spiritual duties correctly because he should have banned anyone wearing a short skirt from going into the church. They were only wearing these types of skirts to deliberately tempt the young boys, he admonished him. Peaid na Brídí was always teasing the 'Crazy One' and joking him whenever he got a chance. When the Great War broke out for example, he told Muiris that he'd read in the newspaper about a new law that the English parliament had recently passed obliging all single men to marry and have children before a certain date. This was to make up for the large numbers of men who were being killed at the front and any man who didn't comply with this law by a certain date would be punished by hanging. Muiris was nonplussed however. He said that he was quite happy to suffer execution by hanging rather than break the vow of chastity he had taken. And this is how the 'Crazy One' spent his life, the poor man, travelling from place to place and spreading the faith, while being the butt of the local joker's wit and sarcasm. He never begged alms but the local women in the houses would always make sure that he had enough to eat. He really loved drinking tea and he'd drink it twelve hours a day if he could. He didn't have any 'meas' (respect) on the tea that was poured into a cup for him, but always wanted it served in a 'jug' or a tin can, so long as it was filled to the brim. He loved the tea to be thick with sugar and bubbling almost. He didn't care if there was a bit of milk in it or not. As long as the tea was really strong, he didn't mind. It would have to be really strong altogether, so strong that the hen could walk on it. Muiris Ó Gormáin is in the graveyard for many years now and not many people in the area remember him anymore. He is buried in Cill Mhuire graveyard. He died suddenly one Sunday as he was returning from Mass. Although hardly anyone remembers him now, there are still many local people who have stories about him in An Gleann still. Although God didn't give him his full senses when he was born, Muiris was still very wise in his own way and there weren't many people who were able for him in an argument. I'm absolutely certain of it that he was a very religious and committed to the faith but Peaid na Brídí used to let on that he was only a chancer and an 'imposter'. May God have mercy on him and may he also forgive all of the people who tormented poor Muiris over the years.

Tadhg Mhichil – County Legal Advisor

Anyone who found themselves with legal difficulties here in Gleann Chártainn long ago always went to Tadhg Mhicil for advice. They had more than faith in his advice than they had in any solicitor. He was a very clever individual, someone who was very wise and far-seeing and there were many people who won their legal cases based on the advice he gave them. He didn't win all of these cases by being scrupulously straight either; he had no problem telling a few lies if he had to in order to get the result he wanted. He hated England with a passion and the way he looked at it was that English rule in Ireland was corrupt anyway and so there was nothing wrong with fighting corruption with corruption, if needs be. He never wanted to get involved in local cases where one neighbour was bringing the other to court unless he was absolutely certain that one person had a cut-and-dried case. Rather than going to court, he used to advise neighbours who were in dispute with one another to sort the case out unofficially rather than bring it to court and put money into the pockets of the colonial government in Ireland.

I still remember Tadhg Mhicil although he was already elderly when I was a young boy and going to school. He was a small thin man with a little rump of a beard just beneath his chin. He had very sharp eyes and spoke in very slow and serious manner. Tadhg Mhicil is dead a long time now but people around here still tell stories about him to this day. I'll try and recall a few of them here now.

One story related to Ned Dhomhnaill returning from the market at Cloichín where he'd been selling young banbhs. He'd had a lot to drink as usual and he was quite drunk as he rode his horse along the road at speed. There was a police barracks situated near Gort an Chuilinn and about a mile on this side of the barracks were two 'peelers' walking along the road, one of whom was the local sergeant. When they spotted him coming, they stood out in the middle of the road and put their hands in the air ordering him to stop. Ned Dhomhnaill paid no heed to them however and they had to jump out of the way at the last minute. They found out who the rider of the runaway horse was and brought him to court and charged him with riding a horse dangerously, refusing to stop when told to do so and with nearly killing them with the horse. Ned Dhomhnaill didn't know what to do so he went to Tadhg Mhichil and asked him for advice.

At the time, there was a police inspector in the southern end of the county named Shoveller who was particularly exercised about poachers and poaching and was always encouraging the 'peelers' to go after them and to catch them if possible. Tadhg Mhichil knew this and his advice to Domhnall Ó Lonnargáin was to say in court that he was riding a young and very temperamental horse that day and that when he was within a few hundred yards of the barracks in Gort an Chuilinn, he'd come across a donkey rolling itself on the ground out in the middle of the road. He was to say that his horse had bolted that day and that he'd nearly broken the reins trying to get it to stop.

The police inspector stopped the case immediately on hearing this. He said that he believed everything that the defendant had said because he himself was more than aware that animals were regularly straying on the 'long acre' and that they were a danger to the public. Within a week, the police sergeant from Gort an Chuilinn barracks was transferred to somewhere else on the other side of the county. Seán Ó hAllaidhe, the blacksmith, had a son – the man who made the really good spades – and he enlisted in the British army. An uncle of his who was in America sent him home his passage-money to go to America, however. He came home one time on 'furlough' and decided that he'd abscond from the army and make for America unknown to the authorities if he could. Before he did this however, his father advised him to go south to Gleann Chárthainn and ask Tadhg Mhichil for advice. Tadhg told this lad that the 'peelers' were under instructions to be 'on constant alert' for soldiers who were at home 'on furlough' in their area and that they were to report anyone whom they deemed had suddenly gone missing or 'absent without leave' from their area. They kept an eye on the ports and the ships also.

The blacksmith's house was situated on the side of the hill about a half-mile from the barracks; in fact, from the house, you had a good view of the police barracks. Tadhg advised this lad to leave for America but to give his red soldier's jacket to his brother as soon as he left and that the brother should wear this jacket as he strolled through the fields for a few days so that the 'peelers' could still see 'him' round-about the place. The brother did as Tadhg advised and when the 'peelers' came looking for him to return to his regiment at the end of his 'furlough', he was already safely over in America. The blacksmith burned the soldier's jacket in the forge-fire and when the 'peelers' asked him where his son the soldier was – he said that he assumed that he was gone back to join his army regiment again.

This next story also relates to Domhnall Ó Lonnargáin from Mónach Buí. He and his young son Ned were bringing ten bullocks to the fair one day and they were passing down by the old-pound when the cattle strayed into a field of wheat owned by old-Peaidí Daltún, the gate of which had accidentally been left open. Before Domhnall and Ned could get all the bullocks out again, they had trampled and destroyed some of the wheat. Daltún got really angry when he heard this and said that the gate hadn't been left open and that the cattle had actually broken down the gate to get in there. He decided to sue them and refused to accept any unofficial compensation so that the case wouldn't go to court. Domhnall said that he was happy to let two other 'independent' people decide how much compensation he owed and that he would pay that amount in damages to Peaidí in and 'out-of-course' settlement rather than the case going to court. Daltún wouldn't accept this arrangement however, and issued Domhnall with a writ in the local district court in Clonmel, saying that he wanted fifty pounds compensation for the wheat that had been damaged. Domhnall called over to Tadhg Mhicil to ask his advice on what to do. The judge who tried the civil court cases there was very honest and direct and he hated any sort of trickery or corruption. Tadhg Mhichil knew this and he decided to play on this aspect of his character. He said to Domhnall Ó Lonnargáin:

'Tell Séimí Céitinn go get you a fairly big salmon. It'll cost you but forget about that; then, give me the salmon. Don't get the salmon until about a week before the court sits, however'.

'And in God's name, what's the salmon got to do with it?' asked Domhnall.

'Just leave it to me, you need to give me three pounds if you win your case. If you lose, I won't charge you anything'.

When the court case took place, it became apparent that the judge had sided against the Daltún's for some reason. He seemed to be very suspicious of the evidence the Daltún's gave and he seemed to believe all of the evidence that Domhnall Ó Lonnargáin gave. The judge found against the Daltún's and they also had to pay the court costs. Domhnall couldn't believe how easily he won his case and afterwards he went to Tadhg Mhichil and gratefully paid him five pounds. Tadhg Mhicil would only accept three pounds from him as that had been their original agreement, however.

'Tell me now', he said to Tadhg, 'what did you need that salmon for anyway?'

'I sent it to him as a present – in the name of Peaidí Daltún!' said Tadhg.

Tadhg had a tiny little dog and the police sent him a court summons because he hadn't paid the half-crown licence for it. The local court sessions would always be held in Baile na hAbhann on the first Friday of each month. Tadhg went to the court and brought his little dog with him. It was a very cold day and when he came to the small bridge in Baile na hAbhann, he threw the dog out into the water. When the dog came out of the water he threw it back in again a few times. Then he placed the dog in the pocket of his great-coat. His case was called immediately as he arrived in court. Tadhg pulled the little dog up out of his coat and placed it on the bench. The poor shivering dog looked like a miserable little thing, like a drowned rat.

'Needless to say gentlemen', said Tadhg in broken English, 'you wouldn't make me pay a fine for a small, miserable creature like this here, would you?' Everyone in the court burst out laughing and Tadhg and his dog were let go home without having to pay any fine.

One day Tadhg was at the fair in Clonmel selling three or four mountain sheep. He and the buyer had an argument but Tadhg wasn't doing very well because the buyer's English was better.

'Turn to Irish, you son of a whore and I'll make bits of you', Tadhg said.

As mentioned earlier, he really hated the English and he was often predicting that the Russians would soon hammer the English in India. The Boer War was on in South Africa during the last year of Tadhg's life and he was delighted when the Boers got the better of the British (John Bull's) army. He was especially proud of the role that the Irish Brigade played in this war. They were reciting the Litany over him as he lay on his deathbed. It was in the evening and he was very weak and there hadn't been a stir out of him all day. Suddenly, he perked up for a minute during the prayers. He opened his eyes and recognised Peaid Philib standing next to the bed. 'Here Peaid', he whispered. 'How are the Boers getting on?' 'Oh', replied Peaid. 'De Wet had a great victory against the English recently. He killed over 5000 of them, and took more than 10,000 of them as prisoners'.

'Whoo-hoo!' said Peaid and tried to raise his hand from the sheet. He went quiet again after that and died the following morning. Peaid made up that story about the war because he knew that it would make Micil happy. Tadhg Micil is in the graveyard clay for many years now but people still talk about him sometimes here in Gleann Charthain. His final words of advice to anyone entering court are still frequently used around here. 'Don't spare the book whatever else you do'.

REFLECTING ON MATTERS
WHILE OUT ON THE MOUNTAINSIDE

Ever since I was a child, I've felt a special connection with the mountains that surround us here in An Gleann. They always weaved some kind of a magic over me and whenever I looked back at Cruachán or An Dá Mhaoil and Cnoc na gCnámh, I imagined the hills almost as living beings with their own feelings and souls. I used to feel sorry for them whenever it rained and especially when their peaks were hidden beneath the snow. Conversely, I thought that they were lucky whenever the summer sun shone down on them. As a child, I tried to imagine what amazing and wonderful things might lie in that exotic country on the other side of the hills. What would I have given to stand on the top of An Mhaol or on the peak of Cruachán looking across at the amazing wonders of that secret land that lay beyond the horizon.

The years went by and when I got older my wishes came true. I did get to climb right to the top of the mountain. I didn't see any Tír na nÓg (Land of Everlasting Youth) on the other side but I did see something else. What you could see from the peaks of these mountains on a fine day was one of the most spectacular views anywhere in Ireland. Stretching from the sea, thirty miles southwards all the way to Greim an Diabhal (The Devil's Bit) sixty miles northwards, the view was incredible. And if you climbed to the peak of the Knockmealdown Mountain on a bright clear day, you could also see the McGillycuddy Reeks at the bottom of the horizon to the west and the Blackstairs Mountains to the east – it was like the whole of Ireland was laid out there before your very eyes. I liked nothing better than to head out into mountains on a fine summer's day or in autumn. At the end of a long week's work and worry, and after my dinner on a Sunday, I often walked up along Gleann na Faille and then climbed the shoulder of Cruachán. The higher I climbed into the sky, the more my worries seemed to fall away. Up there, they melted away like fog before sunshine. And sitting there in the heather and looking at the incredible expanse of the world beneath me, those small worries and cares always seemed far less significant than they had appeared initially. There was a rock near the peaks of Cruachán that was mossy and shaped like a chair; it is still there today I suppose, although it is many years now since I last sat on it. I often spent an hour or two sitting in that chair thinking about what life likely held in store for me. It was a really beautiful place on an autumn day when the heather was in full-bloom and the bees hummed their soothing lullaby around about; or on a sunny summer's day when the larks sang high in the blue sky above me.

Feimhin's Plain lay northwards beneath me like a great map – that same plain that appears so often in the Fiannaíocht tales of old – it was laid out now like an enormous chess board, each square of which became smaller and smaller the further into the distance you tried to see – until, in the end, everything just melted away into the fog of the horizon. This whole scene would quiver gently in the summer heat and the slow scudding movement of the occasional passing cloud. Way off in the far-distance you might see the steam coming from the train that travelled between Cahir and Clonmel; from this height, the train looked like a tiny child's play-thing winding its way across the countryside, a toy moving at a snail's pace. The beauty of the world from this vantage point changed depending on the season. It was also as beautiful in its own way when all the hills were covered in a blanket of snow and I was out searching for missing sheep. In winter it was the black markers made by the stone walls that crisscrossed the fields that were striking.

They reminded you of the patchwork and weave on a great fishing-net. In the beginning of May when the corn was starting to grow and the grass was high in the meadows, the entire plain was covered in a soft green swathe. In autumn, the landscape changed again as the corn ripened and the panorama below became a magnificent golden-green.

Sliabh gCrot and Sliabh na mBan are like two giants watching over the plains then, east and west. To the north, the Bite that the Devil took from the mountains is plain to see between you and the horizon. The Suir river winds its way southwards in the middle of the plain below but just as it seems to be nearing its journey's end, it takes a sudden turn in an easterly direction for a few miles and then northwards again for another few miles until it reaches the sea at Cumar na dTrí Uisce. When the river travels northwards and comes closer to your vantage-point, you can see it dotting the landscape like a series of small lakes. You can trace the Tearra river with your eye too as it runs parallel with the hills and to within a mile of the foot of the mountain. You can follow with your eye also where the Tearra turns eastwards and winds its way north again before emptying itself into the Suir once more at Gob Rinne, just a few miles away.

There is hardly any well-known historical personage who hasn't left his or her mark on the landscape that is Machaire Feimhin, whether for good or ill – from Pádraig who baptised Aongus in Cashel to Briain who beat the Danes at Solohead, to the very last landlord who was driven out of here and killed.

Butlers, Prendergasts, Keatings, Morrisseys and others; they all had possession of these plains here at various stages and they were all very powerful at different junctures of Irish history. The dark ruins of their great castles with their small slitted windows are all that are left today in the meadows and plains around here. That and their surnames that still survive amongst the people here and there also, people who are as Gaelic as any of their neighbours now – the Ryans, the O'Dwyers, the Mahers and the Mulcahys.

Cromwell's soldiers were busy at one time on the plains below also, especially on that day when he travelled over from Youghal and the Irish gave him a real fright at the siege of Clonmel. Some of his followers got control of some of the best land around here afterwards but there are very few of them left around here now, just the remains of the ugly houses they built. The few who are left are much more humble and quiet-spoken than their ancestors were centuries earlier.

Cashel can be seen in the centre of the plain and on a good day, with a telescope, you can also see the ruins of the buildings that Murchadh na dTóiteán once owned. And Cahir, where Brian Mac Cinnéide once built his fort on the great rock – the island in the river – the rock upon which the Butlers subsequently built their fortress – a castle that one of the Butlers subsequently surrendered to Cromwell without firing a shot and Ardfinnan where Ireton held sway; there too is the Newcastle of the Prendergasts, which is an important ford over the Suir and other significant landmarks all around which appear in the annals of Irish history. They are all there beneath you, as if marked out on a giant map.

From the top of An Mhaol and about a half-mile south of Cruachán you can get the best view southwards over the mountains. The sea can be seen southwards also at the bottom of the horizon and so too can a good deal of the countryside that is County Waterford. Cruachán Phaoraig (Power's Mountain) can be seen eastwards of you when looking down over the town of Dungarvan and the Blackwater that runs south from Cappoquin to Youghal and the spire at Melleray peeping above the fir trees and the green fields round-about. When the monks first came to Screathan from 'La Trappe' in France, there was nothing there except western gorse and heather and rocks but they have overseen an amazing transformation there within the last hundred years or so. They have a thriving farm now where there was once just rock and scrub.

When the monks first arrived there, workmen from every parish in the area went up to help them make the place habitable. They dug ditches and built walls and laid pipes down for the water. I often heard the old people here in Gleann Chárthainn say that up to thirty men went south every day for a week to help with the work bringing their own food with them to sustain them.

As I mentioned earlier the view from the top of Knockmealdown mountain is one of the finest in Ireland.

Not only can you see the MacGillycuddy Reeks in County Kerry on a fine day but you can also see the outline of the Wicklow Hills and the Blackstairs Mountains far away on the horizon; this is not to mention the sea to the south of you and the Devil's Bit to the north. And just beside you, on the peak of the hill is another unusual sight, the grave of 'Major Eeles' that strange man who had his gun and two of his dogs buried next to him as his legacy to the world. It is about 150 years since his remains were brought southwards from Youghal where he died, to be buried on the peak of the mountain here.

I observed all of these sights and monuments for years before I really understood their significance. We never learned anything about the history of Ireland when we were at school and it was only when I was growing into adulthood that I began to learn about these aspects of Irish history; and if Seán Mac Craith hadn't constantly encouraged me to read up on this history, I would probably still be ignorant of it to this day.

I couldn't have been more than ten years of age when the daughter of one of my mother's brothers came home from America on a visit. She gave me book as a present – a book in English titled *A School History of the United States*, a fine book with a lot of pictures in it. I read and re-read the book over and over again so many times that I could probably have named all the presidents of the United States from Washington to Lincoln, if I had to. Not only this, but I could have listed most of the big wars and the US army generals who fought in them also. Isn't it a terrible shame that books such as this about our own country are not available to the young people here in Ireland? Whatever someone learns as a child tends to stay with them for the remainder of their lives. I have yet to read a book of Irish history as comprehensive as that book my cousin Nell Ní Fhógartha gave me about the history of the US.

After all of this wandering in my story, I best return to where I was that day, sitting in my moss-covered chair on the top of the mountain. Beneath me I could see two large piles of rocks, one on the hillock just below me and the other about three-quarters of a mile in an easterly direction on Black Hill. There are enough rocks in both 'carns' to build two castles. 'An Clutharacán' is what the people of An Gleann used to call these two piles of rock and the story they had about them was that it was the 'Danes' who had gathered all of these rocks together once to burn them. They had heard somewhere that if you burned rocks, you could get good fertilizer for your land. Once they had gathered all the rocks together however, they discovered that they couldn't burn them as they were sandstone rocks. So the story went; I never believed this however as I just couldn't believe that the Danes were that stupid that they would have done such a thing. They would almost certainly have attempted to burn the rocks prior to gathering thousands of tons of them together in the one place.

Later on again, I heard that these rock-piles were actually the sites were chiefs and kings were buried in ancient times and that they can be found on various mountainsides throughout Ireland. Often, as I sat in my stone-chair on the heights of Cruachán, I tried to imagine what the funeral of one of these chiefs or kings must have been like all those hundreds of years ago. The man laid out on his shield and wearing his best military outfit and his keening women and the members of his tribe following afterwards in the procession – praising him for all his valiant deeds. Then the great fire on the top of the mountain where the body was cremated. It was probably at such a cremation that the first 'wake games' were practiced. To put an end to the funeral proceedings the entire tribe would pile these rocks over the area where the chief was buried. The mountainside must have been some sight on that great funeral day long ago, a noisy clamour of people – as opposed to the lonely silence of today. What great and noble deeds this leader must have performed during his lifetime to be commemorated by his people in such a way. Those who have studied these questions say that these monuments date back to thousands of years B.C. When compared with the pathetic and short-lived monuments placed to commemorate famous people today, these ancient carns are magnificent.

I used to go up to Leacain every now and then to visit my relatives there and I often returned over the mountain again at night. I knew all the old paths and trails like the back of my hand and as long as the night wasn't too foggy or dark, there was very little chance that I would get lost out on the mountainside. If the visibility was poor, I didn't follow the mountain paths but went around by the main road instead. There is something that is both mysterious and awesome about being out on the mountainside at night however, especially on a moon-lit night. The landscape extends out beneath you like a great, dark, blanket with just the occasional glint of light from the windows of a few farmhouses here and there. Sometimes when I stood there for a few moments on the mountainside in the darkness and reflected on life – crazy though it may seem – I imagined that the world and I were rotating around one another on their own special axis. Then, when I glanced upwards at the night-sky, I imagined that the stars had come to a sudden halt and that the mountains and I were spinning around the sky instead. Out there on the mountain, when you looked up at the great immensity of the sky, you had no option but to acknowledge that there must be an omniscient creator out there somewhere, the God of Glory, a thousand thanks to Him.

A strange thing happened to me when I was out on the mountain one time. I went out walking by myself one Sunday during the summer. I was walking in a southerly direction between Bearna an Bhainbh and An Dá Mhaoil where there is a very old path cut into the hillside. People sometimes still travel this route across the mountains even today as it is much shorter than going by road. I saw a sheep far ahead of me on the mountain path; it was about twenty yards in off the path. It was standing very still and just grazing. I thought there was something strange about it, the way it was so still. Initially, I thought that there must be something wrong with the sheep, that maybe it was sick. I walked on and when I came within about fifty feet of it, I noticed a man lying on the ground next to it. Initially, I thought he was asleep but when I came closer I noticed rust on the tacks of his hobnail boots which were facing towards me. I got a real shock then when I realised that the man who was middle-aged, was dead. There were six or seven cords wound around the sheep's neck and one main rope which was wrapped around the dead man's fist. The sheep hadn't been able to move freely for a while and had eaten every blade of grass around where the dead man was lying. I untied the sheep and went home where I reported what I had seen to the 'peelers'. The man looked to me as if he had been dead for a week or so. I had to bring the 'peelers' up to where the dead man was and we brought his corpse back down to Baile na hAbhann on a cart. They held a 'committee' then about what had happened and I had to give evidence to this committee about what I had discovered. The doctor who gave evidence said that the man had died from natural causes. He was a man who used to drive animals from one fair to the next on behalf of the various 'jobbers'. He had attended the fair in Cappoquin apparently and he was bringing the sheep northwards, it seems, to sell at the fair in An Cloichín. I suppose he must have bought the sheep earlier in Cappoquin.

I took a week's holidays at one stage and visited the schoolmaster Liam Tóibín up near Tullamore. The land up there is as flat as a board and I actually missed the hills and mountains after a few days. I felt like someone in a small boat who is out in the middle of the vast and empty ocean.

Whenever the hero or the criminal has to make a run for it, he usually makes for the mountains because it is always safer and easier to hide there than it is on the plains. The mountains have a freedom about them that no tyrant can ever control or tame. I think that mountain people suffer twice as much than others when they are far away from their native area; not only do they miss the mountains, but they also miss their own kind – mountain people.

People with Bad Traits who Lived in An Gleann

About two hundred people lived in An Gleann when I was young. There is barely half that number living here now. Among that small number of people, there were the same mix of good and bad personality traits as you find amongst any group of people, whether they are people who live in a town or in the countryside. The vast majority of the people living here were good-living and devout Christians but some people still had traits that were not so attractive, including dishonesty, miserliness, violence and a propensity for stealing and hurting others – even murder itself.

A small sturdy man named Liamín Búrc – or Liamín na nUbh as he was better known lived here at one time long ago. He lived in a small thatched house about two fields in from Bóithrín na Cille at the eastern end of An Gleann here. He had no-one belonging to him and lived alone. The only land he had was about a quarter of an acre of garden where he grew cabbage plants and onions that he sold to the neighbours. He'd pay the local housewives for their eggs and then he'd go around on Fridays with his donkey and cart to collect the eggs which he brought to the big town to sell on Saturdays. He had the same way of making a living as Ailí Condúin did except that Liam wouldn't have worked even a third as hard as Ailí did. Liamín was a small and happy-go-lucky man who always had funny stories and was welcomed with open arms wherever he went. No-one would have thought that he had an enemy in the world. He did have an enemy however, and a bad one at that.

Micil Ó Néill was out hunting rabbits one Sunday after dinner and as he passed by Liamín's house, he called in as he normally did. When he opened the door, Liamín was lying dead on the floor in a pool of blood, an old axe lying next to him. There was panic and chaos in the village straight away. The 'peelers' arrived and they questioned everyone in the locality about what had happened.

Whenever he went out, Liamín had a habit of locking his front door and placing the key in beneath the threshold of the door. The 'peelers' thought that the murderer must have got the key and entered the house and killed Liamín inside in the kitchen, striking him on the head with the axe. The doctor said that the blow Liamín got broke his skull and that he was killed instantly. The house looked as if someone had searched it carefully. The 'peelers' combed every inch of it and they discovered that every penny that might have been in that house was gone. The big canvas purse that Liamín normally wore on a string around his neck had been torn off him and was lying empty next to his body on the floor. Even the few provisions he had bought in the local town – sugar, bread and tea etc. – had also been stolen.

No-one was ever charged with Liamín's murder, even though the priest said from the altar that anyone who had any information about it was obliged to report it to the police. If anyone had suspicions about any of their neighbours, they kept them to themselves. From what I heard later, a local man was the prime suspect for the murder but they couldn't prove anything against him. The fact that the colonial laws were in force back then and were often corrupt probably meant that people were reluctant to voice their suspicions to the legal authorities at the time. There may have been another reason why people were reluctant to come forward also however, one that I will refer to in due course here.

Whoever the person was who killed poor Liamín, they have now answered before a higher judge than is in this world. May God grant it that this person repented for their sins and was given more time to do so than they gave Liamín Búrc.

Here is a story about another terrible murder that occurred in An Gleann, this time during the Famine, when the potato crop failed. Although this story occurred long before I was born, it is still told by people in this area even today.

A narrow road runs from Bóithrín na Cille southwards towards the main road at Bun an Bhealaigh, close to the old police barracks, near where Cruthúr Garbh used to live long ago. This small road is known as An Bóithrín Dorcha because much of the road is below the level of the ditch and is obscured by the bushes and the furze that grows thickly there. Very few people ever go this road today. About a half-mile in off the road is a sharp turn known as Cúinne na Mine. (The Meal Corner). During the Famine, a poor man lived in a small cabin on that corner with his wife and five children. His children were young and they were suffering a great deal with the hunger. A local farmer ordered the shopkeeper in Baile na hAbhann to give the poor man a hundredweight of meal. The man was returning home late one night, the hundredweight on the back of his donkey when he was set upon and murdered. The meal was stolen. When his wife didn't see him coming home after a few hours she went out the road looking for him and she found him lying dead on the road. According to the old people, it was two local brothers who killed the man.

It goes without saying that the authorities of the day didn't make much of an effort to find the murderers. Hundreds of people were dying every week of hunger and fever back then and life was cheap. I won't give the surname of the people who were strongly suspected of murdering this man. Suffice to say that, none of this family lives in Gleann Chárthainn anymore. These people had no luck for their gruesome deed. Their various farming projects failed – a fact which people ascribed to the curse of the murdered man's widow. Anytime an argument broke out between the members of this family and other people in the locality, the people weren't long directing accusations against them as relating to this horrible murder.

Down through the years, I've often thought about what it must have been like here in An Gleann after this terrible murder. How the poor man's widow found her husband stone-cold dead on the road. I never did hear what happened to that widow and her children in the end. It is difficult for us today to imagine how brutal and terrible life was for many people in that era.

You can say without hesitation that the people who committed this heinous murder deserved to be hanged for their crime but then, when you reflect on the case more carefully, you can have some small sympathy for the predicament of the perpetrators also. The evil one was controlling their actions that fateful night, that's for sure. There wasn't a trace of Christian sentiment left in them; they acted out of an animal savagery but who knows what lengths hunger can drive people to?

You often read stories of people who have been shipwrecked or lost at sea in a small boat for a long time – and that they ate each other in the end. Anyone who hasn't experienced the extremities of such hunger will never understand what thoughts and motivations such people might have in their minds when they decide on such a terrible action.

Some of us can say that we would never resort to such savagery no matter how difficult our circumstances were – but who is to say how anyone might act if they were driven demented with hunger or if it was a matter of life or death?

I can barely remember Seán 'ac Cathail now. He died when I was still going to school but I often heard sean-Risteard talk about him in later years. Sean-Risteard used to say that Seán 'ac Cathail was the most bad-minded and most vicious man ever to live in this area. He always said that the badness in him was in his genes, that it was part of his lineage and nature. Apparently, Seán's grandfather was a killer-for-hire at the time of the Famine. His pay for each murder was five pounds and a bottle of whiskey. I often heard Risteard say this man killed a man once and then used the trunk of his body as a flail while knocking back the bottle of whiskey. Seán 'ac Cathail spent a few years in America and whatever bit of religious feeling that was in him before he went there, it had left him completely by the time he returned home again. He never went to Mass and nor did he bow when he met a priest on the road. He used to laugh at people who went to Confession telling them that they were telling their sins to 'a farmer's son!' Although he would have little enough work to do during the week, he always seemed to find some job to do out in the field on a Sunday; he mightn't have had any meat to eat any other day of the week but he always made sure to eat some meat on a Friday. He was actually mocking the religious beliefs of others all the time. He lived with a nephew of his out near the Tonnóg river, a nephew who – according to all the neighbours – didn't want his uncle anywhere near him, but was too afraid of him to throw him out of his house.

Although Seán 'ac Cathail was elderly enough when Liamín Búrc was murdered some of the locals suspected him of this crime but were too afraid of him to say anything to the authorities. If they had gone to the police about him, they were sure that he would burn down their houses with them inside; they were sure that he would have done this without the slightest scruple. In fact, a few barns were burned down at different times when he was in dispute with the people who owned them and although he was the main suspect for these crimes, nothing was ever proved against him. He was the type of man who wouldn't have thought twice of smashing someone over the head with a rock as thrown from behind the wall. Cruthúr Garbh was assaulted with a rock like this as he returned from the pub in Baile an Droichid one-night. He was left on the road all night and the people didn't find him until they were going to First Mass on the Sunday morning. Cruthúr spent a month in bed, his injuries were so severe. Everyone was sure that Seán 'ac Cathail was the one who had attacked Cruthúr and flung a rock at him from behind the ditch. Apparently, the two men had been arguing earlier in the evening in the pub and Cruthúr had referred to Seán as 'mac mic Sheáin na gcorp' (the grandson of Seán of the Corpses). In the pub Seán had had no choice other than to take this insult from Cruthúr because he knew that Cruthúr would tear him apart piece by piece in a fight. Instead, Seán 'ac Cathail had waited for Cruthúr in the dark and attacked him with rocks from behind the wall when he was on his way home from the pub later that night. Risteard also described occasions where local people had the tails cut off their cows or their dogs poisoned and that these incidents always coincided with Seán 'ac Cathail having some grudge against the people whose animals were attacked. Just the slightest grudge against someone was all the excuse that Seán 'ac Cathail needed to commit some brutal act against them.

The afternoon that Liamín na nUbh was killed, two boys who were erecting a trestle near the side of a house as night was falling spotted a man coming along the road in the dark. It was Seán 'ac Cathail and he was jogging along and carrying some sort of a weapon in his hand. The families of these two boys refused to let them tell anyone else of what they had seen that night. While you can fault them for this, when you consider what type of an individual Seán 'ac Cathail was and the traditional hatred that the Irish always had for the 'informer' one can understand to a certain extent why they didn't report what they had seen to the authorities. Apparently, no-one said anything until after Seán 'ac Cathail was dead. About a year after Liamín Búrc died, Seán 'ac Cathail himself reached the end of the road. I often heard Risteard recount his death in subsequent years. Apparently Tomás Ó Floinn, Seán's nephew needed Risteard to do some kind of a carpentry job for him and he called over to Risteard's house one evening after dinner. Tomás told Risteard that his uncle was sick since the previous evening and that he had taken to his bed. Risteard went back to the house with Tomás and sure enough, Seán 'ac Cathail was struggling with his breathing and he was unconscious. Just one look at him and Risteard knew that Seán 'ac Cathail was dying and he told Tomás go and get the doctor and the priest. Risteard remained in the room with Seán until Tomás returned. The priest put the oils on him and did whatever he could for Seán; Seán couldn't speak or move at this stage.

As night fell, Seán 'ac Cathail's breathing worsened considerably and one of the O'Néill boys read the Litany over him. Risteard was holding the holy candle and making sure that it didn't fall out of Seán 'ac Cathail's fist. At one stage Risteard said that he happened to glance in under the bed and he saw a horrible sight. Under the bed was a big black dog, its eyes ablaze with light. Till the day he died, Risteard swore that he saw that awful vision beneath the bed; he was absolutely certain of it and if I heard him describe it once, I heard him describe it twenty times. Afterwards, when Risteard was at the wake, a terrible gust of wind blew through the locality around midnight, a wind so powerful that it nearly blew the roof off the house. Risteard and a few others went outside into the back meadow at some stage on the night of the wake and they saw another bizarre and frightening vision outside. A small hill behind the house looked as if it was crowded with people and although it was a moonlit night they couldn't tell what kind of otherworldly people made up this crowd.

The night after the funeral, two of Tomás Ó Floinn's sons were sleeping next to one another in the bed when the eldest of the boys woke up screaming during the night. He ran into his parents' room and said that Seán 'ac Cathail had come into the room. His features were twisted and awful and he had a blue light around him. When Tomás and his wife went into the room to the younger boy, he was unconscious in the bed.

When he eventually came around, he too had seen the same terrible vision. They had a Mass said in the house a few days later and that was the end of these peculiar occurrences.

I remember three men in An Gleann who committed suicide during my lifetime here. I was going to school when Peats Thomáisín slit his own throat. Nothing like this had happened in the parish for decades and people were very upset and confused about it for some time afterwards. Peats had been to Clonmel to sell two fattened pigs. He stopped at a few different pubs on the way home and was very drunk by the time he reached Baile na hAbhann where he went into Cit Chaoimh's pub for more drinks. A daughter of his was 'in-service' and working in the pub there and when she saw how drunk he was, she told him to give her whatever money he had left in his pockets. She was afraid that he would be robbed on the way home. He handed her the money and went home. The next morning, when he woke up, he couldn't remember anything about speaking with his daughter the night before and he got into a terrible panic. There was no money in his pockets and he had to pay Langley the rent. He was in a terrible state because he was so worried about the rent. His wife told him to calm down but he couldn't. Later that morning, he went into the bedroom and when he hadn't appeared after a while, his wife went in to see where he was. He was lying on the floor dead in a pool of blood.

Pilib Ó Muirgheasa was the last person here who committed suicide. He was from Flemingstown but had married into the parish here. He married one of the Bál family, a woman who had a good farm of land and who was nearly forty years of age when they married. Pilib was a good ten years younger than her. Her mother was still alive and there were just the two women in the house. Both women were known to be nagging types, especially the older woman. She was said to be the worst in the parish and was constantly cranky. When there was no sign of any children appearing after a few years the old woman began to mock Pilib about it and was constantly tormenting him. Instead of backing up her husband, his wife often joined in. One morning, he left the house to drive the cows home but never came back. When he was gone for a while, the two women went out to look for him. They found his stick jammed into the ground on the riverbank at Poll Fada and Pilib's hat on top of the stick. Apparently, he had jumped into the deepest end of the pool and drowned. They went looking for him but his body didn't re-surface until after nine days.

A few years prior to the drowning of Pilib Ó
Muirgheasa, Tomás Ó Donncha committed suicide. He
worked as a river-bailiff but he had suffered from mental
illness for years and had been in the Mental Home at
various junctures also. For a while before his death, people
had noticed him becoming increasingly disturbed and
talking to himself a good deal as he walked along by the
walls and the ditches. One day he began to strop the razor;
alarmed at his behaviour, his wife and daughter had run to
a neighbour's house for help. The man of the house and his
two sons ran back to Tomás' house but when they got
there the front door was locked. In through the window,
they saw Tomás skinning the flesh from the fingers of his
left hand and laughing manically. The three men broke the
door in but they were too late to stop him slitting his throat
with the razor. No-one found any fault with Tomás for
what had happened as everyone knew he was mentally ill.

Jealousy is a peculiar disease. People often make fun of
others who are overly-jealous in their ways but they
shouldn't mock them in my opinion, as many people who
suffer from jealousy find it very difficult to control this
emotion in themselves. Here are two anecdotes about
people who were particularly jealous.

Séimín Ó Néill was a labourer. He was one of a family of
two brothers, the other being Micil Ó Néill. They both
spent their lives working as labourers on Seán Mór
Breathnach's farm. Séimín didn't like anyone looking at his
wife, although they had five children. The funniest thing of
the lot was that although Séimín himself was a fine
handsome man, his wife was small and butty with a big
nose. She may have been no oil painting to look at but she
was a very kind-hearted person and someone with a lovely
nature. All the neighbours were very fond of her.
Although Séimín would never have dreamed of raising his
hand to his wife, he made her life difficult enough in other

ways, especially because of his incessant jealousy. Supposing they were both outside the house and Séimín spotted a man coming along the road in the distance – even a beggar – he would order his wife to go back into the house. She always did as he said – more for an easy life than anything else. At harvest time Séimín would travel around about the countryside working and also when it was the potato-picking season. He'd return home to his house every Saturday and he would leave on the Sunday evening again and go back to wherever he was working. And yet sometimes he would return to his house in the middle of the night and listen outside the bedroom window to check that his wife was asleep – before returning again to his place of work! The neighbours knew that he did this and they used to joke about it behind his back. It was no joke for poor Séimín to walk five or six miles from wherever he was working in the middle of the night to listen outside his house and then to walk the same distance back again.

Peaid na Brídí and Micil Ó Néill were returning from the pub at a very late hour one night when they saw Séimín making for his own house in the dark. They followed him and they saw him listening at his bedroom window. Micil wanted to grab Séimín and give him a good hiding for this strange 'carry-on' of his but Peaid persuaded him not to. Instead, the two men threw some sods of clay at him to frighten him away. It seems that Séimín had very little control over his jealous feelings as when he was on his deathbed, he made his wife swear that she would never marry anyone else. He was sixty-six years of age when he died.

Seán Ó Donncha lived near Bóithrín na Cille on the other side of the road from Seán Mór Breathnach's house. He was married to one of the Fogarty's from Leacain, a family who were closely related to my mother. This

Fogarty woman was a fine handsome woman and they were married for four or five years but they had no children. Seán was very jealous-minded of her and would never let his wife out of his sight – not even for a minute. Often, when he was working out in the fields, he would run back into the house all of a sudden and check all the rooms and under the beds to see was there anyone else in the house. He also had a big fierce dog that he trained to watch out for any strangers that might approach the house. Anytime he went to a fair or a market, his wife always had to go with him. Before he was married he'd been very fond of card-playing and he went to every house that there was a game in but after his marriage, he wouldn't go anywhere or visit anyone unless his wife accompanied him. What he did from the time of his marriage on was invite three or four old-timers who were card-players around to his house every Sunday night in winter for a game. There was no fear that he'd invite any young men around to the house. Needless to say, the card-players understood exactly what was going on, and whenever the husband would begin giving out about any other local men, his wife would give a knowing kick beneath the table to the two card-players sitting either side of her. Honest Seán went too far with this controlling behaviour in the end, however. He and his wife were returning from the fair in Clonmel one day, their cart heavily-laden with bags of corn and big boxes of cinders. The cart was so heavy that the horse could barely move. The day turned out to be very wet and as they made their way up along Bóthar na Coille Seán Mór Breathnach came up to them with his horse and cart. Seán Mór wasn't married yet at this juncture and he was a fine-looking and handsome man. Passing Seán Ó Donncha and his wife, he said that he could give Seán's wife a lift home in his side-car if they wished as she could then be home much more quickly than if she stayed travelling on their horse and cart which was making very slow progress. Seán's wife gratefully accepted this offer of a 'lift' home and off they went. They had barely gone up the road however when Seán unharnessed the horse and parked the cart with all its provisions at the side of the road and raced after the them on his horse. He overtook them near Baile na hAbhann but he didn't look back at them at all. The horse was white-flecked with sweat by then, he had run it so hard. Seán Mór left Ó Donncha's wife at the gate of her house but when she came to the front door, it was locked and the key wasn't in its usual spot – the hole beneath the window where she always left it. Ó Donncha's wife knew then that her husband was already home as his horse was standing outside the stable-door with its bridle still on. She called out her husband's name a good few times over the next few hours but there was no reply and there was no sign of her husband. She had no choice but to spend that night in a neighbour's house. She went back again to see could she get into the house the next day but there was still no reply. She went around the house looking for her husband again and calling out his name but there was still no sign of him. In the stables, she found the horse stretched out on the ground stone-cold dead. She went up to Seán Mór's house and asked him to drive her back to her family's home place in An Leacain, having explained the story to him. The next day two tough-looking brothers of hers arrived down to the Ó Donncha's farmyard looking for Seán. They were armed with big ash cudgels and they found Séan Ó Donncha out in the meadow. Without a word, the two brothers laid into Seán with the ash-plants and they beat him really badly. He was black and blue all over by the time they were finished with him and they warned him that if he ever treated his wife like that again, they would break every bone in his body. They told him to collect his wife from their family's home place a week from that day and that if he didn't show up, they would beat him to within an inch of his life again.

A year later the granduncle of Seán Ó Donncha's wife left sixty acres to her in his will. The couple sold the farm in An Gleann and they went to live on the new farm in An Leacain. They had three children after this and the beating that Seán Ó Donncha received that day sorted out his jealousy problems for good, by all accounts.

THE 'SOUPERS'

It's a long time ago now since there was any mention of the 'Soupers' in this locality. The people long ago had many stories about them, however. I often heard the 'Soupers' mentioned up in Dic Ó Siadhaile's house and what people once had to do to become members of this religious group. From what I remember now, however, people's memories of the 'Soupers' were already fading even when I was a child and you couldn't be sure of the accuracy of many of their stories about the 'Soupers' or their activities in this area. It was said at one time that you had to spit on a picture of the Virgin Mary to become a member of the 'Soupers' and that you weren't allowed to raise your hat when passing a church or a graveyard if you became one of them. I think that many of these stories were probably just hearsay and myth, however. I remember two families living in An Gleann who were associated with the 'Soup' and anytime there was an argument between the neighbours and either of these two families the 'Souper' jibe would always be directed at them at some stage. A member of one of these families was a fine, handsome and prosperous man with a good farm of land and yet he couldn't get any woman to marry him from any of the three local parishes. He had to travel to some place more than twenty miles away to find a spouse and two of his sisters had to emigrate to America because no-one at home would marry them. And the only stain that was on their name was the fact that the 'Soup' was associated with their ancestors. All of these issues are forgotten about now today and even the old people would never mention something like this anymore. Strange as it may seem, anyone who was interested in reading or writing Irish long ago was sometimes suspected of having been interested in 'Souperism'. Apparently, some schoolmasters who were members of the Church of England learned Irish around the time of the Famine in an effort to convert people to the Protestant religion up around the west of Ireland when the people were dying with the hunger. One of these schoolmasters was named Cramp. Langley had brought him to Baile na hAbhann to teach his children privately on his estate as they belonged to the Church of England. Cramp had a good knowledge of the Irish language and An Gealt ('The Crazy One') often asked him suspiciously why it was that he had learned Irish in the first place. The reason An Gealt was suspicious of him was that he'd heard some of the 'Soupers' had learned Irish in years gone by in an effort to convert the Irish country people, especially in the poorer parts of the west of Ireland. At that time, anyone who could read or write Irish was regarded with suspicion. There was only one man living in An Gleann who could read and write Irish when I was young and even he was the object of suspicion, on occasion. I remember this man well. Pádraig Ó Domhnaill was his name and he was elderly enough when I got to know him. A nicer and more decent man you couldn't meet. He wore a long white beard which reminded me of a picture of Saint Joseph that was in the church in Baile na hAbhann. I heard Risteard Ó Siadhaile say on more than one occasion that the rumours that Pádraig had ever had anything to do with the 'Soupers' was just a load of ignorant and bad-minded gossip that certain people who liked spreading stories about others had spread about him. There wasn't a dishonest bone in Pádraig Ó Domhnaill's body, he said. Pádraig Ó Domhnaill was very interested in history and everything to do with the Irish past. He used to say that the O'Néills and the O'Donnells had first settled in Gleann Chárthainn when the area was nothing but a huge uncultivated area of scrubland and that they were soldiers from the north who had escaped the rout at Kinsale and who had never returned back up North again. I heard that he had a box full of books and Irish-language manuscripts in his house; they'd probably be very valuable if we still had them today but, when he died, his wife burned every book and manuscript that he had left behind apparently. There used to be a copy of *Cúirt an Mhean-Oíche* in the Burke's house in Móin Buí and it had Pádraig Ó Domhnaill's name written on the inside cover of it. I'd say that he had written out his own version of the Irish-language text for sean-Shéamus de Búrc, Tomás' father, who was able to read Irish. I still have this 'manuscript' here in Lios na Faille today. Tomás gave it to me years ago, God's mercy be upon him and on Pádraig Ó Domhnaill.

Méin Bhillí, Pádraig Ó Domhnaill's wife, was a very overweight woman who wouldn't have understood the importance of those manuscripts. It is hard to fault her for what she did when she burned all the books and manuscripts. Maybe she thought that they had something to do with the 'Soupers'.

I often heard tell of a couple of people who 'turned their coats' and converted to Protestantism in times past. Long ago, a man named Greagóir Ó Duinnshléibhe ran a school for a few years at Crosaire an tSean-Phóna. This man had only one arm; his other arm had been amputated from him at the elbow. My grandfather and a good number of his generation attended that school at one time. I remember my grandfather telling me how

Greagóir used to cut and shape his writing-quills from goose-feathers long ago. He would hold the quill in under the stump of his left hand and he could then shape the pen without any difficulty using his other hand. The students used to call this a 'gliugaraí' in Irish. When the National School was set up in Baile na hAbhann, it was said that he went on his knees before the parish priest and begged him to give him a job as an assistant or monitor in this new school. He had a large family and couldn't do any other form of work other than teaching, given his disability. His family would be reduced to beggars if he didn't get his job. The priest refused to give him any job in the new school, however – apparently, on account of him having only one hand. This, despite the fact that he was better-educated than either of the two people who were subsequently appointed to the school. Greagóir and his wife converted to Protestantism and they attended Langley's church up in the 'Great House' from then onwards. The Protestant minister would visit his flock there nearly every Sunday afternoon, and any Sunday that he couldn't make it Langley himself conducted the service. Greagóir's wife hated the priests and Catholicism from then on and even if she didn't have any meat for the rest of the week, she always made sure to have a nice piece of meat roasting over the fire on Fridays and the smell wafting all around the Crosaire, in order to annoy her Catholic neighbours. Langley gave Greagóir Ó Duinnshléibhe a job working as a land surveyor. He would go out surveying the land using a long chain, another man helping him with the measurements. He surveyed every field and farm on Langley's estate and mapped it out in its entirety. As the Ó Duinnshléibhe family grew older Langley got work for the children. A good many people in the area sympathised with Ó Duinnshléibhe's position as he they felt that he had lost his livelihood and it was only right that the priest should have helped him by giving him a job in the school.

Others were opposed to Ó Duinnshléibhe and said it came as no surprise to them that he had changed 'sides'. Wasn't he descended from Máire Ní Dhuinnshléibhe who had allegedly given evidence against Father Nicholas Sheehy[2] whom the British wrongfully hanged in Clonmel more than one hundred years ago.

The neighbours used to say that Greagóir asked to see the priest when he was dying but that his wife wouldn't let him. The two eldest of his children converted back to Catholicism again in later years. I heard my grandfather saying that Greagóir's wife was herself calling for the priest when she was on her deathbed but that she actually dismissed the Protestant minister who came to see her. Her wish to see a priest wasn't acceded to, however. I probably wouldn't remember these stories about Greagóir Ó Duinnshléibhe and others at all now only than I often heard them repeated in later years both by my mother and my aunt Máire. No-one related to Greagóir Ó Duinnshléibhe or his family has lived in Baile na hAbhann for years. None of their children returned to their native place to live, after their parents died. Peaid na Brídí used often say that he couldn't understand why anyone would join the 'Soupers' or what could you get out of it. He used to say that he'd join up himself straight away if there was money to be got for joining – that's if they were stupid enough to give him some money. Honest Peaid was the type who made a joke and a bit of fun out of everything however, and no-one really believed that he was serious when he said he'd join up with the 'Soupers'. One day, he was at the market selling fattened pigs in the company of Seán Mór and Micil Ó Néill. After he'd had quite a bit to drink, Peaid called up to the local Protestant minister's house. The minister was known as an honest and decent man; his name was 'Parson Palmer'.

He knocked on the door and the minister appeared.

'What can I do for you my good man?' he said to Peaid.

'I'd like to join the Soupers', said Peaid.

'Who told you to come here?' the minister asked.

'They say', said Peaid, 'that you give money to anyone who converts to your religion so I'd convert to whatever you want if you gave me enough money to do so'.

'Off with you now, you rascal. Judging by the smell from your breath, "soup" wouldn't be your favourite drink anyway'.

I often heard Peaid repeat this story; he used to get a great kick out of it. I can't remember when I first heard people in An Gleann here talking about the 'Soupers'. That part of the past is over now, and no-one mentions them anymore.

SEÁN MÓR BREATHNACH

Seán Mór Breathnach is mentioned a good number of times in my story here. He was the most prosperous farmer in Gleann Chárthainn when I was young and owned about one hundred acres of land, with the river running parallel to his fields. His house was on the side of Bóithrín na Cille; Today, it is one of those ugly monstrosities or ruins that you see here and there out the country, but back when I was young, this was a fine well-furnished house with ivy climbing its walls, ivy that was kept neatly trimmed at all times. The house is still standing today but it is only used as a barn now. About twenty years ago, the owner of the house – another man by the name of Seán Breathnach, as it happens – built a new house for himself. He removed the walls from around the old house and built a new barn out of them; it is probably the biggest barn in the area now.

It has a huge set of double-doors and an arch and it is so big that you could bring in great quantities of grain into it for storage. The ivy was all removed from the walls of the old house and it is a big ugly ruin now really. The Breathnaigh from Bóithrín na Cille were always well-off; they were prosperous even long ago, when many others were still struggling and poor. That said, they were always very generous people down through the generations and there was never anything miserly about them. I often heard that Seán Mór's grandfather spent large amounts of money buying food for people during the Famine and dividing it out amongst them also. Seán Mór was always very generous to his workers also. He had two other men working for him in addition to Micil Ó Néill and Liam Beilbhí and their fathers and grandfathers had worked in that house also. Whatever he had to eat, they had the same, and he always sat with his workmen when they were having dinner. He'd also give all of his workers a nice Christmas present every year and he always had big rain-coats hanging from a hook in the barn for any of his workmen who had to go outside when it was raining. He treated his workers much better than most other big farmers did in those days. Signs on it; anyone who went to work for the Breathnaigh stayed with them for life.

I remember Seán Mór as a big, powerful man, a man who was quite self-important. He was always very serious about everything and had little time for frivolity or jokes. I don't think I ever saw him really laughing, not even once. He might give a cold sort of smirk or half-laugh sometimes but that was it. People said that he hadn't always been this serious or dour however, and that life had changed him. It was his wife's death just two years after they were married that changed him. She died while giving birth to Eilís, their only daughter and he was never the same man afterwards. For years after this, he just worked from dawn till dusk. It was as if he was trying to forget the tragedy that had befallen him. He certainly wasn't a workaholic because he was short of money anyway – because he was quite well-off. Although he was a young man when his wife died, he would never have dreamed of getting married again and anyone who mentioned this possibility to him, either in jest or in all seriousness, always got short shrift from him. No doubt, his wife had been his one and only true love. Every Sunday without fail, he went to visit his wife's grave and he'd spend a while there in prayer. I suppose his workaholic ways got a grip on him because his sole topic of conversation with other men after a while related to livestock and crops and farm prices generally. He rarely talked about anything else. Although a thrifty and far-seeing man in many ways, Seán Mór was also quite naive in ways. He was very credulous of others and found it very difficult to believe that others could be dishonest or could tell lies.

Micil Ó Néill often said that Seán had been full of fun and a much happier person before his wife's death. Because I never saw Seán when his personality was like this, I found it hard to imagine him in this way. One night Micil Ó Néill told this story up in Ó Siadhaile's house by way of explanation for how his wife's death had changed Seán Mór to such an extent as compared to when he was a younger man. Seán Mór and Micil were in Cloichín one day selling two loads of fattened pigs, about a year before Sean Mór died. They had sold the pigs and were stabling the horses in the Browne's forge. Micil was pacing up and down the shed as he normally did; he was a powerful and athletic man when he was young, a man who could rarely sit still for too long. The man who'd just bought the pigs was sitting on a timber block next to the wall. The buyer was counting out the money and getting it ready for Seán Mór when he noticed Micil.

'That's a powerfully strong young lad you have working for you there', he said in English to Seán.

'You can say that again', said Seán.

'Do you see that gate there?' Seán said. 'He'd jump that no bother'.

This big wooden gate led out into the street and it was about eight feet high.

'Rubbish', said the buyer. 'No-one in the world could jump that gate'.

'I'll bet you the price of these pigs that he'll jump it', said Seán. 'He hasn't a word of English though, so I'll just tell him what's happening'. Seán Mór knew well of course that the buyer of the pigs had no Irish. Micil understood immediately what sort of a 'game' Seán Mór was playing and he began to play the part, throwing off his shoes and stripping down his vest and stretching as if to get ready for the jump. The buyer got 'cold feet' and wouldn't put down the money for the bet despite Seán Mór's best efforts to egg him on; Seán Mór had already placed his money on the timber block as if ready to bet. It was no use, however. When the buyer saw Micil's warm-up antics he got scared that he would lose his money. Next thing Seán told the buyer that he would ask Micil to do the jump anyway – just to prove that he could do it. But Micil was the one now who 'refused'. He said to Seán Mór that he wouldn't do the jump unless he saw the bet-money laid on the timber block. When there was no sign of the money, Micil put on his jacket and boots again.

Here are one or two anecdotes which demonstrate how naive Seán Mór could also be at times, however. He was in the forge one day and he had a terrible toothache. Micil Dhuinn, the blacksmith told Seán to tie a piece of string around the tooth and to attach the other end of it to the door-latch and that this would help make ease the pain. When Micil Ó Néill came in from work that evening – who did he see but Seán Mór sitting next to the fire, a string stretching from his mouth over to the door-latch? 'In God's name', said Micil to him, 'have you lost your marbles completely?' Seán Mór explained to him about the cure that the blacksmith had given him. He said that it was a good cure also as his toothache was already fading. Micil laughed so much that evening that he could barely eat his dinner. Even when Micil told the story again in Ó Siadhaile's house, many years later, he couldn't stop laughing.

They used to hold dances at Crosaire na Cille at one time in summer. The dances were held on Sunday afternoons. Seán Mór's land bordered the road where the dances were held and it was where his milk cows were always grazing. One year, it happened that five or six of his cows had stillborn calves and, naturally, Seán Mór was worried about what had caused this. He was discussing this with three or four other men one Sunday morning as they were waiting for Mass to start. Tomás Brídí, who was always clowning and joking was amongst the men gathered there.

'It's easy to work out what's causing these deaths', said Tomás winking covertly at the others.

'And what is it?' said Seán Mór in a gruff voice.

'The music, what else?' said Tomás. 'Anyone could figure that out. I've heard people saying this a thousand times'. Everyone else there agreed with Tomás and they managed to convince Seán Mór that the music really was the problem. Seán Mór got really stressed about this and he even went to the local priest to try and get the dances stopped there a few days later. The priest told him that what he was saying was ridiculous, but Seán Mór wasn't sure. From then on, whenever the dances were held, he would move the milk-cows to another field.

DANCES AND LOVE

Liam Beiglí was a dancing master. He used to teach dancing in this area when I was a teenager. From Cork, originally, he was fluent in both Irish and English and he spoke with a strong Cork accent. I remember him well; he was a sturdy and powerfully-built man who wasn't overly-tall. He was always clean-shaven, his mop of black curly head of hair flecked with grey. He always wore short pants that stretched just to his knees and although he was a heavy enough man, he was very light and graceful on his feet. He used to come around our area in the years after I'd finished with school, I remember. He would teach dancing down in the Burke's barn in Móin Buí two nights a week and he was in Baile na hAbhann for another two nights. I can't remember now where he'd have his classes on the other nights. They used to carry the big dancing platform or board that they had down at Crosaire na Cille during the summer into the barn during the winter for Beiglí so that he could teach dancing there. Cruthúirín Píobaire played music for him and he had a violin himself that he could play while dancing at the same time. Not only could he play music and dance simultaneously, but he could also call out the instructions to the dancers without skipping a beat. Whenever he taught dancing in Baile na hAbhann, he was the sole musician who accompanied the dancers. I think that out of 'God's love and kindness' that he'd have

Cruthúirín with him when he was teaching in An Gleann; he'd pay Cruthúirín a crown a week for his troubles. When he was ready for some dance-music, Liam would call out 'Music Cruthúirín'. Ever since, 'Music Cruthúirín' is a common phrase as used by the people of An Gleann.

Everyone had to pay three pence a night to learn dancing and there would be upwards of thirty boys and girls there. Whatever money Beiglí made from his lessons, he spent it as quickly again however, on drinking and having fun. In the end, he had problems with his legs and he couldn't teach the classes anymore. He left this area then and people seemed to think that he returned to his native Cork. No-one knows what happened to him after this.

I was about eighteen years of age when I first went to the dancing lessons in Burke's barn. Seán Mac Craith was the one who encouraged me to go and he came with me to the first night of classes. Seán was very interested in Irish dance and music and he encouraged me strongly to learn how to dance, just as he encouraged me to learn Irish. Seán himself was a fine dancer; I'd say he was as good as Beiglí when it came to dancing a double-jig or a hornpipe. I remember one night when the dancing lesson was over Liam Beiglí and Seán Mac Craith danced 'An Londubh' (The Blackbird) for nearly half-an-hour, each movement completely new and original, and without repeating even one pattern or arrangement for the duration. I remember Beiglí shaking hands with Seán at the end of it and saying that his was the best piece of dancing he'd ever seen. Liam Beiglí hadn't a trace of jealousy or begrudgery in him, the poor man. Tomás from Mónach Buí had four children, Séamus, the eldest lad, then Sibéal, Máire and Tomás, the youngest of them. Séamus was around the same age as me and while he and I and Tomás were friendly with one another the way schoolboys of that age are, I was never in their house or in their yard until that day when I began the dancing lessons. Our family, the Burkes of Lios na Faille and the Burkes of Mónach Buí didn't have any interactions with one another and this was something I was aware of from an early age. It would be many years before I learned what had caused the initial antagonism between our two families. We will come to this later in the story. Young schoolboys didn't have many dealings or didn't socialize much with girls their own age back then, partly because girls would have had no interest in the games that young lads played then. The girls had no interest in horsing around, or playing football or hurling. They had their own games but young lads of that age often thought such games effeminate or childish. Coming home from school in those days, you never saw the boys walking alongside the girls. The boys kept to themselves and it was the same for the girls. I'm not sure whether it was like this in all other schools at this juncture but it was certainly like this in Baile an Droichid school. For this reason and although Sibéal de Búrc had already been attending school for a few years before me, I never had any particular interest in her. Sure, I'd see her on the road walking to and from school, but that was about it. I'd say I barely spoke twenty words to her in all the years we were in school together.

It was at those dances in her father's barn that I first got to know Sibéal. She and her sister and her two brothers also went to the dancing classes regularly. And if it hadn't been for Seán Mac Craith, I probably would never have gone to the dances at all, because he kept badgering me to go in the beginning. I wasn't a great dancer; I attended the dancing classes for two years in a row before I was able to dance a double-jig and make a reasonable job of dancing a reel. I was never anywhere near as good a dancer as Seán Baróid or Seán Mac Craith was however. Dic Ó Siadhaile never had any interest in dancing.

In addition to the above-mentioned dances and also the group dances such as the four-hand and eight-hand reels, Beiglí also taught us 'sets'. These 'foreign' dances were becoming increasingly popular at the time and the boys and girls were mad keen to learn them. A few years later and these were the main dances that people did at the Sunday dances and at weddings and on other similar occasions. Only the odd person knew how to dance any these 'sets' perfectly, however.

I still remember well the embarrassment and the shame I felt the first time I ever danced with a girl. Beiglí himself would name each pair and he put me and Sibéal de Búrc together. Sibéal had changed a good deal from how I remembered her when we were at school. She was older and really nice and happy-go-lucky and she did a great job of guiding me through the various steps as I was at that awkward, gangly stage that defines a teenager. I was over six feet tall and she reached up to my shoulder, she was thin and held herself very straight and she was very light on her feet. She had dark-blue eyes and her hair was chestnut-brown and tied up in thick plaits that reached down to her waist. The fashionable hair-style for girls then was the fringe at the front, almost reaching into the eyes; it gave a very bold or sharp look to some girls, especially girls who had a big nose. Sibéal wasn't interested in this fashion, however and she followed an 'older' hairstyle with the plaits. She was right too because she had such a fine head of hair that it would have been a shame to cut it. Sibéal and I danced together regularly after that at the lessons and we gradually overcame some of our shyness towards one another. I was a lot shyer and less-confident than she was then. That's not to say that she was forward or pushy or lacking in femininity in any way. Nothing could have been further from the truth. The winter passed and Beiglí went on his travels again. Anytime I met Sibéal now, I'd have a chat with her, but that was it. Thoughts of love between us or anything like that never entered my mind and I think it was the same for her.

Summer came around and then it was the Feast of Peter and Paul. The weather was beautiful that day. It was a beautiful sunny day, the sky cloudless. I still remember it well; it is as clear to me now as if it was only yesterday. It will always be so, right up until the day that I go into the graveyard. After dinner, I went for a walk across the fields in the direction of Na Faghrach Glaise. In summer there was only a trickle of water in the Falls but whenever we had a few days of heavy rain, the water would crash down with incredible power. The Falls is deep enough although the dip down into it at the sides is not so steep. I can't remember what brought me over to this area, on that particular day because I didn't often go for a wander over in that direction. I did like to go off for a walk alright, especially when I was thinking quietly about something or other. When I needed to think quietly about something or other, I'd often just go wherever my legs would carry me. I was walking along the edge of the falls just a few feet in from the water and humming a song to myself. Next thing, I heard a woman's voice calling out my name. 'Hey! Hey! Séamus! Over here!' The voice was coming from about fifty yards away from me, somewhere down near the Falls. I ran up along the side of the Falls and who did I spot but Sibéal de Búrc sitting down below me about fifty yards ahead of me. She was sitting below me next to the stream. One of her shoes was off. 'In God's name, Sibéal', I said, 'what happened to you?' and I ran down to her. I could tell that she was in some pain by the pale and drawn-out look on her face, albeit that she was trying to pretend that she wasn't too bad.

'I was crossing the Falls and I ran down with the slope here but I stood on a stone and twisted my ankle. I think I've hurt it badly. I've been here for about a half-an-hour and I was trying to work out what to do. I was planning to drag myself up along the riverbank here when I heard you singing. I can't put my foot fully on the ground at all'. She had taken off her shoe and her ankle was swollen very badly so that her stocking was stuck tightly to her foot.

'What'll I do? Should I run over to the house to get help?' I asked.

'No. there's no point in going over', she said, 'because my father and the boys and Máire are all gone off to Cappoquin to the 'Regatta' so there's only my mother at home right now and there's no point calling her'.

'What'll we do so?' I said.

'You're plenty strong and I'm not that heavy'. She gave a little laugh through the pain as she noticed my face reddening with embarrassment. 'And, the house is only two fields away from here. There's nothing else that can be done – other than leave me here for the night! Here, put that shoe into the pocket of your jacket'.

I pulled her to her feet and with my hand around her waist; I lifted her up off the ground. She put her arms around my neck and we began walking across the fields. I felt a pang of longing go through me as I smelled her beautiful hair so close to my face. She was as light as a feather and although she talked to me all the while, I can't remember anything that she said to me or what kind of replies I gave her that day. It didn't take me long to carry her across the two fields but I would have been quite happy to have carried her for another mile or more. Her mother got a fright when she saw us coming into the yard. 'In God and Mary's name, Sibéal', she said. 'What happened to you?' Sibéal told her what had happened from beginning till end. Her mother had to cut her stocking off her with a scissors. Her foot was hugely swollen and her mother thought she might have dislocated something. This was my first time ever inside Burke's house and the woman of the house was very nice to me. She kept insisting that I stay for another while and to have some tea but I said that I couldn't. Sibéal thanked me for helping her and half-jokingly, she said to me not to leave it too long before I called in to see her again. Although she was doing her best to smile, I could tell that she was in a lot of pain. I said goodbye to them and headed for. On my way home that day, I was on a high. I couldn't get Sibéal out of my mind. I saw her beautiful face in front of mine and smelt the sweet scent of her hair again. I relived carrying her across the fields all over again in my mind, every step of the way from the Faghair Ghlas to her house. Previous to this, I had understood nothing at all about love; even in that moment, I was unable to explain the strange mix of emotions that had come over me. I felt as if the world around me was enchanted, as if this day was the nicest summer's day I'd ever seen. Everything about me appeared new and exciting the world was fresher and more pristine than ever. The bushes – even if they were dry and desiccated – looked more beautiful than ever to me in those moments; it was as if their true beauty was now revealing itself to me for the very first time. The cuckoo that was calling from down below in An Gleann; it too was beautiful even if its voice was fading and becoming more faint – as was normal for that time of year. As I got closer to our house and spotted the swallows flitting to and fro high in the sky, I felt so transformed inside that I was sure my aunt Máire or my mother would notice something different about me. If they did, they certainly didn't let on anything, however.

The following afternoon I met Séamas who told me that their father had brought Sibéal southwards to the bone-setter in Cappoquin. Her ankle-joint was dislocated; he had re-set it and bandaged it up. She had to soak her foot in fresh water for the next couple of days to try and get the swelling down; she wouldn't be able to walk on it again for a full three weeks. I didn't go to visit Sibéal for the next three weeks I really wanted to go but I was too shy and I thought that if I did go, everyone would know and my secret would be out. It was a month later before Sibéal was up and walking again. The next time I met her was out near Droichead na Cille and she was hobbling along with the aid of a walking stick. I came across her unexpectedly on the corner of the bridge and I was so surprised that I couldn't get a word out for the first few minutes. I felt my cheeks burning with embarrassment. She was a bit embarrassed too but she was very chatty and full of life. 'I'm mad with you, Séamus', she said 'you didn't come to see me at all, especially after you promised me you would. I suppose you probably forgot all about me'. I can't remember what excuse I came up with for not calling in to see her. She did most of the chatting, I remember. We were talking about this and that at the gate of her house for a while; she wanted me to go into the house with her and to join them for the tea but I was too shy and wouldn't have done that even if you had given me all of Déamar's gold. I understood now that I was in love with her; I didn't think that she fancied me, however, no more than she liked any other boy in the locality. This thought got me down; this time, instead of the world seeming bright and new as on the day I'd carried Sibéal home from the Falls, everything around me was dark. Now, in this moment, the rest of my life looked like as if was filled with nothing but worry and strife. We ran into each other every now and then after this, but we didn't make any arrangement to meet up or to go for a date. Sibéal was always very friendly to me whenever we happened to meet one another and I sometimes thought that maybe she'd like to spend more time in my company. Then, at other times, I would say to myself that I was only imagining this. I was always very careful not to let anything slip when I was chatting to her, however, anything that would indicate to her how much I was in love with her. The Burkes of Mónach Buí had their own seat in the church on Sundays, up on the knave. My family had their seat in the loft directly across from the Burkes on the opposite loft. When I got older, I rarely went up into the loft; instead, I sat in the main part of the church below in the company of my friends. Now that Sibéal de Búrc was up there every Sunday, I began to go up into the loft opposite with my aunt and my mother again, however. I just wanted to sneak a look at Sibéal across from me every now and then. On the occasional Sunday that she wasn't there and I missed her, I would feel depressed for the rest of the day.

I often spent an hour or more sitting out on the fence opposite our front gate staring down in the direction of the Burke's house. Rather than watch the young Burkes out playing as I had done so often as a child, I was now looking down at their house with different thoughts and dreams going through my mind. The summer slipped past that year and autumn came around. Then it was winter and Liam Beiglí came around and the dances in Burke's barn started over again. I went to the dance classes again; I probably wouldn't have bothered with the classes except that I knew Seán Mac Craith would have been upset with me if I hadn't gone. I would have been quite happy just to have gone up there and looked on at the others dancing. As usual, Sibéal was always very friendly and polite with me but then she was like that with all the boys – so I didn't take much solace from this. Rather than trying to impress her more or to spend more time in her company, I felt as if I was actually getting shyer in her company and retreating into myself. That year, I withdrew into myself more than before; I hadn't the same interest in sport or having the crack anymore – or even in hanging around with my two pals Dic Ó Siadhaile and Seán Baróid. I preferred walking alone out in the fields or on the mountain. The two lads noticed this change in me and they used to ask me what was bothering me. I never let on anything to them, however. Instead, I'd put them off by saying that I must finally be getting sense – or something to that effect. That year passed and the New Year came around.

Ned Dhomhnaill's Marriage

That Advent Ned Dhomhnaill got married, an event which generated mixed feelings in me, given the secret love I still harboured for Sibéal. Ned Dhomhnaill's real name was Éamonn Ó Londragáin; none of us here in An Gleann ever called him by his official name. The old people used to say that all of the Ó Londragáin's had always had their own nicknames. instead of their real names. The Ó Londragáin's had a fine farm of land on the southern side of Móin Buí. They were very enterprising people who worked long hours. There was nothing miserly about any of them and – signs on it – everyone in An Gleann got an invitation to the wedding. I was at many weddings down through the years but I'd say Ned Dhomhnaill's was the best of the lot. Then again, maybe I am a bit biased in this regard, and you may understand why in a moment. Ned married one of the Powers from near Baile na hAbhann. His new wife was a fine and beautiful-looking woman. Ned himself was always a fine figure of a man, this despite the fact that he never had much interest in sport or in challenge-games like weight-throwing and the like. Today, weddings are over before you know it. Ned Dhomhnaill and Nell Paor get married in Baile na hAbhann at about three o'clock in the afternoon. They had a coach or 'covered car' from Clonmel and this transported the newly-wed couple and the people who stood with them (i.e. the groomsmen and the bridesmaids); this was the first time the like of this was ever seen in An Gleann. There were two 'side-cars' in the cavalcade, one for Seán Mór Breathnach and his daughter and the other for the bride's family. Everyone else travelled by horse-and-cart and about 12 people travelled to the wedding on their own horses. Myself, my aunt Máire and Seán Mac Craith were at the wedding and we went there by horse and cart. My aunt sat in the middle of the cart on a bag of straw and myself and Seán sat up-front with Seán in charge of the horse. I remember that there were a group of 'bacach's' (beggars) and tinkers gathered at the door of the church and when Ned came out, he threw a fistful of change up into the air amongst them as 'grub'. There was a mad scramble amongst them all to get the money then and they nearly started belting each other at one stage. They probably would have started fighting if it hadn't been that there were two 'peelers' present.

When they left the church, the wedding party raced their horses as fast as they could go until they reached Baile an Droichid. They had to slow down as they climbed the hill at Bearna an Mhadra (The Dog's Gap) but they picked up speed again once they came out onto the level road again and off to Móin Buí. As they passed Droichead na Cille, the riders broke away from the main party and leaped the ditch to race across An Réidh Dhóite galloping on towards the house, everyone shouting and whooping. Two or three people fell off their horses at the ditch. Micil Ó Néill was on a horse belonging to Seán Mór and he and his horse fell into a ditch that was full of water. He was soaking wet and covered with mud and Domhnaill Ned's father had to give him a loan of an old suit of clothes for the rest of the day. The farmyard of the house was like Aonach Bhearna Gaoithe (Windgap Fair), the yard and the barn was so crowded with horses and carts. Everyone unharnessed their own horse, tied it to their cart and fed it some hay from the haystack there. There wasn't enough room there to stable all the horses.

The first thing everyone did then was to sit down for the meal. Seven or eight local women and girls had been preparing the food since early-morning. There was nothing exotic or strange about the food. Huge platters of meat and potatoes were placed in the centre of each table for the guests. There were four types of meat for everyone – beef, lamb, bacon, and roast goose. Three big kitchen tables had been placed lengthwise out in the barn and there was also another table inside in the kitchen of the house prepared for the guests. Even with all of these, there wasn't enough room for everyone, the crowd was so big. Some people had to wait for the second serving of food. Everyone was in great form and cracking jokes and telling stories as they ate, and most of the men were 'maith go leor' (well on). They had gone drinking in Baile na hAbhann while they were waiting for the priest to arrive. When everyone was fed and happy, the barn was readied for dancing. Two of the tables were removed from the barn and the other one was put up in one corner of the barn and three chairs placed on top of it. Cruthúirín Píobaire (Cruthúirín the Piper) and two fiddle players sat on the chairs and other chairs were placed all around against the inside walls of the barn. The fiddle-players started tuning up with Cruthúirín the Piper and when they were ready, they began to play. Out onto the floor came all of the dancers. There were three barrels of porter there and Sibéal's father, Tomás de Búrc and Seán Mac Craith were in charge of divvying out the porter equally to everyone assembled there. They brought the porter into the barn in buckets and they divided it out using tin punts. Most of the older people stayed inside in the kitchen of the house and drank a drop of the 'hard stuff' while sitting around the fire telling jokes and doing their own thing. About midnight, tea was prepared in a neighbouring house for anyone who wanted it. Only a few of the women and the odd man who didn't drink alcohol went in to drink the tea, however. Most of the others preferred drinking the porter and stayed where they were out in the barn, When we came back out into the yard, there were about twenty people gathered around the door between beggars and straw-men; the latter were 'dressed-up' in old clothes and masks and some of them even had false beards on. I recognized Peaid na Brídí amongst them. He was wearing a long beard that was made from roan-coloured horsehair and a hat that had been formed from an old hard hat, the rim of which had been clipped off. The hat also had two goat's horns set into the either side of it, both of which were painted bright-red. He was the spit of the 'old boy' (the devil). He also had two small bells attached to the heels of his shoes and they rang out every time he moved. This wasn't the first time or the last either that Peaid na Brídí took on the role of a 'straw-boy'. A few buckets of porter and plenty of food was sent out to them and by dawn, the younger of the 'straw-boys' had jettisoned their 'funny clothes' and masks and had joined in the dancing inside in the barn. It wasn't long into the night when Cruthúirín fell off his chair and he was lucky that someone nearby caught him before he fell down off the table and onto the floor. Whatever he had drunk had gone straight to his head and he must have got totally dizzy. They brought him into the potato shed and lay him down on a bed of straw, and put a blanket over him. He stayed there asleep for the rest of the night and for most of the next day. Peaid na Brídí took up the pipes and began playing for the dancers. Although he removed his red beard, he was still the funniest sight ever with the funny hat and the horns on it bobbing crazily up and down as he danced and played. They danced 'sets' for most of the night. Two or three sets were danced consecutively before Peaid na Brídí nearly blew the roof off the barn when he whooped and danced

'An Staicín Eorna' up on the table, his horned hat flying up and down and the bells jangling madly on his feet. Anytime they took a break from the dancing, they sang songs as the drink was divided out amongst the assembled people. Although my aunt Máire was a good dancer, she only danced for a while at the beginning of the night. After that she was helping those who were making the tea and calling the girls in from the barn to help out.

Dic Ó Siadhaile was kept busy all night also bringing in turf and water and looking after the lamps that were hanging from the walls of the barn. Seán Mac Craith and Tomás na Mónach Buí went around with a plate collecting money for the musicians about halfway through the night. They collected a good bit of money because nearly everyone there threw a sixpence onto the plate. I was in the kitchen drinking tea alongside Sibéal de Búrc and about four or five other boys and girls when the men came in collecting the money. Seán Mór was sitting behind me right in front of the hearth and I saw him throw two half-crowns on the plate. He had to be seen to give more money than everyone else, of course. To be fair to him, however, Seán Mór was always extremely generous, a man with a big heart. It was just as well that Seán Mór had stayed in the kitchen because if he'd come out to the shed, his daughter and Seán Baróid wouldn't have been as relaxed as they were. They spent the whole evening in each other's company and it looked as if they didn't care if others knew that they were fond of one another. It's just as well too, that the God of Glory ensures that we are always unaware of what lies ahead of us on this earth because Eilís Bhreathnach and Seán Baróid wouldn't have enjoyed that night one bit if they knew the tragedy that fate had in store for both of them only a few short years later. I heard later that Seán Mac Craith and Tomás de Búrc wanted to give a good bit of the money that they collected to Peaid na Brídí but he wouldn't take a penny of it. He deserved it, in fairness, because he played the pipes for most of the night. Peaid na Brídí wouldn't accept any of this money, however. He said to give it all to Cruthúirín as he needed it more than he did. Poor Peaid would never have accepted any money for this, even if he hadn't a red penny in his pocket himself. And now I'll mention Sibéal and I. We danced together most of the night. I didn't dance with anyone else except her and whenever she danced with anyone else, I just stood next to the wall and looked on. A few of the other boys noticed this and teased me about it but I didn't care. Something had changed that night and I felt sure that Sibéal was fond of me after all. It was the first time I'd become convinced of this and it made me really happy inside. When it was about four o'clock in the morning, the 'sets' finished up and Sibéal asked me if I would walk her as far as the gate of her house because she wanted to go home. I said that I would gladly walk her home but asked her why she wanted to leave so early. 'It's a secret', she replied, laughing quietly, 'a secret that I might let you in on some day, maybe'. She got her mantle and we escaped out and down the boreen as far as the main road. The moon was bright and the sky was as clear as day. The night had the look of frost about it. We walked along side one another, step for step, for about 200 yards or so, before either of us spoke. 'You're very quiet?' Sibéal said.

'Well I don't have anything to say, really?' I replied.

'Is there nothing that you'd like to say to me?' Sibéal asked. I didn't respond at all. I knew deep in my heart what I wanted to say to her but I wasn't brave enough to say it straight out. Sibéal stopped still on the road and stared directly into my eyes. 'Séamus', she said. 'You're still just a child. You're in love with me but you don't have the courage to say it to me. Aren't I right?'

The way that Sibéal spoke to me gave me more confidence in myself but I didn't find it easy by any means to put words on what I was thinking.

'You're right Sibéal', I said. 'Since that day when you hurt your foot on the riverbank, I haven't been able to get you out of my mind, day or night. I didn't say anything about this before because I wasn't sure whether you fancied me more than any other boy'.

'Séamus, love', she said, putting her arm around my shoulders, her eyes to the ground. 'Would you be surprised if I told you that it was the same story for me? I've been thinking of you also – day and night'.

She leaned her head on my chest as she said these words and I pulled her closer to me. I smelled the sweet scent of her hair all over again. I didn't say another word. I couldn't, I was too overcome with emotion and my eyes filled up with tears. When she looked up at me in the dark, I saw in the moonlight that her eyes too were tearful. We walked along side-by-side, my hand around her waist. There was music in my heart but we didn't speak another word until we reached the gate of her house. 'You don't need to come any further, love', she said. 'Go on back to the dance now if you like'. 'How could I go back to the dance now?' I asked. 'My heart is leaping with happiness and my mind is in a daze as a result. What does the future hold for us Sibéal? You know as well as I do that neither of our families will be happy about us going out together'.

'You have my word and my hand in relation to this', she said, almost in a whisper. 'You're the only one I'll ever have, and if you agree with me on this, I don't care what either of our families does'.

Hearing these words from my love made my heart jump with joy and I felt my courage return. 'Sibéal, my love', I said, 'I give you my word, here and now in the presence of God, that the only one I'll ever have is you'. This was how we promised ourselves to one another, standing there at the gate, in the early-dawn and by the light of the moon. 'I have to be off now, love' Sibéal said and she put her arms around my neck and pulled my face down to kiss me on the mouth; then she ran through the gate and up the boreen to her house. In all the years that have passed between then and now, I never once passed through that gate again; neither did I recollect in detail every aspect of that magical moonlight morning long ago – not until I came to write this account here now. My mind was racing and confused on the walk home that night. I was a bundle of emotions, a strange mixture of joy and anxiety. What would happen with me and Sibéal? What would likely happen to us when people found out about us? I walked home at a steady pace, praying to God all the while that He wouldn't let me and Sibéal be parted from one another. I was just going through the front gate when my aunt and Seán Mac Craith arrived out with the horse. 'Where did you go?' Seán said. I was looking for you no-one knew what time you left the dance. Why'd you leave the dance so early? That party will go on till morning. 'I was tired of it', I said, 'so I decided to hit out for home'. My Aunt Máire didn't say 'yay' or 'nay' but just stood and stared at me quietly. It occurred to me then that she knew my secret, somehow. She was a very astute and perceptive individual and there was very little that ever escaped her attention. I sensed that there might be trouble ahead for me. I was never a confrontational individual; in fact, I went out of my way to avoid confrontation or trouble. Now that Sibéal had pledged her loyalty to me, however, I didn't care anymore. It was her and her alone that mattered now. The following day after dinner, Seán Mac Craith was gone outside and I was sitting hunched over next to the hearth in the kitchen. I was tired after the previous night and its magic was still singing in my ears. My mother and my aunt Máire were busy moving around the kitchen as they worked on various household tasks. There wasn't a word out of my aunt which I found very disconcerting. I sensed that she was about to say something but I resolved to hold my ground. The sooner the 'issue' was dealt with, the better, I felt. Eventually, my aunt came over and stood next to me and spoke: 'Séamus' she said, 'there was only one girl out at the wedding yesterday that you could have been making a fool of yourself over and that was the daughter of Tomás from Mónach Buí'. I was stunned at this but the way she spoke about Sibéal made me angry. I got to my feet and looked her straight between the eyes. 'No-one has anything but good things to say about Sibéal de Búrc', I replied gruffly. My aunt stopped still and said nothing for a moment. I think she was so shocked at the way that I'd spoken to her because this was the first time ever that I'd stood up to her like this. 'Maybe so', she said, 'but don't you know well how things are between us and the people of Mónach Buí?' 'I know that neither of us are friendly with one another', I said, 'but I don't understand why that is exactly. As far as I'm concerned, whatever happened belongs in the distant past at this stage and we'd be better off forgetting about it'.

'As long as I'm living here', said my aunt Máire, 'her face lighting up with anger, 'no-one related to Séimín of Mónach Buí will ever set foot inside this house'.

Before I had a chance to respond to this, my mother intervened –

'Well now Máire, sure, the two of them are too young to be even talking about matters like this. God knows what's in store for any of us. Sure, these two might have a completely different outlook on this in three months' time, for all we know'.

'Mam and Auntie', I said. 'I'm telling you out straight; I'm giving you my word now that there'll be no change relating to me and Sibéal and how we think about each other. Her people are probably the same way with her now as you are with me. But if the two families continue to be against us, we'll leave you both at it and think of a way to be together anyway – by moving to another place, probably; rest assured of that'.

My Aunt Máire gave me a very sharp look when I said this, but she said no more. I felt that her respect for me had lessened, particularly after the way I'd spoken to her. That was the end of the discussion and I went outside to do my jobs around the yard. I met Sibéal a few afternoons later and told her what had happened, from beginning to end. The only person in her family who had said anything to her was her brother Séamus apparently and he'd just teased and joked to her about meeting me. By the end of the week, everyone in the village was talking about the fact that Sibéal and I had been friendly with one another at the wedding. All country people need is just a hint of a story like this and it spreads like wildfire. If Sibéal's father and mother heard anything about it, they certainly didn't say anything to her about it. Neither did my aunt refer to this subject ever again.

I decided to find out for myself what had caused the row between the two families in the first place. I asked Seán Mac Craith about it first but he knew very little about it other than that it had had something to do with land originally. I thought of sean-Risteard Ó Siadhaile then; if anyone knew about it, then it had to be him because no-one knew as much about the history of An Gleann and its past than he did. I called down to him the following Sunday. When I went into the house, he was making the head for a wooden (tobacco) pipe – he always made his own pipes for smoking. After chatting about this and that for a while, I asked him my question straight out. He told me that he'd often heard the old people long ago talking about this dispute and that he'd tell me as much as he could remember based on what he'd heard. I'll give my own account first here now because the way sean-Risteard related a story could be very long-winded altogether. On the southern side of the boreen that goes from our house down to the main road, are four fields belonging to the Burkes of Mónach Buí. Two of these fields are situated on either side of An Faghair Ghlas. These two fields had belonged to the O'Néill's long ago and Pilib Ó Néill was the last of that family to live down there. He'd had a house once down on the corner of the boreen. There's no trace of that house anymore although there is a spindle-tree growing in the ditch that edges the road which probably dates back to the era when the house was there. These four fields measure just over 12 acres altogether; An Faighir Ghlas actually divides the farm in two. Pilib Ó Néill and his wife lived there originally; they had a son and a daughter living in America, both of whom were doing well for themselves, by all accounts, and when the mother died, the children sent the passage-money home so that the father could join them over there. My great-grandfather and Sibéal's great-grandfather were living in Lios na Faille and an Mhóin Bhuidhe at that time. They were the children of two brothers. The Burkes were all native to Lios na Faille long ago, including Séimín de Búrc's father, the man who was responsible for the big row that occurred in the first place and who inherited An Mhóin Bhuídhe from his uncle – in this case, his mother's brother. As he was leaving for America, Pilib Ó Néill went to both of the Burkes to see would they buy the land off him and, after some negotiations, the Burkes decided that each of them would buy the two fields that were on their own sides of An Fhaighair Ghlas. Everything was agreed and the relevant documents drawn up and ready for signing; and the money was ready to be handed over. However, when the Burke brother from Lios na Faille went to pay the solicitor the fee for his two fields, he was told that Séimín de Búrc had already been to the office and had bought all four fields the previous day. The Burke man from Lios an Faille returned home in a very angry state and went straight up to Pilib Ó Néill's farm to find out what had happened and to give him a piece of his mind but Ó Néill was already gone. He had left already and no-one ever saw or heard anything about him ever again. He then went over to An Mhóin Bhuí to get his revenge on Séimín. He went into the yard and attacked Séimín with an ash-plant. Séimín subsequently brought him to court for this assault and the Burke man from Lios na Faille got two months in prison. In addition, he had to pay Séimín ten pounds in compensation in addition to any legal fees incurred. From that day onwards, there was a deep enmity between both men and if a cow or a sheep belonging to one man wandered onto the land or ditch of another there would be a court case straight away. The solicitors got plenty of 'hard-earned money' courtesy of both men and the 'bad blood' that was between them. The feud abated a good deal only once the two men died. There were no more fights or court cases. Neither family were friendly with one another afterwards and they just kept their distance and had nothing to do with each other from then on.

Unsurprisingly, the Burkes of Lios na Faille felt particularly bitter about what had happened as they had been particularly hard-done-by and got the worst end of the bargain. Throughout the course of my life, I heard and read many stories about the terrible crimes committed because of disputes over land. It is difficult for us today to understand the depth of feeling and the violent emotions that issues relating to land ignited in people long ago. Land was crucial to the survival of the Irish people then as they had no other form of livelihood. For this reason, having some land was really a life or death issue in many ways and many murders and assaults were consequently committed because of land. And right down until today, some country people are so hungry for land that they'll do any kind of trickery or crookedness to get their hands on it. Compared to some of the very brutal acts that were committed in the name of land, what happened between the two Burke brothers was fairly minor really. The next time Sibéal and I met one another I told her what I had heard about the original cause of the enmity between both our families. 'Séamus', she said. 'Maybe it is God's will that the two of us should meet so that our two families can be brought back together again and that this feud between us can be buried forever'. 'May God allow that this be so', I said, 'but it'll be very difficult still to mollify my aunt Máire. She's still very stubborn about all of this although I don't think that she's bad-minded towards any one individual in particular'. The days and weeks skipped by as normal and it wasn't long before the summer came around again. It was the finest and sunniest summer I remember, but also the summer that saw the worst tragedy that ever hit Gleann Chárthainn.

DISEASE AND DEATH IN AN GLEANN

It was at the end of August that summer that the first person in An Gleann got sick with typhoid– God between us and all harm. The person who got sick was the daughter of Liam Ó Cinnéide from the east side of An Gleann. By the end of that week, Liam himself and his son and daughter, were all sick. These were Liam's only two children. The daughter Brídín was about eighteen years of age and she was one of the nicest girls in the parish. The son was a few years older than her. No one, not even their closest neighbours realised at first how dangerous this disease was that the Ó Cinnéide's had contracted – at least, not until the doctor from Baile na hAbhann came to see them. He said that they had typhoid and that it was a very dangerous disease and highly-infectious. He did whatever he could to help them but nine days later, both father and daughter died within hours of one another. They died on the Saturday and the next day, the priest announced from the altar that the doctor had ordered that no-one should attend any wake in the area or visit anyone who was sick, in case they caught the infection. People were also advised not to eat or drink anything in a house where the disease could be present and to boil water before they drank it. People were very frightened and horrified. Within a couple of days three or four other people in An Gleann were struck down with the fever. No-one really understood too much about typhoid in those days. Another thing was that no-one went to hospital then either except poorer people who had no-one else to look after them. Going to a hospital was seen as shameful and as associated with poverty. Back then, people would have preferred to die in their own house than go to a hospital. If it wasn't for my aunt Máire and Seán Mac Craith, no-one would have been there to help organize the burial of Liam Ó Cinnéide's daughter. That poor 'rake' Peaid na Brídí helped out also – like a real man. The day of the funeral saw a tiny crowd of people in attendance, very few of whom could even step inside the family's house; everyone was too afraid of catching the disease. It was a sad and lonely day for the poor widow to lose her daughter and her husband in one go and to be unsure as to whether her only son would still be alive when she returned from the funeral, he was that sick. My aunt Máire looked after the widow's son until his mother returned from the funeral. Her son recovered from the disease in the end and thankfully, his mother never contracted it.

Within a fortnight there were about twenty people in bed with typhoid. The doctor felt that the infection had spread by means of the drinking water. The water levels had been very low that summer because it was so dry and as a result the streams and the wells were nearly all dried up. That said, people got their water from different sources so the doctor's theory as to how the disease had spread may not have been entirely true either.

It was difficult to understand what caused this disease and made it spread because it appeared in houses that were situated a good distance from one another and the neighbours didn't always become infected either. In three or four households, everyone got the infection one after another and in other houses just two or three people contracted it and the others escaped. Máire Baróid was one of the first people in the area to catch the infection and yet neither her mother nor Seán got it at all. None of the Ó Siadhaile family caught it although Dic went to every wake and funeral that took place in An Gleann – this, despite the doctor's orders not to do so. No-one in Lios na Faille here caught the disease – a thousand thanks be to God – this despite the fact that the two people who were in most danger of infection were my aunt Máire and Seán Mac Craith. At Mass, the following Sunday, we heard that Tomás de Búrc from Mónach Buí was on his sickbed and had contracted typhoid. The news spread quickly and within a week it was known that all of the Burkes of Mónach Buí were now sick with it except for Tomás Óg. I was in the yard one day doing something or other – and feeling down because I was thinking of Sibéal who was now also struck down with this awful disease and who had only her younger brother to look after her. Because everyone was so frightened of the disease, few people would venture anywhere near a house where there were sick people in it – never mind going to help anyone who was sick. These dark thoughts were going through my mind when the parish priest arrived into the yard on his horse and cart. He greeted me and told me to call out my auntie, that he had a message for her. I told him that I would keep an eye on his horse and cart for him if he wanted to go into the house but he said that it was safer if he stayed outside. It would be less risky for us given that he'd already been in every house where typhoid was present. I told him not to worry about this because my aunt Máire had been in all of those houses already and hadn't brought the infection home with her but he still wouldn't go in. Just then, my aunt Máire appeared at the door. She invited the priest in and told the priest the exact same thing as I'd told him but he told her he'd rather not come in, citing the same explanation as before. 'I've got a special favour to ask of you Máire', the priest said, 'a

favour that you might do out of the love of God'. I began
to move away from where they were chatting but the
priest called over to me. 'You don't have to leave Séamus',
'maybe, from what I hear, what I'm going to say to your
aunt relates to you also in a way'. He turned to my aunt
again and spoke to her in a tone that was very serious. 'It's
this Máire', he said. 'There are five of the Mónach Buí
people who are in bed sick with the fever – God between
us and all harm – and there's no-one there to offer them
even a drink of water, except for the youngest lad who's
only fourteen years of age; he's the only one who isn't sick
with it. It would be a great act of kindness if you were to
help them. None of the other neighbours will go anywhere
near their house, they are so afraid of catching the disease.
I am very aware of all the good work you've already done
since this fever struck the locality and God will reward
you for your kindness. This is the most urgent situation of
all right now, however. The situation is critical in their
house at the moment and I know that your courage won't
fail you on this occasion. And someone has to take a risk
and try to help out'. My aunt looked the priest straight in
the face and there was fire in her eyes. 'Me!' she said. 'Me
go and stand in the house of the Mónach Buí people! Do
you not realize what you are asking Father?' The priest
raised his hand and interrupted her before she could say
anything more. 'I know exactly how things are between
yourselves and the Mónach Buí people but isn't it time
now to forget about that old bitterness. That old enmity
should have been forgotten about years ago. And Máire,
I'm afraid that you – more than anyone else in the two
families – are the person who's inclined to keep this
enmity alive. This is the only small fault that I can find
with you as a person and it isn't with false praise that I say
to you that you are an amazing woman. Put this small
bitterness aside now once and for all and come down with
me to Mónach Buí where you can perform the most noble

of all deeds you have done, thus far. The God of Glory will reward you one hundred-fold for all your incredible work when the time comes'. My aunt Máire was staring down at the ground all the while the priest was talking and she didn't raise her head for a few minutes until after he had finished speaking. 'I'll go with you', she said finally, 'and they're the most difficult words I've ever uttered in my life, and this is the most difficult thing I've ever done'. 'I praise you to the high Heavens', said the priest, 'you are some woman'. 'Wait one minute', she said. 'I'll stay there as long as I'm needed and there are some small things I need to bring with me'. She sat up on the cart and she and the priest went out through the gate. This was the most surprising sight I'd seen since the day I was born. I was happy beyond belief and I felt there and then that everything would work out with God's help. Sibéal would pull through now because my aunt Máire would be there to look after her and my aunt would take good care of everyone else too. There was a good chance now that the old enmity would be buried now forever. I went back into the house and spoke to my mother about what had just happened. 'It's a miracle from God', she said. 'Máire Lios na Faille going up to nurse the Burkes from Mónach Buí. It's surely for the best. May God keep her free from this awful disease and keep it away from all of us'.

Seán Mac Craith was equally amazed when I told him the full story when he came in from the fields. 'This is the type of thing that your aunt would do. She's an exceptional woman – one in a million', he said.

I know that to do what the priest asked her to do would nearly have killed her and yet she did it because she felt that it was the best thing to do. And you know what; I wouldn't put it past the parish priest to have had two issues in mind when he asked her to take care of the Mónach Buí people – to end the feud in addition to nursing that family back to health. And from what you said, it sounds like he's well-aware of yourself and Sibéal also'.

I've often wondered what thoughts must have gone through the mind of Tomás of Mónach Buí when he saw my aunt arriving in the door to them. But then I suppose that anyone who is that weak and sick doesn't have the energy to be analysing things too much. Tomás, the father, Máire and Sibéal weren't as sick with the fever as were Séamus and the mother. The latter were very sick indeed and the doctor had little confidence that the mother would pull through at all. Afterwards, he said that it was thanks to my aunt that the mother survived at all. Tomás Óg never contracted the fever at all. While my aunt Máire was staying down with the Burkes of Mónach Buí to nurse them, Seán Mac Craith went down each morning and evening to keep their farm ticking over. He milked the cows each morning and afternoon, albeit that it was the pigs who were fed most of that milk. My aunt Máire knew that she couldn't use any of that milk to make butter as she normally would have – given that the disease was in the house. My mother and I were kept a lot busier back home working around our farm for those few weeks and this was probably just as well because the more work that I had to do, the less time I had for worrying about Sibéal, in particular. The days went by really quickly and I had no trouble sleeping at night, I was so tired after the day's work.

Thanks be to God – but no-one here in Lios na Faille caught the disease. Although my aunt Máire, Seán Mac Craith and Peaid na Brídí were at huge risk of contracting the infection, none of them got it. Peaid said that he didn't catch the infection on account of the amount of whiskey he drank at this time. He was in particular danger, of course, because he used to bury everyone who died from the disease. Afterwards, Peaid would say that he had been on a whiskey-high for half of the time that the disease was in the locality.

In summary, 25 people got sick with the typhoid and 5 people died from it, four of whom were strong and healthy men before they caught it. Siobhán Ní Chinnéide was the only woman who died of the disease. While someone was recovering from the worst of the typhoid fever, the doctor said that it was dangerous to give them anything except liquids and drinks. Even if the patient was hungry you were not supposed to give them any food until they were well on the road to recovery; otherwise, you could kill the patient. Séamuisín Risteard, who lived on this side of Bearna an Mhadra, caught the typhoid fever. He fought it off and was over the worst of it but his wife had been instructed not to give him any food at all until he was fully recovered – no matter how much he asked for something to eat. His wife's mother-in-law came to visit her son from Leacain one day and the two women were eating their dinner in the kitchen. It was a Sunday and they were having bacon and cabbage. When Séamuisín Risteard got the smell of the food, he begged the women to give him a bit. His wife wouldn't give him any of it as she was sticking rigidly with the doctor's instructions, however Séamuisín's mother brought him down a plate of food. By nightfall, his fever had returned with a vengeance and he was nearly as sick again as he had been in the beginning. The following night saw a sharp frost on the ground and yet the husband got out of bed; he was delirious with the fever and although he was wearing just his night-shirt, he went out into the back field where he was supposedly counting the sheep. Amazingly, he didn't die from the fever or from walking out into the freezing cold that night. In fact, he lived to be over eighty years of age, this despite being quite a scrawny individual.

SEÁN BARÓID AND EILÍS BREATHNACH

Seán Mór Breathnach had only the one daughter, a girl named Eilís who was about the same age as me. She was one of the nicest girls in terms of personality and temperament that was ever born. Tall and thin, she had curly blonde hair and dark blue eyes and she was always happy and smiling. From what I heard, she was very similar in appearance and temperament to her late mother and as far as her father was concerned, Eilís was the sun and the moon, and the heaven that is on this earth. Isn't human nature strange, however? Despite his enormous love for his daughter, it was actually Eilís' father who was responsible for breaking his daughter's heart and for the fact that she died young. To understand this story fully, however, one needs to go back to the beginning. I have frequently mentioned Seán Baróid during the course of this narrative. Along with Dic Ó Siadhaile, he was a good friend of mine – right from the very first day that we went to school in Baile an Droichid. Sean was a fine, handsome lad when he grew into adulthood; he was athletic and strong and he never backed away from anyone or any challenge – be it an athletic or weightlifting challenge or any other challenge that came his way. Seán Baróid lived on Bóithrín na Cille, about a half-a-mile down from the Breathnach's house. There was just his mother, his sister Máire and himself living there. They had about 25 acres of good land and they were reasonably comfortable. While Seán enjoyed his socializing and sport, he was able to work long hours when he had to and he wasn't; feckless when it came to money. Himself and Eilís Breathnach were very friendly with one another from the day that they both finished school. They were both fond of reading and always swapped books with one another. They loved discussing books and writers and the like. In the end, they fell in love with one another, almost without realizing it. I think the local people realized these two young people had fallen for each other even before they did themselves. I don't know whether Seán Mór heard much about it but even if he had, he would just have laughed. Not for a moment would he have imagined that he'd permit his daughter to marry a man whose worldly wealth amounted to as little as did Seán Baróid's. The two young people were good friends for a few years and neither of them had too many worries in life. Gradually Eilís and Seán came to understand what had grown between them however, and although they weren't engaged to one another or anything – I think that they thought that their situation would sort itself out somehow over the course of time – so that they might marry one day.

Seán Baróid had told me how it was between Eilís and he a couple of times – but I didn't know how to advise him – especially, given that I was in a quandary myself for quite a while in relation to Sibéal. One of the Breathnach's – a man who was a far-out relation of Seán Mór himself – who owned a 60-acre farm that bordered Seán Mór's on one side. This man's name was also Seán Breathnach but everyone referred to him as Seánín Breathnach or Seán Beag. This man was over forty years of age then and he and his mother lived together in the one house. This man was even hungrier for land and wealth than Seán Mór was, but the locals had little enough respect for him. He had the reputation for being miserly and mean, and for not being adverse to a bit of crookedness if he could get away with it. During Advent of that year, a rumour went around An Gleann that Seán Beag wanted to make a match with Eilís Breathnach. This rumour didn't surprise the neighbours too much because they knew only too well what type of people Seán Mór and Seán Beag both were. If you were to consider such a match from a purely monetary and mercenary point of view, it made a great deal of sense. After all, when Seán Mór passed on, Seán Beag and Eilís would have the two farms, both side-by-side with one another – 130 acres of the finest land in the county. Unfortunately, Eilís' feelings about this potential match were barely taken into consideration; no consideration was given to Seán Baróid's view either. For the older generation back then, romantic love was just a past-time as relating to youth; and marriage had nothing to do with past-times. Next thing, we heard that everything was settled and that the marriage was indeed going ahead. The two Seán's – Seán Mór and Seán Beag – were sorting out everything in relation to the land and Eilís' wedding dress was being made in Clonmel.

Dic Ó Siadhaile and I used to meet Seán Baróid nearly every Sunday morning at first Mass in Baile na hAbhann. I didn't see Seán the Sunday of that week and I wasn't outside the house all week because Sibéal had gone to visit her godmother in An Chúil Chluthmhair. As night was falling on the following Saturday evening, Seán Baróid called into me and asked me to join him for a walk down the boreen. While we were walking, he told me about the match Eilís and Seán Beag and that everything was already arranged. There was more to the story than this, however. The previous Sunday, after dinner, Seán had gone for a walk down the boreen that led past Seán Mór's house. He was in turmoil with all the rumours he was hearing about the match that was supposedly being made and he was hoping that he might see Eilís and get the whole truth about what was happening straight from her. He hadn't seen any sign of Eilís for the previous fortnight, although he'd passed the gate of her house every afternoon. When he passed the house that Sunday, however, Seán Mór and Seán Beag were standing outside the gate. He greeted them as he walked past and Seán Mór greeted him also, although it was a fairly cold greeting. He noticed a smirk on the other man's however, and he didn't say 'hello' at all. He was just about five yards past them when Seán Mór called after him:

'Hey Baróid, come here'.

'You want to talk to me?' asked Seán, turning on his heel.

'Yes. To you', replied Seán Mór. 'I'm after hearing that you were running after my daughter. Don't let me hear that ever again'.

'And, just to let you, she's marrying Sean here on Advent Tuesday. The likes of you would really be getting ahead of yourself altogether; imagine a "rambler" like you with your tiny sliver of land; imagine that you'd even consider yourself in the running to marry my daughter; I tell you …'

Seán was angry on hearing these condescending comments from Seán Mór but what made it worse was the dirty smirk on the other man's face. He wanted to plank him more than anything else but somehow he managed to contain himself.

'I can't believe that she'd marry that miserly excuse for a man', retorted Seán Baróid, 'not unless I heard it from it from her (Eilís') own mouth'.

'You'll hear it straight away so', said Seán Mór and he turned and went into the house. He returned a few minutes later with Eilís in tow. Seán Baróid noticed that Eilís was pale and drawn-looking but her lips were pursed and set.

'Eilís', said Seán, 'is it true what your father is after telling me – that you're going to marry slimey Seánín here?'

'It's true', Eilís said, 'and I don't want to set eyes on you ever again. You're only a charmer without shame. And who are you to be talking about sliminess? Who's slimier than yourself?'

Then, without even giving Seán a chance to reply, Eilís turned on her heel and walked back into the house, her head held high and haughty-like.

Seán had no choice other than to walk away sheepishly. He heard Seán Beag skittering behind him and it took him all his power to control himself and not go back and hit him. Seán Baróid said that he couldn't understand what had come over Eilís that she'd spoken to him that. He could understand that she might have to obey her father and marry Seán Beag but what was behind the angry and vicious she had spoken to him? Even worse was the way that she had called him slimy and a charmer and all the rest of it. He couldn't understand it for the life of him and neither could I.

Seán Baróid told me then that he planned on leaving An Gleann forever. He couldn't stay here and look on as Eilís became another man's wife. He would go to America and he requested that I speak to his mother and his sister after he was gone, and explain the whole thing to them. My advice to him was not to do anything rash but to take his time and to try and hide his pain – not to let it be said that Eilís Breathnach had forced him to abandon his mother and his sister. I told him that there was no way that she was worth amount of pain and certainly not the tearing-apart of his family – not after the horrible way she'd spoken to him. I spent an hour pleading with Seán to reconsider, but to no avail. He had already made his mind up that he was leaving An Gleann and nothing would make him change his mind. I asked him when he was leaving and how he was going to travel abroad but he wouldn't give me any details. I asked him to write to me when he got to the US but he wouldn't give me any guarantees in this regard either. He said goodbye to me then while trying to keep the pain in his voice from breaking through. The last words he spoke to me were: 'Séamus, I shake your hand; we'll meet each other again someday when I've put all of this trouble and pain behind me; alive or dead Séamus, we'll meet one another again someday'.

I felt heartbroken and tormented as I turned back down the boreen. Seán Mac Craith was still up when I got in; he was sitting in the corner of the kitchen reading by the light of a lamp although it was almost midnight. He noticed that I was upset and asked me what was wrong. I told him the whole story from beginning to end. It was then that he revealed his own personal story to me for the first time, the personal tragedy that had driven him to leave his native village forever, a story which I have previously related in this volume. Life is cruel and full of great sadness for many people; there is no doubt about it. It is often the innocent who suffer the most. These two men – Seán Mac Craith and Seán Baróid, two of the finest men who ever set foot on this earth – and yet their lives were ruined by two women, who were capricious and unyielding in their ways.

A woman named Mairéad Ní Bhriain lived here in An Gleann once. She lived on Bóithrín na Cille, down a little from the bridge. She was a small low-sized woman who had one son but everyone knew her by the name Donncha Pheigí. Poor Peigí had never been married and she used to get her son jobs, working one day, here, and one day, there. She used to work as a washerwoman or small potatoes, or helping other women get their houses down in the village done up for 'the Stations'. Another type of work she did during the last few weeks of the summer each year – something I'd never seen anyone else do before – was collect gorse-seed. She had a thick stick for this that was twisted into a circular shape – as attached to the mouth of an open bag, and she'd knock the seeds from the furze and gorse bushes into this bag using another stick. A bow was what she called this unusual seed-collecting device or pouch. Once this pouch or bow was full or too heavy for her hands, she'd put the seeds she'd gathered into another larger bag and return home.

She'd spread the stems in big bundles out on bags under the sun to dry and they would soon crack and split. If you were passing her house while this drying process was going on, you'd hear the stems popping and bursting with the heat and if you didn't know what was going on you'd say to yourself – 'what's that strange knocking noise?' She'd thresh the stems that hadn't burst with a lath to burst them open, then sift and clean the seed with a sieve. She was paid a shilling per cartful of seed by a seed-merchant down in Clonmel. Peigí was very honest and very thorough when it came to her work but she had one small fault; she was too fond of gossip and because she did all types of jobs, she found herself working in many houses and bringing stories from one house to the next. There were some women who wouldn't let her into their house because of this but there were others, as you can imagine, who gave her work deliberately so as to get all the gossip. Every argument that happened in every house in An Gleann, you can be sure that Peigí had the full details of it and she was never happier than when she had someone else to share her gossip with. I don't think there was ever anything too serious in most of this gossip. Things that Peigí said did cause rows in certain houses on occasion, however – and everyone would know about it with a couple of days! Seán Baróid had left home without saying anything to anyone. Soon, everyone was discussing the ins and outs of why he'd left, however. Before I'd mustered the courage to call up and tell his mother and sister what Seán and I had spoken about when we'd last met up, his sister Máire called down to ask me if I knew anything about where Seán might have gone. I told her everything I knew. She said that Seán was already gone one morning by the time she and her mother had woken up and that he'd taken his best suit of clothes with him. Poor Máire was broken-hearted and her mother was even more devastated by all accounts. I told them what Eilís Breathnach had done to Seán. Later, when I told the whole story to Sibéal, she began to cry. She was very critical of Eilís and if I hadn't told her, she'd have found it difficult to believe that Eilís was capable of such cruelty and Seán. Near the end of that week, I was going down to Ó Siadhaile's house as night was falling. I was still going over all the bad things that had happened and trying to make sense of them in my mind when I ran into Peigí Bheag at the corner of the road. I greeted her and asked her where she was off to at this was her reply:

'Séamus de Búrc, listen to me for a minute'.

'What's wrong now?' I said.

'Oh, what have I done! What have I done?' she said, her voice trembling. She looked as if she was about to burst into tears.

'And what have you done?' I said. 'Oh. It's this Séamus', and she told me in between tears and weeping that Seán Beag Breathnach had given her a pound to tell Eilís – (let it slip, as it were and as if 'in passing', the next time that she found herself working in that house) – that she had been walking home Baile na hAbhann one afternoon and that she'd spotted Seán Baróid and Caitlín Nic Gearailt, the schoolmaster's daughter, sitting beneath a big hedge near Sean-Phóna and that Seán had his arms around Caitlín and was kissing her. Everyone knew that Caitlín Nic Gearailt was always running after Seán Baróid and following him to football matches and athletic meets and the like. I knew that Seán hadn't the slightest interest in Caitlín and that he was always trying to avoid her. Now I understood why Eilís had been willing to marry Seán Beag and why she had been so 'off' with Seán Baróid when her father had called her out to speak to him that day. I could have throttled Peigí on the spot, I was so angry. I grabbed hold of her and gave her a violent shake – as a dog would do with a rat – 'You devil in human form', I said, 'damn you anyway'.

She roared and wept and went down on her knees in the middle of the road, and begged me to forgive her. 'Forgiveness', I said, 'even God himself wouldn't forgive you for what you've done. The best man who ever stood in this village and the nicest girl ever and you're after destroying both their lives – and all for a measly pound. You deserve to be hanged by rights'.

'Oh, I know that I deserve no better', Peigí said, 'I didn't know that there was any harm in what I was doing. I thought it was just a bit of fun'.

'Listen to me now', I said.

'Go straight down to the Breathnach's house and tell Eilís what you've just told me. Tell her the full truth or as sure as God, I'll break your neck that next time I see you. Be here tomorrow morning at seven o'clock to tell me how you got on'.

I didn't sleep a wink that night, my mind was in such turmoil. I couldn't relax the next morning, not until I went back the road to see Peigí again. She was waiting for me already when I got there and her story was a strange one.

After we'd met the previous evening, she'd gone straight down to Breathnach's house as I told her to do. On arrival into the kitchen, she met Seán Mór, Eilís and Seán

Beag sitting at a small fire in the kitchen. The two men were chatting and Eilís was sitting at the table, her chin propped on her hands and staring into the fire. She wasn't paying much attention to what the two men were discussing by all accounts. Peigí said 'hello' and they greeted her in turn. They told her to sit in next to the fire but she told Eilís to come outside with her for a moment because she had something to discuss with her. They went outside and Peigí told her story, the same as she told me it the previous evening. Eilís didn't say a word when Peigí was finished but just turned and went back into the house. She left the door open and Peigí stood there anxiously, wondering how Eilís would respond. Eilís went up to her room and brought down a big cardboard box that was tied with twine which she placed on the kitchen table. She pulled out a knife from the table-drawer and cut the twine on the box, then opened it and pulled out the lovely dress. 'Did you want to show Peigí your wedding dress?' her father asked her. Eilís didn't answer him, however, but rolled the dress up in a ball and walked over to the fire. She threw the dress into the middle of the fire and shoved it down with her foot. The two men jumped to their feet and roared at her – 'What are you doing?'

She didn't reply but raised the tongs over her and Seáinín's head. Her eyes were blazing with anger and she was as pale as the wall.

'Leave this house, you monster', she said to him or I'll smash your skull in'. Seán Beag stood up and went out the door without a word. Her father grabbed her by the shoulders and asked her what had come over her – had she completely lost her mind? Peigí Beag left then. Two days later, it was all over the village that the 'match' was broken. Everyone had their own theory about what had happened; I doubt that it was Peigí who spread the story around anyway – whoever it was.

On the following Sunday, I went for a walk along the river-bank after my dinner. I was still really confused and upset about everything that had happened with Seán Baróid and the fact that he was gone and no-one knew where he had gone or what had happened to him either. Seán, Dic Ó Siadhaile and I had been close friends since we'd first gone to school and I couldn't help but think of poor Seán all the time now. I was certain that there was no way that he'd ever come back to An Gleann, if he never found out what the true story was; that's the type of person Seán was; he was very headstrong and once he'd made up his mind about something, he rarely changed it. I sat down on the edge of the riverbank as all of these thoughts were circling in my mind. I sat there for a long time and then I heard the sound of footsteps behind me. I looked over my shoulder and was surprised to see Eilís Bhreathnach. She didn't spot me until I stood up as there was a big furze bush between our lines of vision. She stopped and there was a startled look on her face. It was as if she was surprised to see anyone out here near the river. I didn't say anything but just stared at her instead – and it wasn't with love or respect in my eyes either. I can honestly say that I really hated her in that moment after what she'd done to my friend Seán. She was very pale and drawn-looking and had big black bags beneath her eyes. She looked like someone who hadn't slept for a week. She must have read my mind because she ran over to me and threw her arms around my shoulders and buried her head in my chest. She sobbed and wept for about five minutes, her whole body shaking and shivering as my harsh feelings towards her began to dissipate and I began to feel sorry for her. 'Séamus', she said finally. 'I suppose you hate me for what I did to poor Seán. But, believe me, you don't feel anywhere near as bad as I do. Oh Séamus', she said, and there was such an awful sorrow and sadness in her voice, and her face had such a heart-broken look that I began crying myself. 'Séamus, it was because I loved him so much that this happened. When Peigí Bheag told me that false story about Seán, I went into a jealous rage and I was so mad with him that I didn't care what I was doing anymore'.

'Eilís', I said, 'I feel sorry for you, but you knew Seán for that long that you should have known that there was nothing false of dishonest about him. When you called him a "betrayer" and a "charmer", a knife went through his heart. You condemned him without even giving him a chance to defend himself, a chance that the robber, the bandit and even the murderer always gets'.

Eilís didn't answer this at all but just threw herself face-down on the field, and began weeping again. In a few minutes, I caught her by the shoulder and sat her down again and I sat next to her. I told her that she should only weep like that if Seán had died. Eilís calmed down eventually and dried her eyes.

We went over the whole episode again, step-by-step. Eilís had imagined that I would know where Seán was gone but I told her what he had told me – that he was leaving for America, never to return. When she heard this Eilís was really upset. She said that her father didn't like the trick that Seán Beag had played on them but that her father wanted her to get married all the same – and that he was forever going on about the fine farm of land that Seán Beag and she would have when he was gone. When he'd started on this theme again, on the previous day, however, Eilís had sworn to him that she would not marry Seán Breathnach, even if he was the last man left on earth.

I walked back with Eilís as far as the gate of their farm although there was little in the way of conversation on that walk, I remember. We both had a heavy heart. Love is a powerful disease, there is no doubt about it. I had an outlet for my gloom and sorrow that Eilís Breathnach didn't, of course, because once I left Eilís at the gate I made for Móin Bhuíde where I told Sibéal the entire story, from beginning to end. Sibéal was very kind; she sympathized with me about losing my friend and she understood completely how upset I felt.

The days slipped by and the people of An Gleann discussed what had happened in relation to Eilís Breathnach and Seán Baróid less and less. It was noticeable that Eilís was not the same woman anymore. She became very thin and emaciated-looking and only ever came out of the house on Sundays when she went to Mass. Even then, she didn't mix much with the other girls anymore, even those girls who were relatives of hers. Anytime she ran into me she had only the one question for me: Did I have any news about Seán Baróid?

I always told her the same thing – that I hadn't heard anything from Seán – and when Eilís heard this, she would always give a heavy sigh and turn away again without saying another word.

Eilís went to Holy Communion every Sunday and one Sunday in June she collapsed at Mass. They had to bring her outside and it took a long time for her to regain consciousness. That was the last time she was at Mass because she took to her bed when she got home and never rose from it again until she was placed in her coffin. It is difficult to understand but it seems that her father had no inkling of how much Eilís had gone downhill until that day that she collapsed in the church. He hadn't noticed that she had declined greatly, both physically and psychologically in the months prior to that. The doctor was called and from the look that was on his face when he emerged after examining Eilís, everyone could tell how serious the situation was. Within a few days, it was all over the locality what the doctor had diagnosed. He said that Eilís had no ostensible disease or infection but that she was suffering greatly emotionally and that if this suffering couldn't be healed, her health was in danger.

A few days later, I was out working on a ditch near Páirc na nAcra when who came along the road but Seán Mór Breathnach. He greeted me and came to a stop. Then he went straight to the heart of the matter, without any preliminaries.

'Eilís is in danger of death', he said. 'You probably know why she is why she is'.

I could tell by him that Seán Mór Breathnach was in a very agitated state but I didn't have much sympathy for him, to be honest; I held him entirely responsible for what had happened to Seán Baróid. In my eyes then, he was just a big self-important braggart, a person who had no respect for anyone, except the person who was very rich. Now that he had a difficult dilemma himself, his power and authority weren't much help to him.

'What do you want from me?' I said to him, and my tone was less than friendly.

'You were aware that my daughter and Seán Baróid were in love with each other and you know why Seán Baróid left here and no-one's heard anything from him since. I'm the one who's responsible for this tragedy. I was thinking more about how to keep a grip on the wealth of this life, I'm afraid, rather than thinking of my daughter's wishes. Now, I'd spend my last shilling if I could get my daughter cured for what ails her. And I know that there is only one thing that will heal her at this stage and that's to get Seán Baróid back and to marry them with one another'.

'I observed Seán Mór Breathnach closely while he was talking. His demeanour had changed a great deal from the last time I had seen him. He wasn't the same man at all; his tone of voice had changed completely and there was nothing self-important or pompous about him now at all.

Now he was reduced to the state of any ordinary man who is tormented at heart-broken at the turn his life has taken.

You and Seán Baróid were very good friends; maybe you know where he's gone?'

'I don't know anything about him', I said, 'all he told me was that he was going to America'.

'God help us', Seán Mór Breathnach said, pitifully.

I stood there thinking for a few moments and then said.

'If you want to find Seán Baróid', I said, 'wouldn't you be best off giving this job to an attorney who could put an advertisement in the newspapers over in America. Seán told me that he was going to America and he wasn't a man to ever tell lies. I can't see any other way of finding him at this stage'.

'You're a smart boy', Seán Mór said; 'I'll do that right away'. A few more weeks went by and Eilís Bhreathnach was getting weaker every day. When her father told her what he was doing, she bucked up and her health improved a good deal. As the weeks went by and there was no sign of Seán, she began to decline again, however. Her father was nearly mad with worry by this point. He was in and out to the attorney every second day. He couldn't rest until there was some response through the post from America.

I went to see Eilís a couple of times during these weeks and my heart went out to her. All she spoke about was Seán and he was the first name on her lips anytime I spoke to her. Her first question to me was always: 'Have you heard anything about Seán?' After more than three months had passed without any word from America, Eilís gave up the ghost altogether. She was so thin and worn-out looking by then that one sight of her and you knew she wasn't going to last much longer.

I went to visit her one Sunday afternoon at the end of September. She was very weak by then and her father told me that they had thought she was gone on the previous night. They had read the Litany over her and placed the holy candle in her fist – she had rallied a little again, however. The priest called after Mass and gave her Holy Communion and she perked up a lot for a short while after this. When I went to see her, she was asleep and her breathing was so slow that it was difficult to tell that she was alive at all.

It was nearly midnight and I and her father were in the room; two or three of the neighbours were out in the kitchen and the clock there was striking twelve when Eilís opened her eyes and stared at me and her father. Then she looked over at the open door of the room for a few minutes and it was as if she expecting someone to come in the door at any moment. Then, suddenly, she sat up in the bed, as if, for a moment, she was as strong as she'd ever been. She stretched her two hands out towards the door and called out at the top of her voice.

'Seán! Seán! Seán, love! Stay with me! Stay with me!' She tried to get out of the bed then and her father and I ran over to catch her but she fell back on the bed again dead with her two hands stretched out. Poor Eilís was in eternity.

I'll never forget the look of happiness and love she had in her eyes as she called out Seán's name three times; she was like someone who was greeting a long-lost friend after many long years. I'll never forget the mixture of distress and sorrow that was her father's face either.

It was just before sunrise when I left their house early the following morning to return home and I must have cut a sad figure as I made my way down along Bóithrín na Cille. Then, came one of the strangest things I've ever experienced. I was about fifty yards, or less, from the crossroads, the juncture that is Bóithrín na Cille and the main road, when it happened. I was walking slowly and I was very tired and sleepy but the sun was already a bright red ball above the eastern mountains. It was a beautiful, bright day when a man ran out in front of me wearing a strange rig-out – something very similar to the blue and white colours that the Baile na hAbhann football team always wore. It was a very strange sight. Not only did the man make no sound as he passed close to me on the road but it was very strange to see anyone dressed like that out at such an early hour of the morning. I felt sure that I recognized this man as he ran past but he had already disappeared around the corner before it registered with me properly who he was. It was Seán Baróid and his whole face was lit up in that happy, laughing, smile of his that I'd seen a hundred times before and he was looking back over his shoulder at me. I called out his name at the top of my voice and ran after him but he had already disappeared. Within a split-second, I had rounded the corner myself but there was no sign of him anywhere. The road was as straight as a dye and there was no sign of anyone for a half-a-mile in either direction. I was shocked and stunned and stood there for a few moments trying to understand what had just happened. I must have fallen asleep and dreamed the whole thing, I said to myself afterwards. I was probably exhausted after being awake all night. I was more convinced of this than ever, when I awoke the following day after a good long sleep and as the days followed I was certain that I must have imagined the whole thing. And yet a month later, a letter reached me from a priest in the far-west of Canada, a man who was based about fifty miles from the Pacific Ocean. This is what it said in Irish:

Dear Sir,

It is with great regret that I am obliged to inform you of the death of a relative of yours, Seán Baróid, here on Sunday, the 26th of September last. He came here about six months ago and worked as part of a group lumbering and cutting trees in the forests about five miles from this village. There are more than 200 men in this group of foresters who cut down trees and remove the branches from the trees. Then they place the logs in the river and float them down-river to a saw-mill about twenty miles from here. The foresters live out in wood cabins during the week but come into the local village on Saturday night when there is drinking and carousing until the following night.

Just before the men finished work that afternoon, Seán Baróid and another man were trying to free logs that were entangled in the water close to the riverbank, when one man fell into the river. Seán Baróid jumped in and tried to save him. He grabbed a hold of this man but the river-current swept both men away. The flow of water was so powerful here that everyone thought the two men were finished but Seán managed to pull his fellow-worker from the water about a half-a-mile from where the man had first gone into the water.

Seán was highly-praised by his colleagues for this brave action, a high praise that was well-deserved. The man who had fallen in made a complete recovery but two days later Seán Baróid got very sick. The water in the rivers here is very cold at this time of the year when the snow begins to melt in the mountains and so it must have been the freezing water that made him sick.

The doctor closest to the accident was a half-mile away although he was called to the scene immediately. The men promised to gather together whatever money was needed to pay the doctor but the doctor said that he was suffering from severe 'pneumonia' and that he was very sick.

The doctor left him for three days until he hoped that Seán would be out of danger. Seán Baróid didn't recover, as the doctor had thought, however.

I visit this village every second Sunday to say Mass. I arrived two days after Seán was diagnosed with 'pneumonia' and I gave him the Last Rites and he received Holy Communion. When I saw Seán again a fortnight later, he was very low and depressed, however. I got the sense that he didn't care anymore by then whether he lived or died. From the very first day that Seán came to this part of Canada, I was very friendly with him. He was a very devout man and he used to always serve Mass for me here and he always received Communion when Mass was held.

From the first time I ever met him, however, I felt that Seán was greatly-troubled by something or other; he never revealed to me what was troubling him, however. The first day that I met him, however, he gave your address to me and said that if anything ever happened to him, that I should inform you about it. This is the reason for my letter to you now.

As I mentioned earlier, he died on a Sunday. I gave him Holy Communion the morning following that Mass and although he was very weak, I didn't think he looked like he was going to die any time soon. He died unexpectedly at two o'clock that same afternoon. He died suddenly, as one would blow out a candle.

While he never had any interest in the drinking and carousing that happened here every weekend, all the workers here had the highest respect for Seán Baróid. He was an independent-minded man and a diligent worker and while he was sick in bed, his fellow-workers wouldn't leave his side and were competing with one another to stay and watch over him. The man he saved didn't want to leave his bedside at any stage.

You needn't have any worries about his soul as he is now in God's Heaven.

Your friend in Jesus Christ
Eoghan Mac Aoidh, Priest.

As you can imagine, having read this letter, I had a completely different perspective on what happened when I was returning from Breathnach's house early that morning when Eilís died months earlier. When you compare the time differences between Canada and Ireland, I worked out that Seán Baróid had actually died just a few hours before Eilís Breathnach did. Ever since, and even now today as a worn-out, old man, I strongly suspect that Eilís actually saw Seán Baróid that day when she sat up in the bed and called out his name three times before passing away. The same when I saw Seán Baróid on the road home a few hours later. Indeed, hadn't Seán promised me that he would meet me again one day, whether alive or dead – albeit that I hadn't shown much interest in what he was saying at the time. I am certain now that he fulfilled his promise. Looking back on it now, it is easy too to understand that nothing came of Seán Mór's attorney to make contact with Seán in Canada.

Grant that both Seán and Eilís are with one another in the presence of God now and that the happiness that was denied them in this life be theirs for all eternity.

A Final Word

My aim with this book was to describe daily life as lived in Gleann Chárthainn when I was young. I've nearly reached the end of this book now, and it was never my intention to simply tell the story of my life. My life was as ordinary as anyone else's and there was nothing very unusual about it, when all is said and done. As you'd expect of any normal person alive today, I saw good days and bad days and observed both the good and evil aspects of human nature. But as I finally lay down my pen, I need to bring this story to a satisfactory conclusion.

Within the space of a few small years, life in Lios na Faille saw many profound changes. The Christmas of the same year that Seán Baróid and Eilís Bhreathnach died, a brother of Tomás de Búrc from Mónach Buí came home from America. Séamus was his name and he was more than ten years younger than Tomás. He had spent eighteen years in America and needless to say, I didn't remember him from before at all. He was a fine, generous man who was quite similar in appearance to Sibéal. What do you know – but didn't he and my aunt Máire hook up and they got married the following June. He bought a sixty-acre farm that included a house and other outbuildings in Flemingstown on the road to Clonmel. The farm was sold at auction and he bought it for 1500 pounds which everyone said was a very good bargain at the time.

Séamus was very well-off, apparently, because in addition to purchasing this farm and buying livestock for it, he also had tradesmen working on the house and the barns for more than three months before he moved in.

This house is on the side of the main road and everyone from Lios na Faille or Móin Bhuídhe who passed by was always given a great welcome when they called. Nearly everyone who went to a fair or a market called in to the house on their way home. When Séamus de Búrc and my aunt Máire got married and it was Sibéal and I who stood for them. As was the norm that time, they didn't really have any honeymoon in the way that people have a honeymoon today. They went on a trip to Cork for a fortnight, instead. The house in Flemingstown wasn't yet ready to move into by then and they didn't want to get married here in Lios na Faille or in Móin Buí. Sibéal and I wanted to get married at the same time as they did, but our two families objected to this and told us to wait another year to get married – because we were both so young.

It was in August of the following year that we married. We had a great wedding – even better than Ned Dhomhnaill's possibly. Everyone in An Gleann was at the wedding. Peaid na Brídí and Cruthúirín played the music for us and Peaid was as full of fun and as big a trickster as ever. Peaid came as he was this time; he wasn't dressed up as a 'scarecrow' or a 'straw-man' as he normally was on such occasions. He did have the bells on his heels, however, and he danced 'An Staicín Eorna' (The Stack of Barley) up on the big kitchen table as placed out in the barn.

And yet, even despite the happiness and joy of this occasion, Sibéal and I couldn't help but think of the two other people who were now in the graveyard clay already – both of whom were buried a half-a-world away from one another – and how they could have been with us on this happy occasion, if tragedy hadn't intervened. We mentioned Seán Baróid and Eilís Bhreathnach more than once on the evening of the wedding reception; we all said that they were now happy together in God's Heaven, a place where nothing – be it money or pride – could ever divide them again.

Seán Mór only lived for three years after Eilís died. Not once, during those three years did he leave his farm to attend a fair or a market. He only ever left it to go to Mass on Sundays or holy days and to regularly visit the graveyard where the two people closest to him on this earth were now lying side-by-side. He lost all interest in the farm and only wandered along the edge of the ditch when the weather was fine; when it rained, he just sat inside in the parlour next to the fire. The farm was kept ticking over by Micil Ó Néill – because Seán Mór had a great farm manager in Micil. Another Breathnach, a nephew of Seán Mór's from Leacain inherited the farm and all the surrounding land after Seán Mór died.

Liam Tóibín, the schoolmaster married Máire Baróid and spent the rest of his life with us here in An Gleann. He was a big-hearted man and everyone was very fond of him. Máire and he lived a happy life together. After Seán Mór's death, Micil Ó Néill came to work for Liam Tóibín and Máire Baróid and spent the rest of his life working there. Dic Ó Siadhaile married the daughter of Micil Dhuinn, the blacksmith. Sean-Risteard lived until he was a few years short of a hundred. He was as mentally alert as ever right up until the end; he could tell a good story right up till the last few days of his life also. One day, after dinner, he told Dic that he was taking to his bed and that he should call the priest for him because he was going to die soon. Dic began teasing him at first as he thought his father was only letting on; he thought his father was as healthy then as he had been at any other time in the previous five years. When he saw how serious his father was about it, he called the priest as he was told. The priest arrived and prepared him for death, but he, too, thought that Dic was mistaken and that there was no chance that he was dying. Sean-Risteard died the following day, however. His wife Mairéad died ten years before he did. Three years prior to her death, Dic's wife had gone to the town to buy a shroud. She tried the shroud on but said that it was too big for her and that she'd have to return it and get another one. The second shroud was made for her and Dic had to bring it to the priest to get it blessed. She used to hang the shroud out on the bush to air it, a few times a month from then until the day she died. Didn't the people have an incredible faith and belief in God, in the old days. They were not very afraid of death at all. To them, to die was as natural as to be born. There aren't too many people who are like them today, I'm afraid. There aren't many people living today who have the same attitude to death as sean-Risteard Ó Siadhaile and his wife Mairghréad did back then.

The death of Seán Mac Craith was the saddest event we've experienced here in Lios na Faille during recent decades. He had spent twenty-two years living in Lios na Faille and he was one of us. He was only about fifty years of age when he died, and everyone thought that he still had a long life ahead of him. He was out in the loft stacking hay for the dairy when he died. He was called into his dinner, but when there was no sign of him, we went out and found him lying on the ground close to the haystack. He wasn't able to move or to get up off the ground. He was carried into the house and we called the priest and the doctor. They duly arrived and ministered to him. The doctor was of the opinion that Seán would recover, although Seán himself wasn't so sure. He said that his own father had died shortly after collapsing in a similar fashion. The doctor proved right, however, as Seán did make a partial recovery. Seán improved every day and after about a month the strength had returned again to his feet and hands. He looked to have recovered his physical strength except that he wasn't able to talk properly anymore. He would slur some of his words. Six months went by and we all thought that he was improving and getting stronger. One morning when there was no sign of him getting up at the normal time that he did, I went down to his room to see what was wrong. I found him lying unconscious on the bed. His breathing was terrible; it was as if he was about to choke. He remained unconscious like this until he died 24 hours later.

His funeral was the biggest funeral ever to leave Gleann Chárthainn. People travelled by every form of transport available as part of that funeral cortege as it wound its way out Barra an Bhealaigh and southwards to Áth Mheáin to where his relations were all buried. A year later we erected a headstone above his grave and this was only right and good, because as my aunt Máire often said, 'if it wasn't for Seán Mac Craith there would be no trace of the Burkes in Lios na Faille today'.

My aunt Máire and her husband used to visit Lios na Faille and Móin Buí here every now and then, although we were rarely able to persuade our mother to leave her hearth and to go and visit them. Then, when some new children came into the world, my mother felt a new lease of life. From then on, she suffered from depression less often and she was much happier in herself. This was a side of her that I didn't remember a great deal from the years when I was young when she seemed to be more down in herself.

I'll probably miss writing this book when I am done, because when I was describing the people and the places I saw in years gone by, it was as if I was back there again and in the company of those people who are long gone but whom I loved so much when I was young. That said, it probably won't be too long before I'll be joining them myself in eternity – with God's help. My work is done now and the night is drifting in and yet, I have one request of the reader of these words, before I take my leave. Of you who had the patience to read this account of the old life and what happened in An Gleann in years gone by, I have just the one request – that is to say a prayer for the soul of the person who has written this account – old-Séamus of Lios na Faille.

FINIT

1 'Bacaigh' is the plural of 'bacach' (boccough): lit: 'lame' person. The term bacach and bacaigh in Irish is an 'amorphous' term with a wide application and can mean anything from 'beggar', 'poor person', tramp, vagrant, Travelling person, Gypsy, wanderer etc. depending on the context in which the term is used.

2 Nicholas Sheehy (1728–1766) was an Irish Catholic priest who was amongst a group of people executed on a charge of accessory to murder. Father Sheehy was a prominent opponent of the British Penal Laws, which persecuted Catholics in Ireland. Father Sheehy was hanged, drawn and quartered in Clonmel on the fifteenth of March, 1766. Father Sheehy was hanged on a scaffold in Clonmel opposite St. Peters and Paul's Church, after which his head was severed and stuck on a spike over Clonmel Jail as a warning from the colonial government against agrarian violence. He is buried in Shanrahan Graveyard, in Clogheen.

SÉAMUS Ó MAOLCHATHA

Séamus Ó Maolchatha was born on 10 April 1884 in Cruan, County Tipperary. His father Thomas Mulcahy was a farm labourer and his mother was Margaret Burke. Both his parents were from Newcastle in South Tipperary originally and both were native speakers of Irish. Having attended national school in Newcastle, Séamus went to the teacher training college in De La Salle, Waterford and afterwards he returned his own native area where he spent forty-four years working as a teacher in Grange National School (1904–1948). One of the last experts on the Irish dialect of County Tipperary, he shared his information relating to place-names and dialectology with scholars such as an tAthair Pádraig de Paor and Professor Tomás de Bhaldraithe. Ó Maolchatha published short stories and essays over the years in newspapers and journals such as *Scéala Éireann*. He also tried to get an unabridged and unedited form of this book – *An Gleann agus a Raibh Ann* published with An Gúm for many years but his attempts proved futile. Although initially submitted in 1934, his Irish-language translation of *Dualgas Pheadair Bhig* (*La Tache du Petit Pierre*) by French author Jeanne Mairet wasn't published until 1953. Séamus Ó Maolchatha was married to Johanna Prendergast and they had five children, four sons and one daughter. He died in 1968.

Translator:
Dr Mícheál Ó hAodha works at the University of Limerick. He has published many books in Irish and English on the history of Irish nationalism, Irish migrancy and emigration. He is a regular contributor on arts and culture for the Irish-language columns of *The Irish Times* and also writes for the *Dublin Review of Books*, *An tUltach*, *Feasta*, *Beo.ie* etc. Some of his translations from the Irish appeared in the short story collection *Twisted Truths: Stories from the Irish* (Cló Iar-Chonnacht 2011).